I0037695

"*B2B Marketing Fundamentals* is the epitome of a compass in an ever-evolving and changing environment, enabling emerging professionals to navigate the complexities of B2B in a simple and easy-to-understand manner. This must-have book is an indispensable tool for any aspiring B2B marketer worth their salt! Kate Mackie is one of the leading thinkers in B2B marketing, at this watershed moment, in the journey of our craft."
Andisa Ntsubane, 2024 Global President, B2B Cannes Lions Jury

"This book is a masterclass in B2B marketing – comprehensive, insightful and brilliantly structured. Kate draws on her deep experience and proven expertise to guide readers through both the detail and the bigger picture. This isn't just theory – it's real-world, battle-tested advice. A must-read for any marketer looking to build a strong foundation in B2B marketing – engaging, practical and incredibly valuable."
Victoria Fox, CEO, AAR Group

"A much-needed resource for aspiring and ambitious marketers navigating the fast-changing world of B2B. Kate Mackie distills years of experience into actionable strategies and real-world examples that bridge the gap between theory and practice. From building brands to driving measurable results, this book offers practical guidance that marketers can apply immediately to grow their skills, their impact and their careers. Exactly what is needed by ambitious marketers looking to make an impact in the fast-changing world of B2B."
Kristin Gower, Global Client President, WPP

"In *B2B Marketing Fundamentals*, Kate Mackie delivers a much-needed playbook for marketers who want to move beyond tactical execution. The book provides a strategic guide to help navigate the evolving world of modern-day B2B marketing. *B2B Marketing Fundamentals* is a healthy reminder for marketers who get swept up in the day-to-day tactical execution and provides a timely refresh to marketing principles that can help fast-track your career progression and marketing impact."
Chris Peters, editor of *B2B Excellence*

"A masterclass in B2B marketing! This book offers both a deep dive into the essentials and a strategic outlook for the future of the industry. Whether you're a seasoned marketer or just starting out, it will equip you with the tools, frameworks and mindset to unlock the true potential of B2B marketing. A highly practical and essential read."
Ritchie Mehta, Founder, School of Marketing

"*B2B Marketing Fundamentals* offers the reader an important approach and the tools required to succeed in the fast-paced world of B2B Marketing. Building on a true understanding of the market and other key stakeholder needs, readers are challenged to define humanized growth opportunities that drive long-term value for the business and all other key stakeholders. A must-read for all B2B marketers that want to be a step ahead."
Marc de Swaan Arons, Founder, Institute for Real Growth

B2B Marketing Fundamentals

Drive impact across brand, reputation, relationships and revenue

Kate Mackie

KoganPage

First published in Great Britain and the United States in 2025 by Kogan Page Limited.

Kogan Page
Kogan Page Ltd, 2nd Floor, 45 Gee Street, London EC1V 3RS, United Kingdom
Kogan Page Inc, 8 W 38th Street, Suite 90, New York, NY 10018, USA
www.koganpage.com

EU Representative (GPSR)
Authorised Rep Compliance Ltd, Ground Floor, 71 Baggot Street Lower, Dublin D02 P593, Ireland
www.arccompliance.com

Kogan Page books are printed on paper from sustainable forests.

ISBNs

Hardback	978 1 3986 1966 1
Paperback	978 1 3986 1964 7
Ebook	978 1 3986 1965 4

British Library Cataloguing-in-Publication Data

A CIP record for this book is available from the British Library.

Library of Congress Control Number

2025934387

Typeset by Integra Software Services, Pondicherry
Print production managed by Jellyfish
Printed and bound by CPI Group (UK) Ltd, Croydon CR0 4YY

To

James, Edie, Arlo and Digby,

with love and huge thanks

CONTENTS

LIST OF FIGURES AND TABLES

ABOUT THE AUTHOR

Kate is a board level marketer with a proven track record in collaboration, influencing and stakeholder management. She excels at leading global teams to achieve business goals and financial objectives, driving lasting change. Future-focused, she continually disrupts marketing from within to leverage technology and artificial intelligence.

As a key business adviser, Kate adds valuable brand, customer and marketing perspectives to commercial decisions. She is a revenue-driven marketer focused on optimizing results to drive long-term brand value and sustainable business outcomes. Her extensive experience spans professional and financial services, as well as broad consumer marketing and creative consultancy, including sectors such as charity, fast-moving consumer goods, automotive, travel and lifestyle brands.

Kate is a Fellow of the Marketing Society, an alumnus of the Institute for Real Growth and a Fellow of the Chartered Institute of Marketing. She is regularly a judge on awards selecting best brands, awarding agency accolades and ensuring marketing excellence has B2B representation. Kate was included in the Cranfield School of Management 'Women to Watch 2024'. She is an active coach and mentor for individuals, businesses and social enterprises looking to accelerate their growth. She is also a guest lecturer at Cambridge Judge Business School.

Kate lives with her husband, two children and a dog in the wilds of Wiltshire.

All views are Kate's own.

FOREWORD

Marketing is, in my – admittedly very biased opinion – one of the very best professions in which to work. Marketing leaders must adopt a blend of art and science. They need to mix commercial understanding with creative judgment, balancing 'logic and magic'. This combination makes it a fascinating world in which to operate. This together with the critical need for marketers to influence internally as well as have impact externally helps mean that marketing roles, especially as they get more senior, are rarely straightforward ones. They require smart, strong people to do them well, and the best of these marketers are perpetually curious.

If you are reading this book, then you are one of the 'curious ones', which also means that you are smart enough to understand how much we can learn from each other, and that one of the quickest ways to progress in business is by building on the successes and insights of other people's experiences.

As the global chief executive officer for The Marketing Society, I regularly see the best and the brightest marketers using the stories and frameworks of others to help sharpen their thinking and approach. We are a global community of change leaders who work to unlock the best in each other. We believe brilliant marketers should lead the conversation in business. Together, we have the power and potential to grow our organizations effectively. We can lead change not only within our businesses but also in the broader economy and society. Together we achieve more than when we do it alone.

So, I am delighted that Kate, a Fellow of The Marketing Society (an accolade we award to only a few of our most impressive members), has shared her insights and ideas in this great book.

This is an important moment in time for this book to appear.

Business-focused brands have, for a while, been seen by some as less innovative in their approach to marketing. Meanwhile, the very shape of marketing itself has transformed irrevocably; the expectations of business and consumer buyers are converging, competing for attention and driving consumer-grade 'experience expectations'. Add to this the broader contextual disruption facing today's business leaders, and B2B marketing now has much more to accomplish – often with less budget.

As businesses strive to thrive, marketing is a powerful growth lever that B2B business leaders need to understand. The function represents the voice of clients and customers and should be embraced to drive the change needed to optimize towards business priorities. This will only work, of course, if you, as a marketer, can understand and translate to the commercial language of your stakeholders. You need to understand what your business is trying to achieve, its operating model and the broader market trends and context.

Marketers are uniquely positioned to drive both long- and short-term growth, breaking down silos to connect the internal dots for the benefit of your customers. To maximize the impact, your marketing leader needs to have a seat at the top table. This will ensure they can align to the commercial outcomes, connecting data and technology for the benefit of a frictionless customer experience and driving the cultural shift needed to become a truly client-centric business.

As we look ahead, it is increasingly the responsibility of the marketing community to embed the sustainability story, driving demand from both businesses and consumers to drive the commerciality of a greener future. We can drive huge impact and should wield our power wisely. We need to be marketing leaders for the planet.

This book is designed to provide the fundamental process for you as a marketer to build your marketing plan, and act as the commercial story-teller, translating your strategy into a growth story for your business leaders. It provides you with the fundamentals that you can build on to accelerate your career and build your influence within your company. That's a power-ful and exciting outcome for you, as a future changemaker and a change leader in your business.

I love 'frameworks' that help speed up thinking and planning processes (as marketers, there's never enough time in our days or weeks). These funda-mentals will help you ask the right questions, but the answers will be up to you, and the results of working through them, will – I am sure – ignite more great stories of marketing-driven business success that will inspire others.

Great marketing illuminates the path forward and the best leaders bring clarity, warmth and light the way for others. We can't do it alone – and 'the fundamentals' will help as stepping stones to your strategy and success.

I encourage you to embrace this opportunity, invest in your learning and dare to lead. I look forward to hearing what great stories and successes result.

Sophie Devonshire
CEO, The Marketing Society and Author of Superfast: Lead at Speed

PS. If you are reading this and we aren't already connected on LinkedIn,
please do come and say hello, or email me at sophie@marketingsociety.com.
I'd love to know your thoughts on how and where we should champion
B2B marketing excellence more – and what you think of this book.

ACKNOWLEDGEMENTS

I hope you enjoy reading this as much as I enjoyed writing it. The content brings together the experiences across my career, in both B2C and B2B, across agencies and brands. I have met many brilliant people along the way and am grateful for all the support, help and encouragement from folk I met at the beginning of my career through to those that mentor and coach me today.

Writing a book was not on my to-do list, so when Donna Goddard-Skinner approached me, it took me a while to say yes. Thank you, Donna, for persevering. Thank you, Jeylan Ramis and Bobbi-Lee Wright, for all your help in bringing the proposal to life. I appreciate the comments, nudges and backing as I squeezed writing the book into an already overstuffed life. Thank you to all at Kogan Page for your help in making this a reality.

Thank you to all my colleagues along the way. I have learnt a massive amount from you and am hugely grateful for all of you. Marketing is a team sport, and I am so proud to have been on the A-Team throughout my career. This book is written personally, not professionally, which means I will be keeping this thank you short and open to all!

To all the contributors – those formally contributing thoughts and writing to this publication – and those thought leaders in the industry who share their thinking online and at events, your insights make me hugely enthusiastic about the future of B2B, B2C's often more difficult cousin. Special thanks to Elliot Moss, Vonnie Alexander, Lorelei Lenzen, Ian Ewart, Roo Mackie, Tom Steiner, Kat Williams, Sophia Kakabadse and Becca Watts for allowing me to share their perspectives.

A huge thank you to Sophie Devonshire for her brilliant foreword, her never-ending enthusiasm and passion for marketing. Without The Marketing Society, I would not have met many of the inspiring people who have given me the opportunity to test ideas, including Ritchie Mehta, who leads the brilliant School of Marketing. Thanks, too, to Victoria Fox, an inspiration in our Carlson days and a fantastic sparring partner today. Thanks to Vonnie for helping me navigate work and life – you really are incredible. Thank you also to Graeme Robertson, a brilliant mentor from day one.

Thank you to my readers – Ruth Buckley-Finch, Simon Barnett and Juliet Machan – and my constant cheerleaders – the Awesomes (Rachel, Christina and Claire), my bridesmaids Katie and Becky (yes, it is for life) and the

Southport crew (Katherine, Sarah and Louisa). A heartfelt thanks to Paul Jones for his fantastic advice.

Thank you to my friends, many of whom I have actively ignored throughout this process. I appreciate the time you have given me to focus, but really want to see you soon! Thank you also to the extended family of Aindows, Inghams, Holdings and Mackies for bearing with me while I have been distracted.

Thank you to my parents, Peter and Sue Ingham, for reading through everything in forensic grammatical detail – praise doled out in bucketfuls as always – 'at least it is better than your dissertation'.

To Edie and Arlo, I am incredibly proud of the kind people that you are and the agility with which you deal with what life throws at you.

And, finally, James. Who knew that a trip to Australia would lead to all of this? Thank you for everything, I really couldn't do any of it without you. Thank you.

Introduction: The untapped power of B2B marketing

Having spent countless hours working with, coaching and mentoring B2B marketers, there is one question I get asked time and again:

How do I prove the value of marketing in my...

business

function

leadership team

industry?

These individuals feel the need, quite rightly, to justify their existence. Over time, I've become increasingly concerned that B2B marketers are so overwhelmed with day-to-day execution that they are not able to answer this question as well as they should, or worse still, give it any serious thought at all.

Add to this the fact that marketing is often positioned as a cost centre in B2B, which means that many are missing the chance to elevate, and embed, the conversation around business benefits alongside the magic of well-executed creative.

Marketing means business

The modern marketer not only needs to talk the language of the business, they also need to ensure that marketing is a leading voice in developing business strategy. A voice that champions value creation and shapes the levers for both top- and bottom-line growth.

The B2B industry continues to evolve and grow. Kantar's BrandZ report for 2024 shows that the Business Technology and Services Platform category grew by 45 per cent year on year and sits as the most valuable category with an overall value of $2.3 trillion, making up 28 per cent of the value of the top 100 brands.[1]

There is a huge opportunity for the B2B marketer to step up and own opportunities in front of them. They have a duty to their teams, as well as a responsibility to their customers and clients, to bring marketing to the table. They need to educate the business they work with about the potential growth and innovation if marketing is embraced throughout their business. By understanding marketing, driving connected experiences and putting customers at the heart of their organization, the potential for both short- and long-term growth is huge – balancing the science of marketing with the well-trodden art of creativity.

Marketers who can do this will be well on their way to showing that marketing means business.

How this book will help

This book goes back to basics, to the fundamental principles that continue to resonate despite channel fragmentation, technology disruption and a proliferation of potential competitors.

It will help marketers as well as those who work alongside marketing functions. Its aim is to help you understand how best to unlock the power of marketing within the B2B landscape and create real business value.

I will share theory, methods and frameworks I use, or have seen used, to great effect. These are interspersed with external perspectives that will enable you to have a broader understanding of the application of theory to build into your own planning.

Marketers are very good at communicating with themselves, measuring success through functional metrics, many of which are marketing jargon and therefore stop the conversation from rising to a business level. Throughout the chapters focused on marketing detail, I will include a translation into the broader business language – how you can speak to those not in marketing to facilitate their understanding of the impact outside of the measurement and analytics that are common to our function. Aligning with the key performance indicators of your business will drive a different conversation with your organizational leadership and will help you unlock greater investment in marketing. It is essential to mesh the marketing objectives with the broader business objectives so that your programmes can deliver the outcomes agreed on with your business stakeholders.

Defining stakeholders is an interesting task. The definitions of stakeholder groups outside of the traditional set will be discussed in detail in Chapter 4, where we will cover engagement and targeting of the various internal and external groups. The definition of stakeholders follows those identified as part of the Embankment project for inclusive capitalism that looks across employees, clients, financial stakeholders and society, with this latter group including the full gamut of the environmental, social and governance definitions.[2] This business approach to broadening stakeholder thinking aligns with the work coming out of the Institute for Real Growth,[3] a fantastic marketing community and think-tank who have recently published their humanized growth report which comes to very similar conclusions.

The fundamentals

This book is broken down into 10 chapters, starting with the creation and targeting of marketing plans through to the specific areas of focus that will help you to drive impact across brand, reputation, relationships and revenue (BRRR). There has been a significant step change recently with the recognition that the power of a brand is as important in the B2B space as it is in B2C. I think that this is an absolute no-brainer.

We sell to people.

They buy what emotionally resonates with them on many different levels.[4] Selling in B2B is absolutely driven by brand, but the credibility of the brand – and trust in the relationship with the brand itself – is even more important.

I always explain this by saying that no one gets sacked for buying the wrong toothpaste, whereas buying the wrong services, technology, ingredients or raw materials could land you in hot water at work. The B2B conundrum is infusing emotion, purpose and value into something that can range from an intangible outcome in the services industry through to something so tangible it is used to build houses. The increased monetary value marketing can help deliver by aiding the conversion of one-off purchases into an annuity relationship is in the millions.

It is the right time to reach into the untapped power of B2B marketing by elevating the conversation so that you can speak the language of the chief financial officer and be credible in the boardroom.

Any board or ExCo members who have a background in finance or have been part of additional management training will have touched on the importance of marketing. There are plenty of folk I have spoken to who instil fear into a career marketer by saying, 'I love marketing – I did a module at university' as they roll up their sleeves to get into marketing as a hobbyist. This is typically double edged. With enough knowledge to be dangerous, but generally not the up-to-date information to have the marketing conversation in today's context, it's a relationship you need to build on and elevate as a modern marketing advocate.

With strategic B2B marketing gaining traction, we are ahead of where we once were when B2B was previously seen as the poor cousin of B2C, focused only on events and recruitment – both of which have a role to play but are not the be all and end all focus for the function. Many marketing agencies are also recognizing the potential revenues to be made by leaning into the B2B space.

The four main sections of this book cover the following.

Brand

The current themes of many brand campaigns in the B2B space are dry, pragmatic and focus solely on the tangible. This, to me, is utter madness; it is incredibly important that the B2B message is based on a core value proposition that resonates creatively and emotionally with multiple buyers as individuals around the boardroom table will interrogate the positioning, looking for reasons to believe that the message resonates at both a personal and business level.

The definition of a brand, from my experience, is what is said about it and how it makes you feel. The feeling the brand gives you is perhaps the most important aspect of this. You need to show up how you want to be seen. If you are selling technology, your sales team should not turn up with battered phones and laptops, providing an analogue experience that's full of friction. If you do, you will not be seen as a credible tech brand. It is key that the brand experience follows through whenever a potential buyer encounters the brand, enabling the potential customer to feel a connected brand experience at all touchpoints. This needs to extend beyond the marketing function.

A brand is what a brand does, and it therefore needs to be credibly experienced from every angle in order to be seen as sustainable. For instance, there needs to be authenticity across the internal supply chains and policies aligned to the statements made externally. This is even more important when you are dealing with sales of services and larger, enterprise-wide sales. A sales team needs to embody the brand. This is also why a company's culture and employee value proposition are key – connecting the brand with the talent in the business.

Long-term brand growth is key to long-term revenue growth. While there has been a more recent focus on short-term activation, demand generation and the associated metrics, it has often been argued that this overly short-term focus disables long-term brand growth. Brand building is ultimately about getting a long-term revenue effect whereas short-term activation is about the immediate impact.

Les Binet explained in a WARC podcast back in 2020 that smart marketers can build a brand long term and effectively set it in forward motion.[5] Building it for the long term enables a preference to be built for the brand, which then gets converted into cash. He goes onto stress that both the long- and short-term jobs are necessary as they enhance each other and therefore need to be done in balance.

Reputation

It is critical to protect, build and amplify the reputation of a brand, which is connected with brand growth and both short- and long-term revenue. Multiple strands of reputation should weave together to build your story across different channels. We will deal with each in turn, but in this section, public relations is the backbone of the external focus, supported through social media, social influence and other broader influencers. In many cases, these others – like analysts – are increasingly relevant in large-scale, enterprise-level sales.

Mid- to bottom-funnel thinking, where customer behaviour and aligned decisions are moving closer to a sale, either as an individual or as an account, is driven by the search for evidence of the brand's reputation. This is a focus on credentializing the potential purchase: getting the buyer comfortable with their buying decision. This then requires content that brings to life case studies, thought leadership and the outcomes other companies and businesses have benefitted from, establishing the features and benefits that are key to the offer.

Another element of reputation building that is important to B2B, and gaining in greater importance, is the ecosystem built to enable cohesive growth at pace. Ensuring your business has the best partners available to you across industries, leaning on the experts in their fields and amplifying the joint message is beneficial to both parties.

Relationships

Building and deepening relationships is fundamental to unlocking the full value of a customer or client. This becomes increasingly important in more complex sales across an account where the focus needs to align on the entire potential of the purchase as you might be looking to build trusted relationships to drive annuity revenue over multi-year opportunities.

We know that people will always buy from people – particularly from those that they trust. This extends to their sales rep, their account team, business development team or reseller. Marketing helps build the relationship experience throughout the campaign lifecycle, moving individuals from unknown to known via both on and offline channels.

Providing the right content throughout the buyer journey and relating to the needs of the individual helps the seller understand what resonates with the audience. It also signals what type of content they are likely to engage with and, therefore, where the buyer is in the purchase decision. Buyers balance self-navigation of the user journey with guided interventions which help them move to the next best action in their decision making.

As an increasing part of the journey is self-navigated, a brand must eliminate friction and only intervene as signals show interest. Face-to-face events and meetings can help to deepen and strengthen the relationship, providing deeper, more personalized experiences which enable a similarly deep relationship.

Pooling all data – from both individuals and across the buying group at an account level – helps to connect the signals to show opportunities that might exist across an enterprise. Customer relationship management (CRM) tools are key if you are a large, multi-geo brand targeting similarly organized enterprises. Relationships, and ultimately sales, that cross borders geographically and link across siloed functions need to be managed carefully so as to not endanger the next step of the buyer journey.

Data at an aggregated account level also shows the sales teams where, within an account, an individual is most engaged and should be pursued. There are often models in place that highlight these marketing qualified contacts or leads that can then be validated and followed up by the relevant sales teams. This is often a point of contention which we will go into later in Chapter 8.

Account-based marketing (ABM) is a strategy to treat accounts as a market in their own right and is particularly relevant when the sale is relationship-driven and people-based. Strategies are developed to focus on a number of individual accounts or small segments of potentially high value accounts with offers, products and services that are relevant to their needs.

ABM has gained real traction across B2B marketing and is an area of focus that we will work through.

Revenue

The fourth area of impact is, of course, revenue. As we move through the funnel along the client's sales cycle, we track from brand to demand and ultimately enable marketing influenced revenue (MIR) to be delivered. Often, the optimal sale – the end game – is a high value, high margin, annuity sale with ongoing regular sales delivering growth at all levels. To get to this will likely take a number of years of investment and macro effort across brand and reputation, with aligned targeted support at both the account and buyer level to deepen the relationships across the entire buying group before being able to approach the highest value sales.

Working out what the entire target addressable market (TAM) is for your business model will help you understand what share of the market you have and thereby set targets for revenue growth and market penetration.

You will likely be tasked with in-year targets that feel at odds with longer-term investments. Balancing these two is a challenge for all marketing functions. Much has been written in this space as it is an ongoing tussle between those who believe long and short term are opposed. I am aligned more to a term coined by Mark Ritson: Bothism.[6] It is a two-horse race with a balance of investment reflective of where you are currently positioned in the market and what you are trying to achieve. You must look at both short-term and long-term success – ensuring you have revenue today and revenue tomorrow – tracking through MIR as a key indicator of success for the impact on top line growth. Looking at the influence of marketing on lead conversion with a focus on shortening the sales cycle and ensuring that all processes are as streamlined as possible drives bottom line margin. In tech-enabled markets, building assets, initiatives and programmes that can be built once but used for multiple opportunities releases time, effort and ultimately capital to be focused on the next potential sale.

The handshake between the sales teams and marketing teams is integral to success – an interlocked single strategy targeting the right buyers to deliver the optimal outcomes. A successful co-created plan enables the marketing team to warm up the market, driving awareness of new products, solutions and services, moving the buyer closer to the point of purchase, which will range from a one-off transaction to an ongoing annuity relationship which requires continuous nurturing to advance the growth potential.

Marketing measurement

Wherever your plan ends up and whatever your tactics are, you must ensure that you are able to report against your objectives. By ensuring you can report and measure across all areas of impact on a regular basis, you will be able to:

1 demonstrate the worth of the investment in marketing

2 pitch for what you need with agreed metrics

3 drive a clear understanding of the function as a source of value creation.

When used in the correctly connected way, marketing is a growth lever for the business to drive predictive revenues with clear return on investment (ROI) and demonstrable long-term growth metrics. Using marketing wisely is integral to business success. We will work through this as we touch on all areas of impact throughout the rest of this book.

Impact of AI

I will also touch on the current thinking and influence of artificial intelligence (AI) on marketing. This is an area that is moving fast, with Generative AI exploding into common usage. I will cover how you can approach this, the fundamental principles of application and the basic strategies you need to apply alongside the work you need to do with your data, processes and creative thinking in order to leverage AI to its current potential. However, due to the speed at which this moves, there will be newer applications and tools that disrupt these functional applications that are not covered here. I will also embed the use of current marketing technologies into the conversation, which come with the same caveat.

With marketing being touted as one of the functions most likely to be disrupted by GenAI with particular focus concentrated on the areas of search, content development, advertising targeting and digital, there is a drive to embrace the upside and efficiencies in front of us – with some individuals thinking that this will result in a declining need for marketing professionals in the future. I challenge this thought as I do believe that there will be a continued requirement for right-skilled marketers who are able to interrogate the wealth of signals being shown by our customers. Individuals who are able to dive in deep to the heart of their businesses and challenge the functional expectations and commercialize the B2B marketing function will be in high demand.

There are great lessons to be learned from our B2C brethren, particularly those in FMCG-focused companies who often operate with full financial responsibility for their brand. There is a greater necessity for insightful, value-focused individuals who can use AI to drive towards optimal business outcomes.

Personalization at scale has been talked about ever since the inception of e-commerce and as an area of focus with its increasing sophistication from the early 2000s. This is now coming to fruition – and in a way never considered previously – both driving greater creative opportunities and opening up unique challenges.

This book will cover the pitfalls, the watchouts and the best practices to take advantage of where we are today, starting with the fundamentals which includes a focus on the foundational approaches we all need to take. The first step is clean and well-organized data structured for use across all customer touchpoints, ideally at both the individual and connected account level, to enable targeting across a business's buyer demand unit – a term coined by Forrester in 2020 to indicate those within a business who are the group of multifunction buyers that will ultimately cover any purchase.[7] I will go into the detail of this approach, with strategies specific to this B2B need, within Chapter 4.

We know that buyers in the B2B context do not follow a straightforward path to purchase, and this becomes more difficult where a complex service-based sale is the approach as it takes many influencers, decision makers and procurement professionals to get a deal across the line. This means internal marketing teams need to work hand in glove with the sales, business development and account teams to drive the maximum value from prospective customers and clients.

I should also explain why I feel I have permission to pick up a pen in this space. My background was originally in integrated agencies focusing on financial services from both a B2B and a B2C angle across the full spread of banking, wealth and asset management. Along the way I also worked across many B2C/FMCG brands, delivering award-winning initiatives across everything from an on-pack promotion for Anchor butter – 'Make a Moo' – and social media campaigns promoting travel across the Emerald Isle with Tourism Ireland to encouraging dog owners with a 'Nicer to neuter' charitable programme for Dogs Trust.

I've worked my way through integrated networked agencies, across data and digital specialist boutiques where I focused on huge brand launches, innovative app developments and digital experience delivery. As an account-focused client server in agency land, I took a sidestep into two of the largest B2B brands, firstly GE and then to my current professional home at EY. This has helped me understand that the translation of objectives to outcomes remains core no matter which audience you are targeting.

'Back to the fundamentals' has been my long-beaten drum. Every human makes purchase decisions for uniquely different reasons, but they all send buying signals we can read and respond to as long as you set up your plans and programmes in an optimal way so the data can be rolled into insights at both an individual and account level.

I also regularly mentor and teach at the School of Marketing. I find that those without formal training often ask where to start and what I would recommend as a starting place. This book gives the fundamental approaches that I follow, gleaned through years of experience – both successes and failures. I am sharing them here for the benefit of the next generation of marketers. Selfishly, this means I can explain it in detail once and then direct people to the same place to answer the questions regularly asked.

References

1 D Walter. Kantar BrandZ: 2024 Most Valuable Global Brands, 2024. www.kantar.com/campaigns/brandz-downloads/kantar-brandz-most-valuable-global-brands-2024 (archived at https://perma.cc/PH3Z-C4MQ)

2 Coalition for Inclusive Capitalism. The Embankment Project for Inclusive Capitalism, 2021. https://coalitionforinclusivecapitalism.com/wp-content/uploads/2021/01/coalition-epic-report.pdf (archived at https://perma.cc/7WYB-5K6K)

3 Institute for Real Growth. IRG Impact Study, 2023. instituteforrealgrowth.com/Impact-study.html (archived at https://perma.cc/R5ZL-8QJ8)

4 System 1 Group (2024) https://system1group.com/methodology (archived at https://perma.cc/7U96-4WLF)

5 L Binet. Les Binet on why long-term marketing matters in the age of short-termism, WARC, 10 January 2020. www.warc.com/newsandopinion/opinion/les-binet-on-why-long-term-marketing-matters-in-the-age-of-short-termism/en-gb/33073. (archived at https://perma.cc/38BY-97C5)

6 M Ritson. 'Bothism' is the cure for marketers' fascination with pointless conflict, Marketing Week, 3 September 2020. www.marketingweek.com/ritson-bothism-cure-marketers-fascination-conflict/ (archived at https://perma.cc/HB5T-DYFV)

7 Forrester Best Practice Report. Demand Unit Waterfall™ Target and Active Stages: Business Requirements, 2020. www.forrester.com/report/demand-unit-waterfall-tm-target-and-active-stages-business-requirements/RES171631 (archived at https://perma.cc/VCV4-Z8HL)

1

Marketing as a business function

Marketing is not a back-office function.

Instead, marketing is a core business function focused on promoting and selling products or services, engaging customers, creating brand awareness and generating leads and ultimately revenue. It involves nurturing individuals from unknown to known audience members and engaging them through to a sale.

Back-office functions are those that support and empower the organization to operate more effectively and efficiently. These functions can include information technology, human resources, finance and operational management. They are designed to optimize the internal processes and infrastructure, providing the tools, systems and support necessary for the core business functions like sales, marketing, product development and customer service to carry out their roles successfully. The distinction is that marketing is outward-facing (focused on the market and customers), while business enablement or back-office functions are inward-facing (focused on internal processes and capabilities).

It is important to note that marketing should focus on reducing the operational friction of their part in the sales process, but this is in service of the client and is focused on the user experience.

The main drivers within the marketing function ultimately align to two key outcomes. The function drives top-line revenue growth by increasing sales. It should also make the sales process more effective and more efficient to reduce the friction and drive bottom-line margin. Both sets of outcomes are key to elevating the strategic importance of the function. In light of these areas of focus, we need to reframe the way a business thinks about their marketing function. In many B2B industries, marketers are more likely to be seen as a cost centre rather than a centre of value creation. But, by doing so and viewing marketing as a cost centre, you are missing out on the potential impact of an important lever for growth.

This is a space B2B can learn from B2C. In B2C the power of marketing is clear and well understood, with direct links to revenue. The more traditional FMCG companies – the Unilevers and P&Gs of this world, in particular – train their brand managers to treat their individual brands as businesses in their own right, with full responsibility across the brands' profit and loss (P&L) from new product development through supply chain management to marketing support.

Understanding the world of your CFO and finance function is the key to being taken seriously as a commercial marketer. Being able to speak the language of finance and translating how you look at growth is foundational. You must be able to connect the hard financial outcomes to the marketing metrics and buying signals within your gift to control.

Knowing where all facets of the marketing function are positioned on the P&L will also guide how you set up marketing investments to effectively deliver optimal cost management for the longer term over multiple years. For instance, brands are intangible assets that take years of investment over time to increase their value. This value is often only realized when a brand is bought, sold or licensed. The consistent and ongoing influence of your brand drives absolute sales growth and revenue metrics – proving this is the basis for driving a highly successful relationship with your leadership team. How to explain this impact, alongside the increased impact of the brand on other intangibles like culture, employee engagement and trust, will be covered in further detail in Chapter 5.

P&L: A profit and loss statement is a financial report that shows how much your business has spent and earned over a specified time. It also shows whether you have made a profit or a loss over that period of time. A profit and loss statement might also be called a P&L or an income statement.

OpEx: Operating expenditure/expense refers to the ongoing day-to-day costs incurred while running a product, business or system. These costs span the course of a year and need to be spent within that time frame.

CapEx: Capital expenditure/expense refers to the major long-term costs of acquiring tangible assets to be used over an extended period and can be amortized (paid-off) over a longer multi-year period of time.

Marketing investments: Can be seen as a combination of both OpEx and CapEx depending on the investment itself. You should speak with your CFO and understand their position and how they are treating the marketing spend. Working with the CFO when building your budget asks can help make the ask more palatable!

Uncovering the objectives across your business

The first step in building a strategic marketing plan is to understand what your business is striving to achieve. Understanding the long-term company vision, corporate values and purpose alongside the detailed business objectives is fundamental to you being able to set aligned marketing objectives that will help drive successful business outcomes. It is also important to understand what is driving the leadership team, both their collective and individual areas of focus across your business and, often more importantly, their personal objectives.

Vision: The hill your business is trying to climb. The desired future state.

Purpose: The reason your business exists. Its position in the world and how it drives forward.

Values: The way you deliver your business – your moral compass.

There is a movement towards businesses focusing on driving long-term business objectives that align with more than just the short-term gain of the shareholder – looking at people and planet as well as profit.

A strategic approach was developed by the Embankment Project for Inclusive Capitalism where a broad group of companies came together to identify and create new metrics to measure and demonstrate long-term value to financial markets across four areas of value: financial, consumer, human and societal. The 2018 EPIC report goes into detail around the development of this thinking and the increased growth seen as an outcome of focusing business objectives on the holistic long-term value a business can drive.[1] In 2022, BlackRock CEO Larry Fink wrote a letter to the CEOs of the businesses BlackRock invests in, stating: 'In today's globally interconnected world, a company must create value for and be valued by its full range of stakeholders in order to deliver long-term value for its shareholders.'[2] With this stance becoming more prevalent, understanding the objectives of your business across the four areas of value is key.

Another player in this space, but more specifically focused on marketing, is the Institute for Real Growth (IRG). The global IRG Impact Study shows that overperforming companies drive a new kind of growth that addresses the needs of all stakeholders – colleagues, customers, communities and the capital markets – and refers to this type of growth as 'humanized growth'.[3]

As an alumnus of the 2021 IRG100 Leadership Program, which is an executive programme that connects 100 marketing and growth leaders, helping them drive greater impact across all stakeholders, I can see that the focus of humanized growth is not dissimilar to that of long-term value. Consolidating the two approaches gives us a foundation from which to think about holistic business objectives and how marketing objectives might align.

Looking at the consolidated value metrics, business objectives can be allocated to these four areas of focus.

Financial/capital markets

Revenue – Sometimes referred to as top-line sales or as turnover it equals the total amount of income generated by the sale of goods and services. Most businesses are looking to maximize their revenue.

Expenses – The total costs incurred in running the business and delivering the goods and services. Businesses often have objectives relating to cost control. These are looking at how you drive efficiencies – economies of scope or scale – alongside driving down costs or expenses themselves. Freeing up costs enables investments in other areas that future proof your business. This type of strategy is often referred to as 'save to invest', as over the long term it will drive more efficient costs. For instance, investing in a single customer data platform across a business not only reduces the cost of siloed data platforms but will also enable better connectivity, plus a more effective and efficient customer experience.

Profit/margin – The money left over once all expenses incurred in running the business have been paid. Revenue minus expenses equals profit margin or net income and is often referred to as 'maximising your bottom line'. Creating efficiencies reduces costs and expenses, therefore increasing margin which can help make your business more profitable without increasing its overall revenues. The rise of AI-driven business models across all industries is forcing companies to look at their operating models to optimize the balance of people and technology to drive long-term commercial success.

Sustainable growth – A sustainable growth rate (SGR) is calculated as the optimal growth a business can deliver, or sustain, without additional capital investment. We often also refer to sustainable growth where growth is determined in terms of the broader impact across people, profit and the planet – a more ethical and purpose-driven approach to success akin to driving long-term value, with a focus on expanding the business in a stable way for the good of all stakeholders.

Consumer/customer

Market share – In order to understand what you might be aiming for as an appropriate market share you should assess the market, define your target audience and understand the target-addressable market for your product. The business objective would be to optimize and increase your share of this base. This is often looked at in terms of increasing the number of customers alongside increasing your share of wallet, so you would look to target both net new customers and look to create upsell opportunities within your current base.

Customer value – A business might focus on increasing value from their current base of customers to optimize the efficiencies of customer acquisition. This could be looked at as an increase in deal size or scope, so both upsell and cross-sell opportunities. You should also measure the customer lifetime value (CLV) so that the true cost of acquisition can be calculated over the entire relationship, with the customer and the total value of the relationship understood. Sales and marketing strategies can then align to the most cost-effective channels and programmes that recruit the clients with the highest CLV.

Customer experience – Understanding the full detail of your customer lifecycle will enable you to align all functions internally to maximize the experience received during the relationship you have with a buyer. This can then be measured with customer satisfaction and Net Promotor Scores (NPS). This is a critical area to measure within service-based organizations which have larger deal sizes and dispersed client relationships. We will cover the detail of marketing planning around a client lifecycle in Chapter 3.

Sales – Your business will likely develop specific sales targets by category, product line, industry and geography, alongside any combination of these factors. The sales organization will aim to directly increase sales metrics against these targets. The marketing function should work closely with the sales teams and account teams to enable efficient lead generation and focus on upsell and cross-sell within current buyer groups. There may also be attention placed on the churn metrics: how quickly do people fall out of a buying group or choose not to renew a particular product or service? Minimizing churn would align with a focus on customer retention to reduce the spend on customer acquisition. This is hugely important across all buyer groups and the full client lifecycle.

Human/colleagues

Employee satisfaction, engagement and retention – Productivity increases when employee satisfaction is high. When your employees are engaged it reduces the employee churn, enabling retention which minimizes talent acquisition costs.[4] Depending on the focus of your business, your people might also be your product, this is particularly true in professional services, e.g. legal or consulting firms.

Learning and development – Your business will likely have goals aligned to the learning and development needs of your workforce, often driving a focus on new skills in the market. For example, it is top of many leadership agendas to ensure that employees know how to augment their skillsets with AI to take advantage of the efficiencies that technology can unlock. Your people are also key to your brand as they are embedded in delivering your clients' experience. It is therefore imperative that your workforce has the relevant skills to drive client satisfaction.

Culture – There is much written around the impact of culture on both top-line revenue and bottom-line margin, with those businesses investing in a positive employee-focused culture outperforming businesses that don't invest in this space. Two drivers of workplace culture are the purpose and brand – both need to be embedded within the culture so a consistent employee experience is delivered, the 'say-do' gap is minimized and the business can acquire and retain top talent.

Diversity, equity and inclusion (DE&I) – Your business might have objectives that promote inclusion throughout all intersects of diversity, ensuring that you have a workforce that is representative of the population in which you operate. Diversity and Inclusion has grown to include E – Equity – where social inclusion is also a focus. This is often reflected in recruitment strategies that include expanding university recruitment lists to encompass non-traditional campus hires, delivering apprentice-style programmes and measuring social mobility within the workplace. These

DE&I programmes should interlock with your marketing so that you have an authentic and credible position in the market. Diverse and inclusive procurement and supply chain strategies also need to be developed and embraced by your marketing operations teams and embedded in your agency strategies.

Societal/communities

Regulatory/compliance requirements – If your business is regulated, you will have to comply with the regulations driven by your industry and geographic footprint. These will have a broad impact on the governance of your business, your reporting timetables and what you can and, more importantly, can't say in the market. Depending on your geographic footprint you will also need to comply and report on the data regulation requirements for the markets that you operate in.

Quality – This is a key area to measure in many industries and categories. Quality metrics look at how well your products and services deliver to the customer requirements, safety standards and industry regulations. There are specifics within manufacturing, for instance, aligned to the industrialized production of standardized outputs, with minimal defects and minimal returns. In the services industry this aligns closely with client experience, but in some cases – e.g. financial services – will also apply to the services delivered.

Environmental, social and governance (ESG) – These standards are set to measure the impact of a business across the three ESG pillars. Environmental looks at the impact of your business on the planet, social on people alongside the wider community you operate in, with governance focusing on your impact on the capital market and alignment with corporate governance. There is often alignment with corporate social responsibility (CSR) programmes and sometimes also with the United Nations 17 sustainable development goals (SDGs).

This is not an exhaustive list, so you should make it a priority to understand how your business measures itself, how it defines success and what other functions are targeted with delivering.

Business objectives should include measurable targets that are set up to measure progress on the road to achieving the larger business vision. To enable successful execution any objectives (business, personal or marketing-specific) should be SMART.[5]

Specific: What are you trying to achieve? Who will need to be involved? Why are you focused on this space? Is the objective clear?

Measurable: How are you going to measure success? What will it look like when you succeed?

Achievable: Is the objective within your gift to deliver? Is it attainable from your starting position with the time, resources and support that you have?

Relevant: Is the broader business context in support of the objective? Will this aid the long-term vision for your company?

Time-bound: When will you deliver the outcome? Have you set target dates for reviews along the way?

Working out the regularity of reporting will depend on your business requirements. In a regulated industry such as finance or healthcare, you might need to report in alignment with the Governance needs and the cadence of the management committee meetings, e.g. board and executive committee, that will need to have oversight and approval of your functional strategy and execution plans.

Understanding your stakeholders' personal objectives

The other range of objectives you need to understand are the personal objectives of your leadership team. Personal business objectives are goals that each individual sets to achieve their business plan, making the most of their own abilities and aligning with their career aspirations. Getting to the heart of what the members of your leadership team are looking to achieve professionally and personally will help you drive more effective stakeholder management. In the same way, it is also useful for the team you lead to know your own personal objectives as team members can then align their own goals which in turn ensures greater connectivity across the function.

Personal business objectives can be within many different areas of focus. Three broad groupings are as follows.

Career progression

An individual might have specific areas that they are focusing on to drive their career forward to the next role or rank. Ensuring you are aware of this motivation and that the business plan is enabling this goal will bring greater alignment.

Personal brand

Each individual leader will have areas of their personal brand they are looking to amplify. Interlocking business programmes with the relevant individuals as spokespeople or experts will help build both the brand of the individual and the business. We will go into detail around building and driving a personal brand within Chapter 10.

Personal growth and upskilling

Building the right team can help accelerate execution. Knowing the areas of growth or learning that an individual is focused on and ensuring that they can both play to their areas of strength while developing new skills and gaining relevant new experiences will give a greater chance of success for the business.

We often talk about this as having 'skin in the game' – tying an individual's personal investment into a broader plan. This will drive the individual to act for the good of the plan and its aligned objectives so that you all share the potential upsides and downsides of success or failure. There is a great book by Nassim Nicholas Taleb, *Skin in the Game: Hidden asymmetries in daily life*, published in 2018, that goes into this detail on a broader scale.[6]

How is marketing measured?

Understanding how your business will measure marketing will drive how you set up your team. The specific approach your business ascribes to you and your function will determine who you need in your team, the model you need to set up to deliver the outcomes required by your business' footprint and what type of leader you need to be. It will also determine what you should build as management reporting – aligning your metrics to those that matter is mandatory if you are looking to be taken more seriously by your commercial colleagues.

As the marketing leader, you will need to set up detailed programme metrics so that you can optimize the channels, creative messaging and timing of your short-term programme activation alongside the longer-term brand metrics. These detailed marketing-focused metrics do not automatically translate to the rest of the business. The science of marketing is a functional language that those outside of the department do not understand.

As a communicator, the expectation is that you can translate detailed, complicated business issues and potential solutions into creative messaging. You need to apply this skill to enable you to sell marketing to non-marketers. I would hazard a guess that you are currently confusing your leadership team or taking them down blind alleys of vanity metrics. Education and a level set to the broader leadership team is key. This is a multi-pronged story that needs to be consistently told to all those that interact with your function.

While many of your business leaders will have done a module on marketing within their broader business degrees or MBAs and will understand the basics, you will need to define the value proposition your marketing team delivers to your business to ensure that you are being viewed as a growth lever. Driving an understanding of the value you deliver will also ensure that you are personally measured appropriately and therefore suitably compensated.

There are several areas of focus that you might lean more heavily towards depending on the life stage of your business, the industry you are in and the type of customer you serve.

Sales focused

Many newer businesses are more heavily focused on sales delivery and the role that marketing plays in the end-to-end process. Performance marketing, with lead generation as a key metric, will be a huge part of the playbook in this case.

Product focused

Companies that are heavily focused on their products will need a team with deep domain expertise in product marketing. Building value propositions, defining features and benefits and building out the detailed marketetecture will be core to the marketing plan.

Brand focused

If a business is more established and the category is well understood by the buying audience, a focus on brand will be key in driving a differentiated understanding of your offer. You will need to build in a greater level of investment for both your masterbrand and any relevant sub-brands.

Customer focused

A highly mature, or perhaps new and enlightened, business will build their operating model around a customer need. With a single-minded focus on the buyer, it will be key for your team to enable a frictionless experience and really understand the drivers of their purchase behaviours.

Setting your marketing function up for success

The focus of your function will also be hugely impacted by where and how your marketing function reports. This will underpin how the function is perceived within your business and, importantly, what the additional unsaid focus will be. There are several more common reporting lines depending on how the business values and measures the impact of marketing. These will determine how you as the marketing leader or team are able to build your function.

Marketing into the CEO

When marketing is combined with brand and communications – a brand, marketing and communications (BMC) function – it would normally line into the top of the organization. The control of the brand internally and externally alongside the power of communications and engagement naturally elevates the combined function, even where the real value of marketing is less well understood. This ensures that internal and external communications tell the same story to their relevant audiences while also protecting the brand – which is particularly important in a regulated industry such as finance, pharma or professional services – with both the industry regulators and broader stakeholders. Where there is the potential for regulatory issues to arise the BMC function will likely include public affairs or be closely linked via the legal or risk functions.

Marketing into the Chief Commercial/Revenue Officer

Often marketing and sales are in the same group or function and both report into a commercial leader/Chief Revenue Officer or similar. In order to balance the sales and marketing pendulum and not swing too far in either direction, an equally ranked leader should head each side of sales and marketing, set up as peers with a relationship established around a mutually developed and agreed plan. The challenges that can be faced in this set up are that marketing becomes beholden to short term sales targets and the longer-term, brand build investments are sidelined. This is often exacerbated if marketing reports solely into a sales leader. The reverse is also true, so the CCO or CRO needs to be able to balance the demands of both short term sales revenue and long-term brand build.

Marketing into other areas of the business

There are always other options, depending on what the focus of the function is, and it could be argued that this is a predictably circular conversation. If the marketing function lines into the product lead or customer lead, there is likely to be a greater focus on this area of expertise. Similarly, if the head of the function has a particular specialism, this personal objective is likely to seep into the focus of the function.

As your business matures and as its operating model shifts and changes to align to the needs of your customers or end users, the position of the function may move too. Business thinking waxes and wanes – with specifics coming in and out of focus depending on macro-economic forces, geopolitics and the market demands. Being able to position your function for success is key to navigating any disruption and ensuring you can optimize the outcomes for your customers.

Marketing operating models

Few of us will have the time and space to build the optimal marketing model from scratch, however many of us will be tasked with transforming or evolving the function. When you are given the task to drive change, or if you are part of the team defining the future, a simple approach to tackling this is by running through three sequential steps (Figure 1.1).

Strategy

Knowing the vision and mission of your business will enable you to define the role of marketing within the operating model.

FIGURE 1.1 Three steps to take to build your operating model

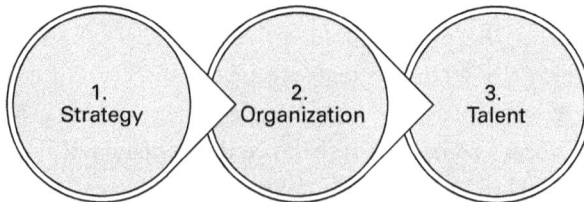

1. Strategy
2. Organization
3. Talent

What are the outcomes being influenced by the function?

How mature is your brand within the category?

Where in the value chain does marketing play?

Are you responsible for the holistic client experience?

Is it in your gift to deliver change and optimize the outcomes for the customer?

Do you own, or can you influence, after-sales customer service and longer-term relationship development?

The convergence of brand differentiation and customer experience has always been well known in the B2C world where it is often the biggest differentiator in a commoditized market. In retail banking, for instance, when customer rates are pegged to government-driven interest rates, the only real difference is the experience, with many banks aiming for the most frictionless experience possible.

In B2B, the marketing function owns the marketing communications and external position of the brand, but there is often a large proportion of the brand experience delivered in a more fragmented way through account teams, service delivery teams, customer/product success and many other fragments of the business.

Understanding how you can influence these broader teams will determine part of your structure, for instance internal communications will be key to driving the marketing message and ensuring the voice of the customer is heard throughout a more heavily fragmented business in a service-based industry. If you have an employee base that includes people focused on manufacturing or in a depot managing the despatch of products, you will often have to think through a highly segmented internal brand message that travels from the executive level to the shop floor and is applicable to all.

Organization structure

Building your team to ensure you have strategic flexibility to be able to adapt to new inputs, new insights and new customer needs will give you greater agility, relevance and longevity. To do so, you will need to move away from a linear value chain to a more collaborative model where domain experts can cycle in and out of a project at the right time. Depending on the scale of your business, you may need to think about dispersed geographic teams that ladder up to a common infrastructure where the handshake and interlock with the central team is key. You may be focused on driving a multiplicity of campaigns in numerous markets at any one time so will need a strong campaign team with channel management experts. There will likely be a need for strong domain expertise in the product or services space that sits adjacent to those with a focus on strategic optimization of the detailed plan. Throughout, you will need to ensure you have connected data and a deep understanding of your current and future client needs aligned with a core team who live and breathe the brand.

There are myriad ways to set up your organization, but the overarching approach comes back to these three basic models.

OUTCOME-FOCUSED STRUCTURE

Enabling your team to focus on driving growth with a clear outcome ensures a clarity of thought and prioritization that could otherwise end up layered within a functional or segmented organization. There will need to be soft networks within the harder-lined pillars where disciplines connect to ensure cohesion, e.g. a digital headcount within customer acquisition will need to work closely with a similarly tasked individual in the customer retention space to ensure the lifecycle of a customer feels unified. (See Figure 1.2.)

FIGURE 1.2 Outcome-focused organizational structure

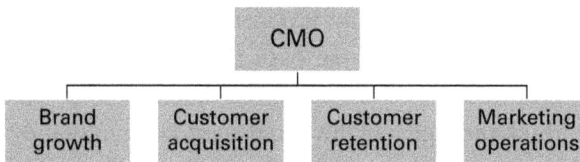

FUNCTIONAL-APPROACH STRUCTURE

This is a common approach that is built around the specialized skillsets found within the department and requires large, cross-team collaboration to deliver an end-to-end programme. (See Figure 1.3.) There will need to be a large amount of infrastructure set up to ensure the hand-offs across a campaign are understood and smooth. The product marketing teams will be key to planning the strategic plan across the broader pillar groups.

FIGURE 1.3 Functional-approach organizational structure

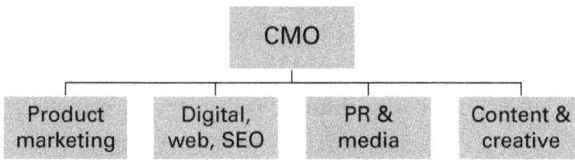

SEGMENTED/PRODUCT-FOCUSED STRUCTURE

A structure delivering to different segments of the business will need to replicate the specialisms within their own team, which means there can be costly duplication in each aligned team. The upside is that there is deep domain expertise and understanding of the product close to the business with new products and versions which are likely able to get to market more efficiently. (See Figure 1.4.)

For larger businesses, layering in multiple business units, geographies and sub-brands with their own aligned organizations will drive greater complexity, often moving to matrixed models that have layered leadership teams. The additional governance required needs to be resolved so that it does not slow down decision making and that teams closest to the client are able to move at the pace required by the market. Data-driven decision making is inherent in large-scale enterprises that allocate budget against functional outputs but, as in any creative industry, the balance of art and science is key.

FIGURE 1.4 Segmented/product-focused organizational structure

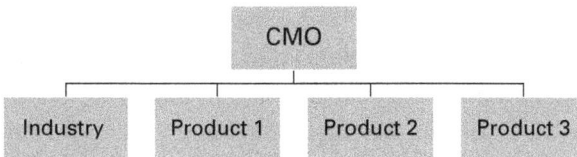

Talent

Making sure you have the right people with the appropriate mindset and skills in your team will enable you to have the agility and flexibility needed to reach your strategic destination, which will inevitably evolve as you move forward.

Today the conversations are all around the technology skills needed in your team. This is clearly an important topic and something we should cover; however, these skills will be outdated more quickly than we can print the list of 'hot' skills to invest in. The human skills that will be augmented through technology are much more important to consider and bring into your teams. With the advent of AI at scale, and a move to no-code and low-code development, this is absolutely where we should focus. Interpreting data and signals to drive real-time actionable insights and using technology to drive enterprise-level scale for the implementation of insights is the game changer. You will need people who can apply technology to a business problem, uncovering the optimal outcomes.

Curiosity and cognitive flexibility are paramount as they underpin an openness to learning and give the individual a high tolerance towards ambiguity, which will empower both the individual and the broader team to operate at the highest level. The ability to work in the grey with the information available also protects the individual from burnout.

Building collective intelligence

Culturally you need to set up your team for success. This means defining the values of your team, thinking through how you will build trust and transparency, how you will drive a functional reward and recognition programme and how you will provide equitable access to professional development. You will also need to ensure you build a feedback loop so that you can understand what lands and what needs to pivot. To build psychological safety, each individual needs to feel that they have a voice and are empowered and safe to voice their thinking. People need to recognize they can share and that their voice is relevant to the conversation. The added upside of operating in this inclusive way is that you will avoid building an echo chamber. This does not mean that everything is shiny and bright all the time with no conflict. Instead, it means that you embrace honesty, building from a platform of productive disagreement to get to an aligned outcome where all voices have been heard, concerns have been mitigated and a plan has been built together.

It has been proven that the more diverse the group, the more intelligent the collective is. To harness the collective intelligence, you will need to embrace a broad spectrum of opinions which means you need to build a safe space for discourse and disagreement. The 2023 McKinsey Diversity Matters Report shows that companies committed to diversity show a '39% increased likelihood of outperformance for those in the top quartile of ethnic representation versus the bottom quartile'.[7]

Collaboration and dot connecting

The marketing function is frequently seen as a dot connecting function. They are often the team that owns the voice of the customer and is the group that needs to be able to benchmark against external competitors and understand what drives an optimal customer experience. To do this they must be incredibly well connected through the business. When the function is across the full spectrum of marketing, including communications, a clear understanding of the business of your business will be foundational.

Collaboration points can be officially built into your planning cycle, where you as a function will report out against the agreed annual plan. It is wise to build in a moment to review the next period of execution, integrating any changes that might need to be made to reflect the business metrics being achieved. In larger organizations, the plan and aligned objectives could be spread across a number of geographies – global, areas, regions, countries and territories – rolling up metrics and insights to the business as a whole. In a smaller business, ensuring you have those around the table that are empowered to make decisions will help enable a smoother process. Whatever the scale of your business, getting marketing a seat at the right table is key – this will only be achieved if your leadership have a commercial understanding of the impact you and your function can have. You must show how marketing acts as a lever for both short- and long-term growth.

Budget and investment asks

Unless you are incredibly lucky, you will likely need to pitch for budgets or additive investment in order to deliver on the myriad asks on your plate. Marketing is always handed a lemonade budget with a champagne ask. Preparing for your pitch is key. You need to understand:

Who you will be pitching to – what are their personal and functional objectives and how does your plan support them?

What are you pitching for and why – what is the impact of the investment ask from a business perspective?

How will you stack up against the competing asks – what are the key business objectives you are aligning to?

What do the leadership team need to plan in for ongoing continued investment – this one is key particularly when the corporate memory is short and the investment ask crosses multiple years.

When you pitch for your annual budget, it is imperative that you understand the competitor landscape – who is spending what in your space and what are the industry benchmarks. These benchmarks should also underpin the ask. The focus of the function will determine the metrics you need to use and the expectations that will need to be managed around ROI both for the short and the long term.

In larger organizations you may need to build out a multi-function ask to ensure you have covered all players in the project. This will likely need to include external costs alongside internal headcount alignment and any additional people or recruitment costs. The latter is often the first thing removed from any allocated budget but has a huge knock-on effect. When a project is under-resourced it is unlikely to be positioned for success and will be detrimental to your team morale. Do not try and spread the resources thinner. Focus on doing fewer, bigger and better. Easy to say, incredibly hard to align and execute.

Power of influence

Contrary to many B2C businesses, marketing is likely to have less direct power to determine the focus of the business but will have a greater need to lead through influence. In B2C, marketers are more likely to be seen as having a straight-line link to drive revenue so they are at the core of decision making – reflected in the seniority of the roles and individuals recruited, alongside the hard coded marketing training across the business. In B2C, the balance of power is also more comparable to other functions and BMC will not normally be seen as an order-taking service function; it will be seen as a front office revenue driver.

In B2B (or B2C if it applies) where direct power is limited you will have to lead through influence. This will take more soft skills and will personally demand more resilience, more patience and, most importantly, more storytelling. We will cover the softer skills in Chapter 10 and will dive into the detail needed to get both the investment and support needed to be successful.

The indirect power held within the marketing function is also driven by the ownership and management of the channels to market. As the marketing team, you own the message in the market, you can direct how your prospective audience experiences your brand and can optimize towards both short- and long-term metrics.

It is proven that engaged employees drive business growth. With a combined BMC function, you also own the channels internally to garner support for the business messaging, collaborating with other functions to ensure that your employees are fully engaged towards realizing the vision of your business.

COLOURING IN DEPARTMENT

Brand, marketing and communications functions need to move away from being seen as the colouring in department. The balance of art and science is key. Yes, there is a spark of creativity that you are unlikely to find in other departments in quite the same way, but you need to back it up with behavioural science, customer insights and marketing-influenced revenue metrics.

When I started at GE Capital and had to present regularly to our ExCo on the new retail brand, the leadership team would lean in, rub their hands and say 'what creative are you going to share today?' It was only by showing the team the financial metrics we were able to drive from our creative executions, and that we had effectively built a well-oiled lever to enable the team to drive retail savings as an efficient alternative funding source, that we gained further respect and understanding.

While it may be an outdated perception of the function, using creativity as a route to leadership engagement can be successfully balanced with discussion around the short- and long-term revenue impact so that you can have the optimal marketing conversation that will push the credibility of the function forwards.

SUMMARY

To understand what you need to deliver and how you can build a marketing plan aligned to the business objectives, make sure you:

Define and understand the vision, purpose and values of your business.

Understand the business objectives. How are they measured?

Make sure you also understand the personal objectives of your stakeholders. What is driving them both personally and professionally?

Where does marketing fit into the objectives?

Are you reporting to the same outcomes?

Think about your operating model and understand how your marketing function is funded.

Where does your investment come from?

Are you set up for success? Does your functional operating model enable you to drive alignment to the business objectives?

Are you connecting dots across the business?

Where do you have direct or indirect power to influence the future strategy?

Coming up next:
Back to the fundamentals of marketing. Where do you need to start?

AN EXTERNAL PERSPECTIVE
Building on a famous name to become a famous brand

The below is taken from a conversation with Elliot Moss, Partner and Chief Brand Officer from the law firm Mishcon de Reya.

Mishcon de Reya became known as the law firm representing Princess Diana when she split from Prince Charles in 1996. However, at the time, divorce made up only a small fraction of the business. It was recognized by the firm that rather than only being a famous name, they had the opportunity to become a famous brand, leverage their reputation and open the aperture to show the broad scope of legal services they provide to both individuals and businesses.

Elliot joined in 2009 from the advertising agency Leagas Delaney, tasked with driving both business development and powering the brand's growth. In his first five years he helped drive 100 per cent growth across the firm.

He notes that there are specific challenges to driving a successful strategy within professional services, where fee earners need to be involved in marketing and marketing teams must provide real evidence of capabilities to gain the authority needed to direct the focus of marketing investment. The partners need to recognize the benefit of a firm wide 'brand we versus brand me' approach as marketers help build the future revenues of the business.

In order to gain authority, he believes there are a number of steps marketing teams can follow:

1 **Know the business of your business** better than any one partner. Know the strategies and the different markets as well as the numbers and be able to tell the commercial story.

2 **Advocate well** for yourself, your teams and your strategy. Use clear metrics, corroborated by external independent sources to get the business behind you.

3 **Creative ideas drive differentiation.** Building a brand is about having a consistently emotive conversation. Creativity engages. Dullness does not.

4 **Show your workings in the margin.** Don't hide how you build your strategy – share the strategic, commercial and creative workings so that your thinking is credible.

Elliot used this approach to great success in 2012 with the launch of an innovative branded content strategy. Working in partnership with Jazz FM, he set up the weekly radio show Jazz Shapers. Each week, the show focuses on the entrepreneurs shaping the business world in conversation with Elliot around their business and their leadership as well as their music choices.

It is a strategy that has led to tangible ROI in brand awareness as well as financially. The target audience for the firm's growth were, and continue to be, 'ambitious families and enterprising businesses', with bold attitudinal similarities. With 40 per cent of the listeners of Jazz FM crossing over with BBC Radio 4 – the flagship BBC news and intelligent speech-based public radio station – it gave an opportunity to penetrate this affluent and educated audience. To gain internal support, he ensured that Management was on side, explaining the business case and the predicted impact of the investment. The programme is now in its 12th year.

This content initiative is part of a wider marketing strategy that has helped Mishcon de Reya grow to more than a £300 million business, with 17 per cent year on year growth for 2023/24. Elliot has been a partner since 2017 and sits on the Group Operations Board.

Elliot Moss
Mishcon de Reya, Partner and Chief Brand Officer

References

1   Coalition for Inclusive Capitalism (2018) The Embankment Project for Inclusive Capitalism. coalitionforinclusivecapitalism.com/epic/ (archived at https://perma.cc/A2HX-RKQE)

2   Fink, L (2022) Larry Fink's 2022 letter to CEOs: The power of capitalism, BlackRock. www.blackrock.com/dk/intermediaries/2022-larry-fink-ceo-letter (archived at https://perma.cc/E6RF-DH7S)

3   Institute for Real Growth (2023) Institute for Real Growth 'Impact Study'. instituteforrealgrowth.com/Impact-study.html (archived at https://perma.cc/23ZS-P7DX)

4   Gallup (2023) The benefits of employee engagement, Updated 7 January 2023. www.gallup.com/workplace/236927/employee-engagement-drives-growth.aspx (archived at https://perma.cc/8L78-WGXT)

5   Doran, GT (1981) There's a SMART way to write management's goals and objectives, *Journal of Management Review*, 70, 35–36.

6   Taleb, NN (2018) *Skin in the Game: Hidden asymmetries in daily life*, Random House, USA.

7   McKinsey & Company (2023) Diversity matters even more: The case for holistic impact. www.mckinsey.com/featured-insights/diversity-and-inclusion/diversity-matters-even-more-the-case-for-holistic-impact (archived at https://perma.cc/EW5X-9ZUB)

2

Back to brilliant basics

Marketing has been around for millennia. The beginning of marketing is in line with the inception of selling. When one market stall tried to stand out from the next, they developed early brands – named themselves and shared reasons to buy from one over the other with their audiences.

The first records of marketing practice have been found in clay tablets in Mesopotamia, under ash on walls in Pompei and as signatures to brand Greek pottery. It could be argued that the first coins minted were advertising channels for prominent people, sharing symbols of achievement and reminders of great leadership. In the 1920s, Variety reported that 50 per cent of cinemas showed advertising programmes.[1]

Radio, TV, and then telemarketing channels had all become commonplace by the late 1950s. The American Marketing Association (AMA) was the first marketing group set up in the 1930s which also published the *Journal of Marketing* – the first academic marketing journal of its kind. The first Cannes Lion Festival of Creativity followed a few decades later in 1954 to 'champion creative excellence with the goal of providing a global destination and the definitive benchmark for creativity that drives progress'.[2]

As the channels developed the theory did too. It was in the first half of the 1900s when marketing principles, frameworks and models started to take hold. The first marketing-focused degree was offered by the University of Michigan in 1902. Key proponents of early marketing thought were beginning to be published with two of these early publications setting the standards for the future and defining some of the brilliant basics that still apply today.

- E Jerome McCarthy's seminal book *Basic Marketing: A managerial approach* in 1960 – this included the 4Ps theory, which we will discuss later in this chapter.[3]

- Philip Kotler, the 'Father of Modern Marketing', published the most successful book in this field, *Marketing Management: Analysis, planning and control*, now in its 15th edition which popularized the 4P model.[4]

Marketing as a profession grew and developed at the same time. The initial heyday of consumer advertising in the 1960s and 1970s has been well documented, brilliantly brought to life across seven seasons of Mad Men, a TV drama focused on one of New York's most prestigious advertising agencies located on Madison Avenue.[5]

The 1980s saw the advent of database marketing, relationship marketing, desktop publishing and early forays into e-commerce, which took a strong hold in the early 1990s. CRM (customer relationship management) and marketing communications were both defined in the 1990s, alongside terms such as marketing automation, search engine marketing and digital marketing.

The proliferation of digital channels, media and the advancements of social media all hit new heights in the 2000s. Myspace and LinkedIn launched in 2003, Facebook in 2004 and X (formerly Twitter) in 2006. Integrated marketing started to be talked about more strongly in this period with channel planning crossing above and below the line.

MOORE'S LAW

The principle is that the speed and capability of computers can be expected to double every two years.

Geoffrey Moore's 1965 prediction has held relatively true although the initial thinking was aligned to the number of transistors in a circuit, which is now beginning to slow slightly due to physical space and size as we are approaching atomic levels.

Moore's Law has played out in relation to processing power and other technological progress, impacting marketing in the explosion of marketing technology, tools and channels available.

The biggest disrupter we are working with today only officially launched in 2022 – Generative AI – which underpins ChatGPT and other large language models (LLMs) such as Dall-E, Midjourney, Firefly etc., and is yet to reach peak maturity. And, with Quantum computing potentially impacting at an enterprise level in the next 5–10 years, we have a host of deep and disruptive changes just over the horizon. The convergence of these technologies will crack open data processing at a scale in ways we are yet to consider.

With huge change in the near future, both soft skills and the fundamentals of marketing are increasingly important. They apply across all technology developments, becoming the compass to guide through the mass of choice. This chapter will go back to basics to level set a foundational understanding before we head into deeper topics in the latter parts of the book.

Marketing fundamentals

A personal area of frustration for me is that although we are marketers, we confuse the market with our inconsistent definition of marketing, which is the exact opposite of what we do for our brands where creating consistent clarity is key. We go to great lengths to argue about new models, throwing additional marketing jargon into an already confused vernacular. If we cannot agree on what and how marketing can add value, how on earth do we expect our audiences – particularly those that sit across the boardroom table from us – to approve our budgets!

I believe that we need to align to common foundational theories, professionalizing the function in a similar way to those in the finance function, but with a key difference: the space for serendipity and creative thinking. Formalizing the single language of marketing science will enable us to focus on driving known value from baseline investments and ensure we get the funds needed to amplify creativity and drive long-term growth. Table 2.1 lists some of the language used.

TABLE 2.1 A few fundamental definitions to start us off

Above the line (ATL)	Mass targeting of customers using advertising channels to broadcast messages through TV, radio, newspaper/magazine print, out of home/billboards (OOH).
Below the line (BTL)	Targeted messaging to a smaller group of potential customers using narrowcast channels such as direct mail, email, targeted digital, sponsorship and account activation.
Integrated marketing	Combined planning across ATL and BTL to ensure the messaging is integrated across all channels, providing a consistent brand story to the customer.
Omnichannel marketing	Focused on holistic customer experiences, deepening the relationship across all on and offline channels – moving to the next level of communication at each customer touchpoint.

(continued)

TABLE 2.1 (Continued)

Direct marketing	Directly targeting a known individual customer with a message tailored to an anticipated need and response, often containing a way for the individual to respond – covering multiple channels like email, post and targeted, in-feed digital advertising.
Customer relationship management (CRM)	A strategy which includes processes and technology that enable a business to organize, operate and often automate customer interactions to deepen the relationship and lead to the next sale.
Marketing communications	Often used as a catch all for communications across all audiences, messages and channels from ATL/BTL, including internal communications.
Search engine marketing	Driving traffic to your website through both organic (SEO) and paid search (PPC) with the latter being driven by the ad copy on your search ads.
Search engine optimization	Optimizing your website to gain prominence in organic search results, including driving trust and authority through links from other sites.
Content marketing	Focused on creating and distributing content for targeted audiences, including podcasts, thought leadership, articles and blogs. B2B often uses content marketing to engage audiences around particular areas of technical expertise to drive deeper consideration of their offers.
Thought leadership	Distinctive insights that are used as part of Content Marketing to drive an appreciation of your business as a thought leader in your industry. Can consist of survey outputs, blogs, reports and white papers that enable a client to experience the expertise available through your business.
PR (public relations)	Often includes media relations, crisis management and corporate communications. PR is the management of your message with key stakeholders such as the media, broader business stakeholders and the public to elevate and manage the reputation of your business in your industry.
Social media marketing	Specific marketing strategies that use social media to interact with your customers and prospects to build brand, cement your reputation, drive traffic to your site and ultimately increase revenue.
Marketing automation	Technology that can be set up to manage and automate routine workflows and marketing tasks, based on customer interactions to move them through pre-planned journeys that can be centrally orchestrated and optimized.
Account-based marketing	Targets individual accounts as a market in their own right, using marketing strategies specific to the known needs of your high value accounts.

(continued)

TABLE 2.1 (Continued)

Customer data platform (CDP)	Enables a single customer view (SCV) of an individual, unifying all data sources into a single database so that marketers can understand buying signals across multiple platforms and create targeted campaigns to move an individual to the next best action. The B2B form of a CDP also enables aggregation of individual data at an account level, so that buying signals can be grouped and understood by the account teams.
Channel and partner marketing	Marketing focused on building relationships with partners who help sell and distribute your sales. This can include alliance partners, e.g. technology companies who are co-selling your products as they are involved in the technical delivery as well as intermediaries who also benefit from a customer purchasing from you.
Marketing mix	The comprehensive marketing plan across channels, often seen as optimizing the elements of the 4Ps.
Artificial intelligence (AI) – Generative AI – Artificial general intelligence (AGI)	AI is a type of technology that includes machine learning (ML), natural language processing (NLP) and robotic process automation (RPA). It enables computers to simulate human intelligence and can solve problems from vast underlying data sets. Generative AI is a summarisation tool at speed. It digitises large data sets, looks for patterns to predict what is most likely to come next but does not understand the content it is trained on. Artificial general intelligence is the next step in AI where the machine begins to understand the outcomes, by comprehending context and applying human cognition, not just replicating actions.
Quantum computing	A combination of computer science – which is based around bits of data existing as a 0 or 1 – and quantum physics. Quantum computing uses theories from physics where a qubit can be both a 0 and a 1, plus anything in between all at the same time, so that multiple outcomes and options can be understood simultaneously. Combining AI with Quantum is a convergence point in the future that will enable a huge number of possibilities to be understood and the optimal outcome delivered with massive potential in everything from healthcare research, to cybersecurity while also driving a truly personalised customer experience.
Metaverse	The metaverse refers to immersive online experiences delivered through virtual or augmented reality where users, often using a self-defined avatar, can interact with each other alongside businesses in real time.
Blockchain	A blockchain is an open ledger where all transactions are transparently recorded, stored and verified within a peer-to-peer network. Blockchains exist as either public, where anyone can access the information, or private, where they are only available to authorised users.

Marketing planning

The sole purpose of marketing is to get more people to buy more of your product, more often and for more money than your competition.

Increased B2C expectations drive increased demand for connected, frictionless, personalized experiences in B2B to align with their expectations of a consumer grade experience. To do this, there is a need to reorientate teams across the end-to-end customer experience. With accelerating shifts in technology and data, we need to balance hype with the benefits the technology might unlock (think Metaverse). We need to use technology, data and automation efficiently to drive growth and increase total customer lifetime value. There is also a heightened demand for effectiveness from limited budgets. It is therefore an absolutely foundational imperative that you, as a marketer, understand what tools and levers to pull to drive ROI and growth for commercial success.

WHERE TO START

The five step approach I follow for all planning is:

1 Define the objective

What are you trying to achieve? What is the business objective? How will you measure success? Ensure that you have a clear understanding and agreement with your stakeholders.

2 Find the human insight

This is key. No matter the brand, the product or the service, what is it that you are looking to solve for your buyers? What is the emotional need or customer insight that you are aligning to? The deeper the emotional understanding of why someone might buy your product or service the greater the connection you can build to your brand.

3 Connect to the brand truth

How will your brand, product or service deliver to the human insight? How does your offer differentiate? Why you versus the competitors? Why should the customer believe you? How will it connect to the human insight you have uncovered?

4 Think about the experience (not just a single journey) across all audiences

We often think about tasks within a plan – producing content, creating an advert or defining a product overview for an event. All tactics and tasks need to be thought about as part of a broader journey and across all potential buyers in the business you are targeting.

> **5** Execute, measure, test and learn
>
> A plan is better in the wild than on your desk. Getting the execution plan live
> and optimizing it as you go will make it more effective. Knowing real
> responses to your messaging and tactics will help you gain greater insight
> in what you need to adapt and change. Building a measurement framework
> to understand the impact and expected outcomes of your plan with
> industry/channel benchmarks will help direct the focus of what you may
> want to test.

When you think about your tactical plan and align to the relevant marketing metrics, remember to translate these into the language of your business so that you can report out to business leadership on the execution of your marketing approach. You should align your reporting cadence with that of your leadership group, so that you always have the latest data available to share within the wider reporting tasks.

Unpacking how you take these steps towards a plan means you need to understand and build the optimal marketing approach to the audience you are targeting. This will often start by considering the marketing mix.

The marketing mix (otherwise known as the 4P model)

You need to start by getting the foundations right. This will help you build the most effective marketing plans grounded in the reality of your brand.

Applying the 4Ps will help you take the initial steps to working this out. Despite being initially communicated in the 1960s and worked through in detail in the 1970s, they remain core to marketing planning.[6]

There are many marketers trying to add additional Ps. You may hear of models that add people, process, physical evidence, probe (research), purpose, promise, principles, personas, positioning, proof points, pride, passion and patience to get up to 12 Ps, however I feel that these are all a bit more of a stretch.

Starting with the initial four – and getting to the core of these – will include the majority, if not all, of these potential additions. I think we distract ourselves with the continuous efforts to outsmart the fundamentals. These additive Ps are all facets of the core: how you define your product includes pride and passion; personalization is key to every promotion; patience is an attribute all marketers should have at their core. Instead, I believe we need to drive accreditation of the core marketing skills, so our seat at the boardroom table and the commercial value we bring is truly understood.

FIGURE 2.1 The 4Ps align to make the marketing mix

Let's look at each of the Ps within the marketing mix model as shown in Figure 2.1 and take them in turn.

PRODUCT

Product refers to and defines the product portfolio or services mix and covers everything from the physical product itself (functional benefits, features, aesthetics, lifespan) to the broader product (packaging, brand name, including ancillary services like guarantees) to the total product (emotional and immaterial benefits, values, purpose).

Understanding the needs of your customers will lead to the development of the optimal product. Really digging into what they tell you and uncovering the benefit they are looking for will help your teams deliver the right outcomes or solutions to the customer. Henry T Ford is often quoted as saying, 'if I had asked my customers what they wanted they would have said a faster horse.' Understanding that his customers wanted to go *faster* meant that he created a car with incredible *horse-power*.

Keeping the lines of communication open to enable a continued understanding of your customer needs – either through ongoing quantitative research surveys or deeper qualitative focus groups – will ensure that you continue to understand the evolving requirements of your customer base and can optimize your product towards these for the future.

We will cover how you might think of your product portfolio in terms of branding in Chapter 5 as there are several potential options to think through depending on your audience needs and the investment your business has available.

PRICE

The fundamental purpose of marketing is to create an increase in the perceived value of your goods or services with your potential customers versus your competitors in the market. The price reflects what your customer will pay for the perceived value you are delivering for them. If the price is high compared to your competition, the customer will expect a better product which will impact all areas within the product from packaging through to after-sales servicing. If you have matched your price to the perceived value of your product and its associated benefits, you should be able to maintain added value pricing that can survive a commoditized market where your competitors might discount to gain market share.

The basic underlying price is defined by supply and demand: what is the total baseline cost of your products or services with all allocated overheads and running costs. Price is the only P that directly generates revenue – the other three are all costs that will help justify the price. The price itself can be adjusted as needed to reflect the elasticity per channel of distribution and is often optimized for the business over time depending on its objectives (volume, share, profit, etc.).

Pricing models will differ for tangible versus intangible products and services. In B2B service models where people are your product – e.g. in professional services like law, consulting and accounting services – the rates per hour of individual specialists working on a client's business will be agreed upfront and aligned to value delivered or specific deliverables that will be completed. SaaS models (Software as a Service) – where software is sold as a subscription – lead to long-term annuity revenues based around usage. The majority of IT companies have a combination of hardware, software, cloud and aligned services to ensure a balanced business model.

PRICE ELASTICITY

A measurement of the change in demand relative to a change in price.

Most customers are sensitive to the price of goods and services, and the assumption is that there will be greater demand if the price is lower and lower demand for a higher priced product.

If the demand is price **elastic** it is sensitive to change and an increase in price leads to a decrease in demand with the opposite also true – price decrease leads to a demand increase.

Conversely if the demand is **inelastic**, it can withstand change and an increase in price leads to an increase in demand.

PLACE

The place is where your business customers buy a product or service. The product needs to be accessible and available to the customer, wherever they are at the point of purchase.

If you sell online you need to think through the entire purchase journey pre- and post-sale. How easy is it to buy your product? Is your site mobile friendly and easy to use? You should work through the full journey and ensure you remove the friction at all steps of the purchase. Is it easy to find, buy, receive and return your product? Are your distribution channels enabling the purchase? The means of getting the product to that place must be easy for your buyer. You should also look at how your product is displayed on-shelf, whether that is in an online or offline environment. Thinking about the position in the store also needs to be part of this plan.

As noted elsewhere in this book, a brand is more than just the marketing around a product or service – it includes the full experience of the brand and includes all elements that touch the customer. Call centres, support services and after sales all need to embody the brand and be considered as part of your focus on *Place*.

If working with resellers or partners, you will need to understand how you are being sold. The resellers are an extension of your brand and need to be experienced in the right way. This is often driven through reward programmes that should focus on aligned metrics to your own sales teams to drive consistency of messaging and experience.

Byron Sharp, from the Ehrenberg-Bass Institute for Marketing Science, refers to the ability to access the product as physical availability, which includes both on and offline channels. It is about making your brand *easy to find* and *easy to buy*.[7]

PROMOTION

This is what we are most well-known for in marketing – the promotion of a product. It includes all forms of communication around a product and needs to be distinctive, consistent and give the customer a reason to buy your product or service over a competitor.

We know in B2B that 'up to 95% of business clients are not in the market for many goods and services at any one time'.[8] Therefore, the long-term brand build needs to focus on the mass audience, differentiating at a brand level and driving brand salience so that the buyer is primed and ready for the moment they are looking to purchase.

BRAND SALIENCE

The degree to which your brand is thought of or noticed. Strong brands have high brand salience and weak brands have little or none. Without brand salience people would not choose your brand at the moment of purchase.

Research from Ipsos has shown that at the moment of choice brands are recalled based on both memory and attention salience.[9]

Memory salience: the mental network a brand has in a person's mind as well as the mental availability of the brand. Will people have your brand in mind at the moment of choice?

Attention salience: the ability of the brand to capture people's attention at the moment of choice.

As noted previously, Byron Sharp refers to the ability to recall your brand and recognize it quickly as mental availability. It is about making your brand *easy to mind* through distinctiveness and clear brand signals, such as distinctive brand assets, messaging and experience. According to the LinkedIn B2B Institute 2021 publication 'How B2B Brands Grow', it 'requires distinctiveness and clear branding, while brands seldom compete on meaningful differentiation. This means that marketing attention should be focused on building these assets so that a brand is easier to buy for more people and in more buying situations.'[10]

Distinctive differentiation should be the focus of your promotions – both for the long and the short term. Building long-term brand salience for those not in the market and ensuring that those ready to purchase find it easy to buy through immediate promotions in the right channels.

SWOT analysis

To gain greater insight and help make decision making easier, a foundational analytical approach to apply is the SWOT analysis (see Figure 2.2).

It is a tool that can be used across your business, a product portfolio or a single product to help you identify the next steps you can take to drive growth within your own business context.

This works best when you can bring in both internal and external viewpoints. Once you have the final map you can then look at where strengths match opportunities and understand how you might need to mitigate weaknesses in areas of threat.

FIGURE 2.2 The SWOT analysis: Uncovering opportunities

	Positive	Negative
Internal	Strengths	Weaknesses
External	Opportunities	Threats

Marketing funnel and buyer demand unit in B2B

The traditional marketing funnel was built for B2C, where a single buyer moves through the layers of the funnel towards a purchase.

- Awareness – moving from not knowing your brand and its associated products and services to being aware of them and how they might help.
- Consideration – investigating further, finding out more about your brand, enabling the buyer to build a longlist of providers they might want to understand more from.
- Preference – the buyer starts to build a shortlist ahead of their purchase decision, preferring your offer over other providers.
- Purchase – the point at which the sale is made and the contractual deal is done.
- Loyalty – maintaining the relationship with your brand, choosing to continue buying your products and services over your competitors, often with adjacent products and services.
- Advocacy – speaking on behalf of your brand, driving advocacy with other potential buyers.

This foundational thinking can be applied across B2B both to the individual and to a group of buyers. You can start to look at the movement of a buying group through the funnel, engaging across the group and moving each individual towards conversion. However, there are added obvious intricacies as we look at the larger buying units.

Within B2B there is also a greater focus on loyalty and then advocacy post-sale with the potential for one buyer's story to be used by others to credentialize their own decisions.

FIGURE 2.3 The traditional marketing funnel

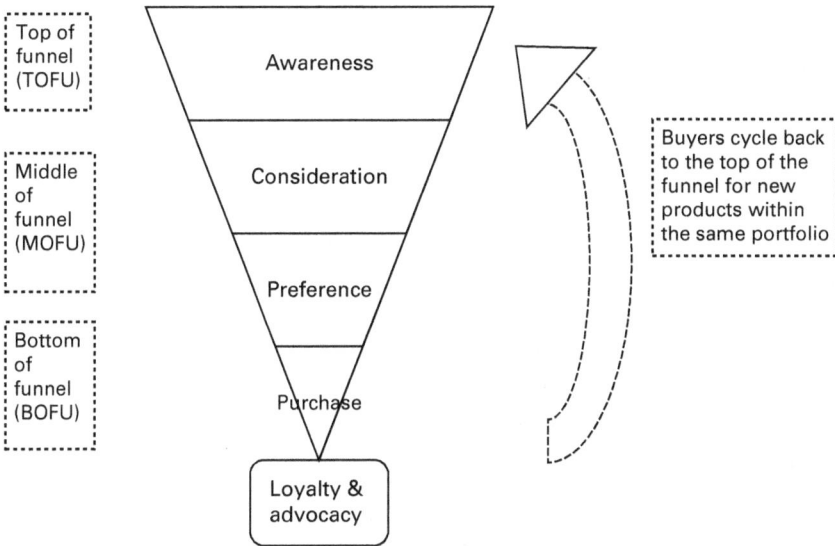

Across any funnel both content and messaging can be segmented to align to the three sections noted on the left of Figure 2.3; a brief overview is below. We will come back to content development in more depth in Chapter 7.

Top of funnel (TOFU)

Content should be focused on driving awareness and interest in the brand, product or service. You are looking to capture attention, educate and start the customer experience. Building an audience at the TOFU is critical to driving conversion to the next best action through the following phases of the funnel.

Middle of funnel (MOFU)

The messaging and content used mid funnel needs to deliver the next level of engagement, deepening the understanding and nurturing the potential buyers onwards. Optimal messaging will focus on encouraging a relationship ahead of a purchase, driving the prospective customer to be qualified as a potential buyer.

Bottom of funnel (BOFU)

At this point in the potential purchase, content needs to authenticate the decision being made to buy from you. This means that success stories that show the impact of your products and services are needed, alongside other incentives to buy. If you are selling a product, the urgency of the decision can be dialled up with discounting or other incentives. In a longer more consultative sale, confidence in the future relationship is key, particularly where the success of the purchase can impact the careers of your buyers. Why are you the right partner to work with? You need to demonstrate how you have done this before for other players in their industry or with their specific challenge.

In large-scale B2B sales the funnel is not as simple. While an individual can move through a funnel in a linear way there are many more individuals in the buying group who all need to be nurtured towards a purchase. These individuals can be in many different phases of the buying cycle, so need to be managed as an overall buyer demand unit.

The SiriusDecisions Demand Waterfall, first introduced back in early 2006, is one that many revert to when managing demand generation at scale.[11] This follows the process of the sale as the key stages in the route to a purchase rather than the journey of the individual. Within each of these steps there can be many different people as part of the decision-making group. The individual buyers will move through the traditional funnel in their thought process moving from Awareness to Consideration to Preference, which is influenced by the messaging that they are targeted with as an individual. The buying group may all reach different stages in that thought process at different times, so as a brand you are looking to drive a mass understanding across the buying group which enables them to move collectively towards a sale. We will go into a lot more detail on this in Chapter 8.

The process steps within the waterfall are more aligned to the procurement process than the thought process. Looking at Figure 2.4, I have built out the lead generation journey. In the consideration phase, buyers will build a long-list based on their combined mental availability of a brand – 'who do we know' and then shortlist from this collective list. This is where an **unknown** buyer might start the process of research. As they travel through their research journey, there is the opportunity for you to gather their details as they become a **contact** in your system. They might ask for information directly or perform general research on and off your website, visiting trade shows and learning more about potential supplier's offerings.

A **marketing qualified lead (MQL)** is the next phase which is reached when requirements from your lead scoring model are hit. This model is defined by you around the high value actions that an individual might have taken indicating buying signals. These can be seen both individually and across an account landscape.

FIGURE 2.4 The sales and marketing lead generation journey

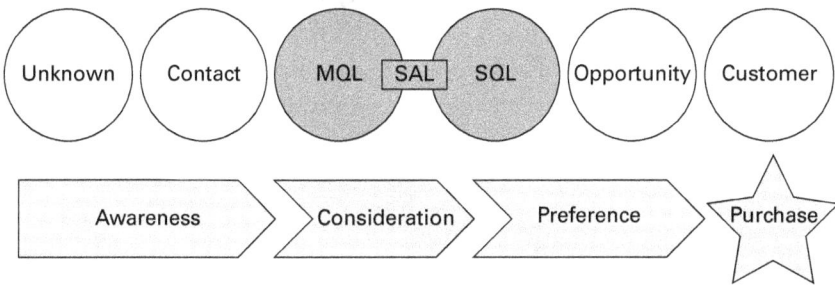

The **sales accepted lead (SAL)** is where your sales team acknowledges that the MQL has the potential to turn into a sale. This is often the handover point between the sales and marketing functions and can be the most difficult to agree on the correct process and parameters. Once accepted, the **sales qualified lead (SQL)** enters into the pipeline as a potential **opportunity** and, if successful, the opportunity will become a **customer**.

Many marketing automation and CRM systems are set up to deliver against buying stages and have them as the de facto off-the-shelf setting for the customer journey. While there are absolute benefits for this model it does not consider the revenue opportunity across an enterprise.

In enterprise level sales you need to roll the individual data up to the account level so that you can see the potential buying signals at an account level. There is a move to augment marketing qualified leads (MQLs) with marketing qualified accounts (MQAs) when the size and scale of the potential opportunity requires it.

Aggregating account data at a marketing level requires marketing technology. There are many options for doing so, with a variety of aligned costs. The volume of data we can collect around both an individual and an account continues to increase. This level of data requires a customer data platform (CDP) that collects, collates and unifies customer data at both an individual and an account level so that you as the marketer can build optimal models that include customer lifetime value at both an individual and an account level and can start to understand the total potential revenue available.

You need to build mental availability across an entire account, across the whole buyer demand unit, so that both your direct and indirect buyers are positive about you as the supplier of the product or service. This is especially needed when you have large indirect and influencer populations at multiple levels of decision making. For example, technology buyers will exist in the IT function but will also sit in dispersed roles across the business as experts in specific technologies. Their opinion of you as a technology partner will be key to the sale. You are looking to move everyone to a supportive perception of you as the supplier in this space, so will need to think about mass market messaging to hit those individuals across an enterprise level account who may be indirect influencers but not direct decision makers. We will go into this in more detail in Chapter 4.

Customer journey and customer experience

The traditional approach to a customer journey is one that aligns to the marketing funnel where an individual moves from A to B to C, moving from awareness into consideration and then preference in a straight line towards a single sale. As humans are incredibly unpredictable, a straight line is likely best looked at as an approximation to the steps in the sales process. You need to build a detailed understanding of the steps in your own brand-specific buyer journey aligned to your product or services purchase cycle. As you do this, you are likely to uncover both the known steps that your brand is involved in and also other self-navigated steps in the journey, where the buyer conducts their own research, seeks to educate themselves and talks to their own networks about their purchase decision.

With this latter point in mind, focusing on the entire customer experience is likely to be a more fruitful approach. You can drive greater mental availability for a brand with a consistent experience delivered over time, using memorable brand assets that are optimized to deliver your brand message and align to your values. Many of the self-navigated steps in a journey can only be influenced by a broader programme of brand experience – the halo effect of mass advertising will continue to increase brand salience. Within the customer experience, advocacy from other buyers is important. Your prospective buyers will be looking to understand the experience of others and therefore the entire after-sales or key-account management experience needs to be included.

Marketing toolbox

As a marketer you need to know what is in your toolbox and what you can leverage to deliver the outcomes you are tasked with and the strategies that you are driving. Conducting a regular audit of all tools, technology and training will ensure you know what you have available. A well-maintained approach to measurement and analytics will also ensure you have your latest internal benchmarks available and can use them as a foundational element in all campaigns you create.

It is imperative that you start with the brand basics – brand guidelines: a toolkit with logos, fonts, colours, image library, tone of voice etc., all lined up to deliver your overall brand across on and offline channels.

It is useful to have a centralized suite of creative templates that cover the use of your brand in different situations with aligned training so that the people within your business that drive the brand experience all have the same guidebook to work from. This can then be updated depending on any new channels, ways of working or new technological developments that come your way. With the advent of Generative AI as a creative enabler, this backbone of brand essentials can be used to train the relevant LLMs to be able to produce activation assets from master creative executions. It is useful to consider how you structure your brand guidance so that it can be used as a data set for training technology models.

At the beginning of this chapter, I mentioned Moore's Law – aligned to the exponential increase in available technology. Digital tools continue to proliferate and there are a huge number of tools solving every imaginable problem. Building out your Marketing Technology (MarTech) stack needs to be aligned to the business, marketing and communication objectives. With so many tools available, you need to know what problem you are trying to solve, what you want to be able to report on and how this all aligns to the needs of the business and your customers so that you can build your optimal stack.

Maintaining strong data foundations that align to a single dictionary will enable you to layer processes, asset creation and deliver optimal experiences through the appropriate user interface. Structuring your marketing operations teams around this will also increase the efficiencies you will be able to drive as you plug the jigsaw pieces together – ideally through native application programming interfaces (APIs), so that you have out-of-the-box configuration that can be updated in new versions and releases in real-time by the vendor.

Brand marketing and performance marketing

I believe that you need both brand marketing and performance marketing programmes to run concurrently, particularly so in B2B. Brand marketing to drive mental availability, focused on driving the long-term emotionally-driven affiliation with the brand that will help drive brand equity over time while most buyers are not within sight of a purchase. Balanced with performance marketing to enable the immediate buyers in the market – the 5 per cent – to have physical availability of your brand. The balance of investment across the two needs to be reflective of the importance of each to your business. However, in the 2017 analysis 'Media in focus: Marketing effectiveness in the digital era', Les Binet and Peter Field found that the ideal ratio of investment is 60 per cent brand marketing and 40 per cent performance marketing.[12] This balance exists across all channels. Taking search as an example, on-page SEO or organic search works as a mass enabler keeping your brand in the relevant rankings whereas PPC would pick up these individuals in the market to buy your products and services, so investment in both is needed. This 'bothism' means that you are protecting your long-term brand value while also enabling short-term revenue.

Marketing skillset

Alongside the toolbox of kit, you must develop a future-ready workforce, plugging skills gaps in new areas of technology, data, analytics and insights, all the while balancing the demands for improved employee experience driven by an inter-generational workforce and the increased desire for a work–life balance. It is therefore fundamental to the success of your function that you maintain an investment in learning and development so that your teams can stay up to date with the latest thinking. We will touch on this further in Chapter 10 as we look at some of the skills needed to optimally manage the function.

Ensuring your teams are able to keep up with an increasing proliferation of technology and tools is hard. Often the skills gaps within your team mean that you are not using the full potential of your technology investments. Building out a marketing ecosystem that enables you to lean into experts in both technology implementation and execution is useful. You can then build the balance of insourced and outsourced skills augmented by your marketing ecosystem.

Marketing ecosystems

Depending on the size, scope and scale of your budgets, plan and geographic footprint, there will be myriad options for you to consider as you refine your individual marketing ecosystem.

The world is moving quickly so having a core group of contributors within your ecosystem will help you stay ahead of anything impacting the marketing function. It will also enable you to balance the work you need to deliver internally and externally, while also pulling in specialists who add huge value to your strategy, delivery and execution. They will connect you to best practices in their area of focus and are deep experts in their areas of specialism, so

FIGURE 2.5 Agency specialisms to bring to your ecosystem

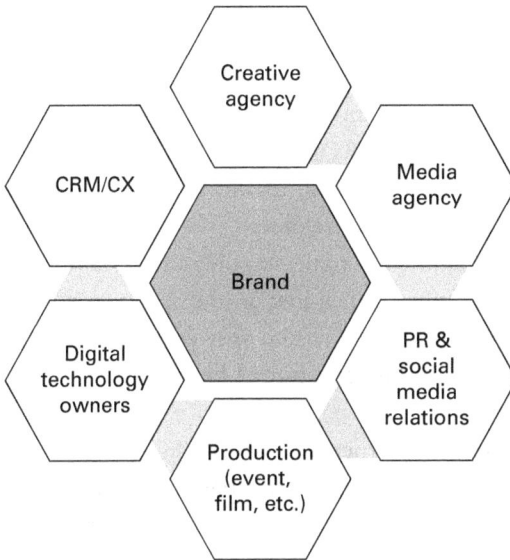

they will be able to advise you of what is coming over the horizon. Figure 2.5 shows the type of collaborators you will likely need in your ecosystem. Each of these specialists brings their domain skills to bear on your issues as you build out your marketing plan.

Getting the best out of your agencies

Empowered agencies that can work as an extension of your team will deliver more distinctive and more impactful creative work. A close relationship will enable seamless execution and they will be key to your function's success. You need to invest in the relationship across your whole team to ensure that all members of the marketing function can access the right level of support for their task.

Each agency or provider you work with will have an area of specialization where they are able to make the most impact. It is worth working with your ecosystem players to build out an aligned understanding across the ecosystem so all are fully aware of, and embrace, the swim lanes that they work in.

I spent over 10 years working for agencies, from large creative networks (integrated, digital and social) through to CRM (digital, data and direct) boutiques. I have now spent over 15 years on the client side. I understand the power an aligned agency group can play from both sides – clarity in the role and scope of the brief for each player helps them do the best in the space that they occupy.

Depending on the projects that you are delivering, it may also be useful to bring all of your ecosystem players together on a regular basis to review the past metrics, achievements and look to the future. This is particularly important if you are working on a fully integrated initiative, e.g. a large rebrand, campaign or product release.

The key to driving a clear understanding of the task at hand is the brief. This can take many forms depending on the agency you are briefing but will need to include some key thoughts and answer several foundational questions. Table 2.2 shows the topline questions I believe you need to answer as part of the agency brief.

Briefing your agency partners together on larger briefs can often be useful but remember agencies often charge based on time and materials. The former is key – every hour you are brainstorming with an agency will cost you, so make sure you have your thoughts aligned ahead of jumping in. Manage expectations on both sides, understand the rate card of the people you are working with and ensure you know what you will be expected to pay for. You do not want to end up distracted in discussion over the time

TABLE 2.2 The agency brief

The agency brief	
Objective	What is the business trying to achieve? What is the aligned marketing objective? What is the communication objective for the agency?
Target audience	Who are you targeting and why? What do you know about them? What is the value proposition you are trying to convey? What do you want them to think, feel and do?
Single minded proposition	What is the single most compelling thing to be communicated to a customer to make them consider purchasing from you?
Task	What is the expectation of this brief? What will success look like?
Scope	What is the budget? What is included from a geographic/channel/delivery perspective?
Timing	What is the go-live date? What are the next steps and timelines for the agency to hit?
Bear traps	What should be avoided? Anything that is a definite no?

spent on a project instead of focusing on the creative outputs. In larger organizations you will likely have approved rosters of agencies to work with, where the initial financial discussions are managed by procurement. It is wise to start here to understand the approved agency strategy.

Accessing best practice

Building your personal and professional network in marketing will help you understand how the industry is changing, how others are reacting to that change and will help you identify potential knowledge gaps.

There are some great organizations set up to share thinking, thought leadership and best practice which are worth joining or following. The majority are open to both B2C and B2B and, as we've noted previously with the convergence of consumer grade experience expectations, there is a lot to learn on both sides. (See Table 2.3.)

It is useful for marketing recruitment to have your brand show up at industry awards, whether that is an award for being a great place to work from a talent perspective or as an organization that is doing impactful, distinctive work. Both will increase the perception of your marketing function as one where others might see themselves thriving.

TABLE 2.3 Inspiring and useful marketing networks

American Marketing Association (AMA)	Strives to be the most relevant force and voice shaping marketing around the world.	www.ama.org
Chartered Institute of Marketing (CIM)	Supports, develops and represents marketers, organizations and the profession all over the world.	www.cim.co.uk
LinkedIn B2B Marketing Institute	A LinkedIn think-tank that researches new approaches to B2B growth.	https://business.linkedin.com/marketing-solutions/b2b-institute
The Marketing Society	Inspires, accelerates and unites a global community to raise marketing's positive impact.	www.marketingsociety.com
WARC	Provides insight, intelligence, expertise, case studies, benchmarks and guidance to help marketers navigate any challenge with confidence.	www.warc.com

So, where next...?

In these first two chapters we have looked at understanding the objectives of your stakeholders, uncovered the 4Ps relevant to your business, looked at the situational analysis with your SWOT matrix, conducted a review of your toolbox and built an understanding of your marketing ecosystem.

As we start to look at setting the marketing objectives for your brand, the next step is to understand the needs of your audiences aligned to the products and services within your portfolio. This will then give you the human insight that you can start to build your marketing plan around, aligned to deliver to the broader objectives of the business.

As you work through the steps in these chapters, make sure you review the business objectives that have been shared in light of what you now know. They can often shoot for the stars without much detail, such as 'increase revenue by $XM'. You need to get to the granular breakdown of how this will show up on the balance sheet – the source of this additive revenue will help you define what it is the marketing function can influence and what it is directly responsible for. Understanding where any new growth comes from will help you build the marketing plan aligned to the reality of the brand truth. Marketing will always be a function in high demand so ensuring you focus on the measures that really matter will help you enable the business to hit both their long-term and short-term revenue goals.

SUMMARY

- Marketing planning

  - o Uncover the business objectives and understand marketing's role in delivering to the agreed outcomes.

  - o Find the human insight – we will work through this in Chapters 3 and 4.

  - o Connect to the brand truth – build the right value proposition for your brand, product or service.

  - o Think about the experience – all touchpoints in the customer journey are influenced by the application of your brand.

  - o Execute, measure, test and learn – your thinking is better in the wild where you can optimize rather than on your desk, so get it out quickly!

- Set the foundations of your brand with the 4Ps model
  - Consider your role in all four: product, price, place and promotion.
  - Aim to build brand salience across the full audience or buyer demand unit.
  - Make it 'easy to mind and easy to buy'.
- Think about your opportunities and threats using a SWOT analysis
  - What can you do differently to mitigate any weaknesses?
  - How can you align your strengths with your opportunities?
- Consider the traditional funnel
  - Do you have a single buyer or a buying group?
  - Depending on your business model you might need to sell to multiple individuals at the same time. Consider the influencers – more on this in Chapter 4.
  - Think through your buyer journeys and understand any gaps, aim to optimize the holistic experience.
- Build the marketing toolbox across your internal talent and processes augmented by your external ecosystem so that you can drive your strategy forwards.

Coming up next:
Strategic planning in B2B

- Finding the white space to operate.
- Planning across brand, reputation, relationship and revenue.

AN EXTERNAL VIEWPOINT
B2B marketing or just Back 2 Brilliant basics?

In old school direct marketing, we were taught that you had to get the right message to the right people via the right medium at the right time. It sounds so simple, but it is a carefully curated combination of art and science, which was one of the reasons I loved it so much.

It used to remind me of maths.

It was either right or it was wrong – and you knew very quickly which of those it was because there was no hiding from results – but you could work creatively to solve the problem.

Over the years, direct marketing has morphed into CRM and increasingly we talk about the whole *customer experience* – the sum of a customer's interactions with your brand – or, as I prefer to refer to it, Customer. The principles have remained the same albeit with a little more modern-day complexity thrown in. We are now swamped in data, and technology is everyone's favourite under-utilized resource.

I firmly believe that all things related to the customer should be the most important marketing topic in the boardroom. Sadly, they are not. Brand is Customer's much sexier cousin and often gets all the attention.

And while brand is important, and increasingly so in B2B marketing, decisions – consumer or business ones – are still made by people. The difference is that in B2B marketing that decision-making process is often more complex.

If we unpick the 'old school' mantra a little, we get the following.

Right people: There are multiple stakeholders with different mindsets and motivations who must be reached and influenced individually which makes the challenge of doing excellent B2B marketing that much greater. This is where adopting segmented strategies is critical and using observed and volunteered data over modelling is much more reliable and accurate.

Right time: Long term prospect cultivation is key because the purchasing cycles are often longer, more complex and more unpredictable. That means that creating mechanisms to identify purchasing triggers becomes essential, ensuring that you are there to influence at every stage from awareness to post purchase.

Right message: Substantiation is important not because decision making is rational but because the emotional risks that surround it are so high. Reinforcing rational arguments before, during and after purchase is essential. It might not be what drives choice, but it is what makes choice possible.

Right medium: Even in relatively small businesses, decision-making units can be surprisingly large. Therefore, being able to reach and influence each of these individually and efficiently requires an understanding not only of their mindsets and motivations but also of their habits so that you can reach them in a way that is efficient and timely using multiple touchpoints. This is where your tech platform comes into its own making sure that the message is delivered in all channels.

Interestingly over time, consumer marketing – especially service marketing – has increasingly adopted many of the techniques that used to be the preserve of B2B marketing.

B2B marketing forces us to **be creative** rather than simply **do creative**. We cannot simply hide behind a big idea or hope that this will carry us through. Our efforts need to work harder, to convince more people to buy into our product, service and, yes, our brand. It makes us better marketers. The thing about B2B marketing that no one tells you is that it really does rely on marketing excellence, and it is unforgiving otherwise.

Vonnie Alexander
NED, Board Member, Executive Coach, Lead Consultant CRM/CX – AAR.

Following a 15-year career in the marketing, advertising and communications industry, Vonnie set up award-winning agency Kitcatt Nohr Alexander Shaw and grew the business before selling it to Publicis Groupe 10 years later. She now coaches leaders and their teams, consults and advises in the marketing services industry and beyond.

References

1   Marketing Museum (2024) Historical timeline marketing.museum/marketing-history/ (archived at https://perma.cc/7BCW-RJAB)
2   LIONS (2024) About us, www.lionscreativity.com/ (archived at https://perma.cc/WQV6-EPF5)
3   McCarthy, EJ (1960) *Basic Marketing: A managerial approach*. McGraw-Hill Inc., US
4   Kotler, P (1967) *Marketing Management: Analysis, planning, and control*, Prentice-Hall, Upper Saddle River
5   Cunningham, JM (2024) Mad Men, Encyclopædia Britannica www.britannica.com/topic/Mad-Men (archived at https://perma.cc/BAQ9-EAZK)
6   McCarthy, EJ, Shapiro, SJ and Perreault, WD (1979) *Basic Marketing*, Irwin-Dorsey, Ontario (pp. 29–33)
7   Sharp, B (2011) *How Brands Grow: What marketers don't know*, Oxford University Press, UK
8   Dawes, J (2021) Advertising effectiveness and the 95–5 rule: Most B2B buyers are not in the market right now, Ehrenberg-Bass, Institute for Marketing Science. marketingscience.info/advertising-effectiveness-and-the-95-5-rule-most-b2b-buyers-are-not-in-the-market-right-now/ (archived at https://perma.cc/4J3F-53WS)
9   Rademaker, D and Joosen, B (2016) Brands don't buy brands – people do, Ipsos, 23 September 2016. www.ipsos.com/en/brands-dont-buy-brands-people-do#:~:text=The%20order%20in%20which%20a,at%20the%20moment%20of%20truth (archived at https://perma.cc/SX7Y-XTNC)

10 Romaniuk, J, Sharp, B, Dawes, J and Faghidno, S (2021) How B2B brands grow, The B2B Institute at LinkedIn. business.linkedin.com/content/dam/me/ business/en-us/marketing-solutions/cx/2021/images/pdfs/final-how-b2b-brands-grow-white-paper.pdf (archived at https://perma.cc/AYZ3-JD5J)

11 Sirius Decisions (2006) Sirius Decisions demand waterfall https://www.forrester. com/blogs/demand-waterfall-modular-system/ (archived at https://perma.cc/8H4E-L5QQ) [Last accessed 30 January 2025]

12 Binet, L and Field, P (2017) *Media in focus: Marketing effectiveness in the digital era*, IPA, London

3

Strategic planning in B2B

In the first two chapters we worked through how you might set up your team for success as a function as well as getting a detailed understanding of your business objectives and where your leadership is looking to focus. We can now start building the marketing plan, knowing that we need to look at a balance of budgets with a portion for long-term brand building and another portion for short-term activation. This proportion will differ depending on the objectives, maturity of your business and current market awareness of your products and services.

Business to business, or B2B, focuses on selling to companies versus household consumers, with the latter known as the B2C model. B2B combines a huge spectrum of companies ranging from manufacturers to distributors, to service providers and business consultants, selling everything from tangible widgets to intangible services. For ease, when we look at the broad range of companies we can divide them into a number of types.

1 Manufacturer sold via distributor

These companies produce products that are smaller scale and sold in a commoditized way, either as part of another product or to build something else, e.g. building materials or widgets sold within other products.

2 Manufacturer sold via a retailer

Products that are sold to a business to sell on to a household consumer are sometimes known as following a B2B2C model. They are often white label consumer goods sold through licensing agreements, or white labelled for a retailer to sell on as their own branded items.

3 Manufacturer sold directly to buyer

These companies often produce products that need to be maintained, serviced and have agreed service level agreements for uptime or usage.

They are often SaaS (Sold as a Service) and are supported with after-sales care and include IT products, solutions and finance packages.

4 Professional services

Services can be provided to businesses, business owners and sometimes individual consumers. These types of service include law, accountancy and consultancy and are often delivered on a time and materials basis with fees agreed. The extent of the fees can also be based on the impact, outcome or value delivered to the buyer.

These four types of a B2B company will all have different approaches and strategies depending on what you are looking to achieve in the industry and specific category you operate in.

Going back to the 4Ps

Product

There are consistent requirements for product development strategies. New products must align to the need of a customer or a business. They should provide measurable value (tangible or intangible) that can be communicated as part of the product detail.

Brands with history and heritage should use these anchors as credible proof points that enable them to continue the ongoing conversation with audience members, including both previous and prospective buyers and influencers. Embrace the brand built on the core portfolio of products and services, look at extensions and adjacencies for new product development (NPD) and acquisitions. Build a complementary portfolio that enables a customer to move from an entry-level product across the entire portfolio through upselling (encouraging the buyer to buy more or the next product up) and cross-selling (encouraging the buyer to buy adjacent products or add-ons).

Price

This will depend on the market you are in, your competitors, the price elasticity of the market and cost of the product alongside the financial targets you are looking to deliver.

Place

You will need to determine the distribution strategy by building a plan that is focused on delivering your product or service in a place that can be easily accessed by potential buyers. Understanding your geographic footprint, the online vs offline plan alongside the needs for any intermediaries, will be key to ensuring you have covered all the necessary details.

Promotion

The approach will need to be built to support the product benefit and value proposition, targeting your buyer so that the price feels appropriate for the value delivered. It should be focused on driving trial or usage, based on the potential category entry points where your buyers might enter the sales cycle. These points of usage may differ by audience segment and so should be thought about both during audience segmentation and as you look at how your product is used and how relationships are built with your brand. Mature brands are likely to need support to maintain and drive new growth, for instance redefining new usage points or benefits in differing categories.

Industry understanding

Understanding your industry gives you greater power in your decision making and planning as you will know the macro forces most likely to impact you and your business. Thinking through the adjacent segments in your industry will give you greater insight into influences that you may be able to leverage. Convergence of industry dynamics across segments is also interesting to think through. For instance, digitalization is converging the needs and expectations of buyers across multiple segments, with new entrants disrupting them with slightly different business models.

Steps to understanding your industry:

1 Ensure you know the industry that you are part of. Think through what your buyers consider you to be – does this match what you are aiming for? The convergence of technology firms with other industries can make this more complex than it seems. For example, Funding Circle is an online lending platform that connects small and medium enterprises looking to borrow with investors who want to lend. Defining their industry is difficult as they are not a bank, but they provide access to similar funding and are regulated by the Financial Conduct Authority (FCA). They are a technology-driven platform-based company, but this isn't what they sell. As a commercial lender they provide finance and so need to consider all competitors in this space alongside adjacent providers like commercial banks.

2   Understand who your customers and competitors are. Defining who your current and future buyers are – both from a business and individual perspective – is key to understanding what they buy and how they are likely to buy it. More on this in the next chapter.

3   Size the market. What is the target addressable market (TAM) for your industry? Looking at the full size and scale of your industry will give you an idea as to whether you have the right share of the market, what headroom there is to grow and who you will need to unseat as a competitor with your target-buying segments.

4   Work with, and across, your industry so that you can both understand and influence the organizations that regulate, license or assure you and your competitors. It is useful to do this at all levels and within all functions of your organization. For example, many bodies that support marketing will have smaller groups that are focused on your segment of an industry or sector – make sure you connect with your peers.

It is increasingly important for you and your business to understand the industry you work in and the adjacent or convergent industries that are both influencing and taking share through providing potential substitutes for the buying need you aim to satisfy.

The rise of direct to consumer (D2C) business models are disrupting some segments' channels to market, retailers and those that manufacture white label products. It is a model where new customers are marketed to directly. Customers buy the products directly from the manufacturer who in turn delivers the product directly to them, cutting out retailers and physical stores. Many businesses in this sector are also implementing subscription plans for their buyers, particularly those in fast moving consumer goods (FMCG), e.g. Dollar Shave Club for shaving and Glossier for beauty products.

Market dynamics

As mentioned previously, we often focus on the latter P – promotion – as the key part of marketing, but the other three are incredibly important in determining where you need to direct your promotional investment. You also need to understand the full market context, and one of the foundational tools that is regularly used is the PESTLE analysis.[1] This acronym can be broken down as political, economic, social, technological, legal and environmental factors. It can be used to assess the external factors that might impact the context of operating your marketing plan, giving you a greater understanding of what might influence your buyers or impact their buying choices and behaviours. A useful way to think about the impact is by going macro to micro – what is impacting the world, your industry and then your organization.

When you have fully reviewed all the external factors and thought through the individual elements that could impact at a macro level, across your industry and then your organization, it is worth looking at the relative importance of each, thinking through any mitigation you can put in place and also anything that you can flip to a positive. For instance, when pitched in the right way, the scarcity of a product can drive up the desire to buy it as the competition increases.

Table 3.1 shows a completed template for a fictional building manufacturer who sells through distribution centres to companies who build houses.

TABLE 3.1 Completed PESTLE example

	Macro-trends	Industry	Organization
Political	50% of the global population is going to the polls – geopolitical disruption might impact supply chains globally. *Other factors to consider: Government, trade and tax, regulatory changes.*	Access to technology might disable some supply chains and impact distribution in the manufacturing industry.	Delivery of products might be delayed by impacted supply chains – may need to think about how customers can pre-order and how we manage waitlists.
Economic	Cost of living continues to remain high despite inflation stabilizing in most countries. *Other factors to consider: Interest and exchange rates, unemployment.*	Building trade may falter and less house building will be planned during high inflationary period.	As a manufacturer there may be less demand for the products from the business distributor – may need to think of other channels to market – B2C for home improvement?
Social	There is an increased focus on multi-generational living. *Other factors to consider: Sociodemographic, lifestyle and consumer behaviour.*	This focus is driving a different approach to house planning – looking to build annexes to large family homes.	Different need for materials – need to think through full impact on products produced – if larger houses become the norm does it affect demand?

(continued)

TABLE 3.1 (Continued)

	Macro-trends	Industry	Organization
Technological	AI and tech are disrupting design processes, driving different consumer expectations. *Other factors to consider: Emerging tech, cyber, supply chain automation.*	House builders are enabling greater personalization in new build house planning, with less uniform designs and more integral technology built into the house.	Focus on building a greater understanding of potential options that can be built into the product portfolio – with specific options for integrated technology builds. Investigate more options within 'just-in-time' supply chain planning – where the timing for delivery of materials is just at the start of the scheduled production.
Legal	Environmental regulations are coming into play in all manufacturing processes, looking to drive less wastage and usage of more sustainable materials. *Other factors to consider: Regulation, anti-competition laws, corporate governance.*	House building regulations are changing to become more sustainable – this is however impacting cost and supply of materials.	Need to ensure that all obligations are met within product manufacturing and that it adheres to sustainability regulations.
Environmental	Demand for sustainable materials is increasing, with new awareness at both a consumer and business level of the broader requirements. *Other factors to consider: Sustainability, climate, regulations, ESG.*	House builders need to consider how they react to both the increased awareness of consumers and business demand – while balancing the increased cost of materials.	Potential to revisit the packaging of all materials – remove unsustainable practices, looking at different baseline materials, e.g. sustainable sources of wood etc.

Overall, this manufacturer of house building materials will need to consider building further focus on sustainability through a review of the materials used, supply chains and packaging. Working closely with their distributors to ensure alignment to regulatory requirements and end customer expectations will help build a unique product message. Getting ahead of these requirements with their buyers could help drive relationships and advocacy for the manufacturer within their industry.

Finding the white space

We often talk about 'finding the white space' – this is a term that refers to the search for a unique market position. How can you build and position your offering so that you limit the competition around your specific space. Understanding how your competition approaches the market is key. What are they selling that competes for the same attention of your audience, at the same usage point or with a similar product benefit? How are they differentiating and what strategies are they using to deliver sales?

Understanding the terms in Table 3.2, and reviewing your own position, will help you think through the potential white space around your competition.

TABLE 3.2 Terms that are useful when thinking through your positioning as you look to find the 'white space'

Industry/sector	A sector is a division of the economy which groups multiple industries, e.g. the energy sector has an oil and gas industry within it.
Market capitalization	Market capitalization is the total trued-up value of a company based on its share price.
Total addressable market (TAM)	Full size of the market demand for your product or service (across the full competitor set).
Market share	Your business' share of the total addressable market.
Share of wallet	Your business' share of a target buyers spend in the space.
Segmentation	A full market segmentation is a way to look at all the buyers in the TAM – which companies are buying the product/service, their buying needs and behaviours. Segments can be purely behaviourally driven or sociodemographic, and it is most often a combination of the two.
Target audience	The audience segments you are targeting with your product/service. Can be further segmented for you to ensure optimal targeting.
Value proposition	The unique promise you make to your buyers about your product or service.

Building a deep understanding of your sector and industry, the issues that will impact it and the competitors in your space will help you identify what makes you unique. Your uniqueness, when combined with the individual benefit to a customer, should be your focus and at the centre of your plan. Defining your objectives within the context of your market dynamics will enable you to understand what you are able to control and what you will need to allow for.

There are a lot of resources that can help you understand your industry and what you might need to be aware of, either from upcoming regulation, competitor changes and shifts or potential disruptors who might play in your market. Make it a personal objective to stay connected with your peers across the industry, join connected networks and ensure you are connected to your industry influencers and analysts. There are many online networks and groups on LinkedIn and other social media platforms that can help you connect with thought leaders easily, enabling you to edit your feeds to highlight upcoming trends. Staying up to date with the news agenda is key to keeping your analysis up to date.

A deep understanding of the macroenvironment, achieved through your PESTLE analysis, needs to be combined with an equal understanding of the microenvironment. One of the commonly used frameworks for doing this is Porter's Five Forces, thinking developed by Michael E Porter of Harvard Business School in 1979.[2]

The industry you operate in is dynamic – it changes over time as new entrants enter the market, new products are launched or competitors increase their sales and marketing motions. Bargaining power of both suppliers and buyers are also forces that can drive the potential success of your business – too much of both together and the margin you are delivering will be non-existent and your business model becomes untenable. A detailed understanding of the forces that impact you will stand you in good stead as you think about your industry.

Existing competition

Current competition is often understood the best – it is what is happening right now within your industry. Your customers are already making choices between you and your competition. Understanding why they are buying from you over the competition is key to understanding what your USP (unique selling point) is, what you need to protect and what concerns you might need to overcome.

Some questions to ask are:

- What are your competitors' business strategies?
- What is their current portfolio? How do they support it? Where are they investing for their future?
- What are their marketing strategies and sales motions?
- How do they position their products/services? What is their value proposition?
- What do your customers think of them? Why do they buy from you and not your competition?

Replacement product or service

A replacement of your product or service is where a different way of doing the same thing becomes possible, often where new technology disrupts an old process, e.g. Blockchain's open source ledger is a substitute for long-form bookkeeping and a potential substitute for traditional accounting practices. In this case, understanding what the optimal market dynamics would be for a replacement to take real hold is key.

Some questions to ask are:

- How easy is it to disrupt your business model?
- Are there replacements for the same need already available that could become greater competitors if market dynamics shift?
- How easy is it for your customers to move to a replacement?
- How likely are your competitors to offer a replacement?

New market entrants

New market entrants are new providers doing exactly the same thing as you do – but with a different brand or proposition. Often these new providers are brand extensions from adjacent categories, trading on the power and attraction of their current offering, who are looking to optimize a similar buyer group in a new space. By being aware of what your customers consume in categories adjacent to yours, you can ensure that you have an eye on potential new entrants or directly competitive brands. One example of these extensions and new entrants is clear if you look at advertising and marketing agencies. These agencies advise businesses on their marketing practices.

Recently, professional service consultancies are moving into this space by acquiring agency networks and elevating the conversation from a creative to a functional or enterprise level in line with other services the consultancies deliver. These new entrants are competing head-to-head with more traditional providers and changing the conversation in this market.

To understand the dynamics in your industry some questions to ask yourself are:

- Who do your current buyers trust in adjacent categories?
- How transferable are adjacent brands?
- Are there any barriers that would make entry to your category difficult or prohibitive?
- Are the distribution channels open to new providers? How might your customers buy differently?
- How easily could your suppliers switch to support a new entrant? Would it make your business model more difficult to operate?

Buyer price sensitivity

You need to understand how sensitive your buyers would be to price changes. An industry with multiple options that satisfy the same need puts the bargaining power in the hands of the buyer, whereas an industry with few options puts the bargaining power in the hands of the seller. Commoditized products or services are generally more price sensitive, with customers switching depending on price and access to the product – if it is reasonably priced and able to be found easily, customers can switch easily and therefore have the power.

Questions to ask in this space are:

- What are the costs for buyers to switch?
- Are buyers sensitive to price changes?
- How easy is it for buyers to access alternatives?
- Is there room in the market for growth – are there enough materials for new entrants?
- Are you aware of the customer need you are fulfilling? Could there be replacements?

Resource/material scarcity

If resources are scarce then suppliers are in a better position to bargain over prices. This includes the service industry. When specific skillsets are rare, the cost of hiring the right talent needs to be factored into the pricing. Suppliers of finite raw materials, components and ingredients can create barriers to entry for new entrants if the contracts are tied up with current manufacturers.

Things to think about in this space:

- How accessible are alternative suppliers for current materials?
- Have you considered alternative materials for your products?
- How flexible is your workforce? Are they able to upskill?
- Are your competitors able to absorb costs in a different way to you?

Understanding the micro dynamics that can influence the success of your business will underpin your broader marketing strategy. Combine this with the understanding of the macro impacts for your industry and you will start to be able to define the business impact. How important is each factor for your organization and what can you do to mitigate any negatives or position yourselves to embrace any upsides?

As a marketing function, you should also look to work closely with your corporate strategy function (if you have one) or the individual in charge (sometimes the CEO or CFO) to feed into the strategy for the business. The marketing function is the voice of the consumer or client and consideration should be given to their changing needs. Without this, the data and insight you have will not be recognized.

Planning inputs

If you are following through the chapters in order, you will now have a number of inputs to use to build your optimal marketing plan:

- Business vision and objectives – overall what is the direction of your business
- The opportunities that align to your strengths
- The broad market context you operate within
- The micro context in your industry and for your business

You can start to think about what your long-term marketing vision will look like, aligned to the long-term business vision. You will need to build the plan centred on the role marketing will play to drive long-term growth for the business, balanced with an understanding of where you will invest to deliver leads in the short term. You will also need to factor in what you should do to engage the business to optimize their role in delivering marketing programmes by defining clear collaboration with the sales teams to drive a connected commercial focus.

If you cross multiple geographies or have global and local teams working together, the elements you are responsible for might be more prescribed. For instance, the global team might be responsible for defining the corporate brand positioning, the brand guidelines and the overall direction for a global brand campaign to drive awareness of the organization's overall offering. The in-country teams might be responsible for campaigns that drive consideration of specific products within specific audiences. Both teams will work closely with business leadership and sales to define the target outcomes and will likely have to contribute to one integrated plan so that the global impact of marketing can be understood.

Whatever your remit, global, local or everything in between, ensuring you are fully aware of the objectives will help you weave the right strands of focus for the outcomes of your marketing plan: brand, reputation, relationships and revenue. Each needs to be thought through as you define the success for your function and business.

Building a successful plan

It is important to define the objectives and the measures of success for your marketing plan across these four outcomes in a balanced way so that you are driving both successful short-term revenue objectives and long-term brand growth aligned to the vision of the business.

Short-term objectives and plans

In a tougher market, the business focus tends to centre on driving immediate revenue, to get footfall into the retail unit or to ensure the phones ring to generate leads. These tactics need to be able to show movement within one to three months.

The most straightforward and immediate approach is to look at driving incremental sales from your current customers. They know you, understand what you do and already value the benefit you help them deliver. They just need to be persuaded to buy more, and that can be through upselling or cross-selling, working with the business development and key account teams to turn leads into revenue. This can be a 1-to-1 approach, where you specifically target those potential buyers who you know are in the market due to market triggers or a clear understanding of buyers' needs and your relationship with them.

Looking across your geographic footprint and product portfolio is key to ensure that where you are driving interest aligns with where you have immediate supply. If you drive short-term interest where you have insufficient products or services to deliver immediately, then you are driving interest to your competitors by elevating your buyers' need.

This becomes more difficult the larger the company or business. If you have teams across multiple departments with slightly varied objectives, it can be difficult to know who is driving the near-term revenue. In cross border teams it can be even harder to understand how to attribute any success.

Some examples of short-term initiatives to increase immediate leads, sales and revenue include a focus on driving an increased conversion rate – moving people from awareness to consideration to purchase as quickly as possible through any one of the below.

- Price promotions – to sell more – can convert those not in the market to buy now and in bulk.
- Product/service trial promotion – to enable customers to try before they buy – free access for a limited time that then converts to paid access; complimentary meetings to consult on an issue; sampling of a tangible product.
- Seasonal content campaign – aligned to immediate need drivers such as industry triggers or timelines, new regulations and the broader news agenda.
- Upsell or cross-sell product campaigns – encouraging the buyer to buy higher value or additional products.
- Short-term media – e.g. search engine marketing (SEM), programmatic display, social media – with performance marketing objectives aligned to a pay per click (PPC) model, you can invest a known amount in the media spend, optimizing quickly as costs and behaviour changes.

While your goal is to drive short-term success, you need to be mindful of long-term needs. For instance, you do not want to move to commoditize your product or reduce your position to be that of a discounter in your industry. You need to balance the short-term desire for revenue with the long-term positioning of your brand and should choose your tactics on this basis.

Medium-term objectives and plan

The medium-term focus needs to be on driving consideration of your products and services, building an interested base of potential buyers. These tactics need to show success within the next 3–12 months, depending on the resources you can divert to execute the initiatives.

The main approach is to protect your customer base, expanding your footprint within current customers and engaging with new prospects to continue to refresh your lead data as old customers attrite. Customer acquisition is based around demonstrating why you are the right choice over your competitors, showing them the impact buying your product or service can have to the buyer and end user.

This may be more of a 1-to-few approach, where you are targeting groups of segmented customers identified through a needs-based assessment. You can then use targeted messaging to drive home the 'why you' value proposition benefits that align with the potential customers' specific issues.

Some examples of tactics that can drive ongoing consideration for your products and services, while encouraging potential customers to become buyers, include:

- Content campaigns – demonstrating the value and expertise of your company.
- Case studies and impact stories – what did using your product or service achieve for your customers, how effectively did you solve their issues or align with their needs?
- Email nurture campaigns – using a combination of content, case studies and event invites to deepen and strengthen the relationship and nurture prospective customers to become buyers.
- Round tables/webinars – bringing customers and potential customers together to influence the conversation and demonstrate your experience and expertise.
- Medium-term investment in website optimization – looking at the end-to-end journey and ensuring that you stop any leakage from the sales cycle, plugging any holes in the processes you provide.
- Digital campaigns with media placement aligned to the issues that you solve – featuring case studies and impactful content.
- Trade tie-ins – industry alignment with events, press and web content that are targeted at potential buyers in your industry.
- PR and influencer relationships – driving positive sentiment in both on and offline media and press titles.

Medium-term tactics can be easily used for short and long-term objectives – with messaging tweaks moving towards either a larger brand or revenue focus to drive the success you need. Many of these initiatives need to be planned with a fair amount of lead time for asset delivery so you can determine the optimal message. You can also optimize your assets with A:B testing across content, email subject lines, messaging and creative content; ultimately rolling out the best performing to the segments of your audience as relevant. This will not only give you flexibility but will also make your spend more efficient.

Long-term objectives and plan

Long-term is all about building brand awareness by creating memory patterns to drive recall and recognition at a brand level. These should align with the emotional needs that can be used as levers to drive sales. Building these strong foundations will make short- and mid-term investments more efficient as they can use the levers and memory patterns as shortcuts within their initiatives, either through the brand assets, e.g. logo, visual and audio brand mnemonics, or through the continued associations that you build through creative consistency.

Driving the long-term brand is an investment that will drive revenue improvement. We will talk more about this in the coming chapters, but it is proven that long-term focused advertising and initiatives drives an uptick in sales, enables price inelasticity (demand is not impacted by price increases) and thereby allows you to price to protect your margin. The brand is an intangible asset on the balance sheet but can be something you report on – brand value as a long-term metric is a key proof point of your investment.

The emphasis on long term is a mass, one-to-many approach with a broadcast focus on your initiatives, attempting to target the full market for your products and services in the most efficient way. At scale, the messaging will need to feature the full extent of your offer. This does not mean including everything you do in the execution, but instead means pulling a hero product or service to the fore or homing in on the brand message that is true to your business and aligns to the overall benefit you deliver compared to your competitors.

Some examples of tactics and initiatives in this longer-term space include those that will succeed over time, from both a brand and infrastructure perspective.

- Branded advertising – featuring the hero message for your business.
- Longer-term relationships and sponsorships – with trade bodies, influencers and press titles.
- Business community engagement – building business communities around the issues you solve in industries and geographies that you operate in, allowing two-way conversations between the brand and the buyer.
- Corporate social responsibility (CSR) programmes – local community outreach to build your brand locally and align with your business purpose to give credibility to any claims made, or environmental focus discussed.
- Buyer relationship focus – CXO programmes driven around the needs of buyer segments (CXO refers to a Chief X Officer, with X interchangeable for the function they lead) – e.g. Chief IT Officer (CIO) buyer programmes that are directly related to the needs of the technology buyer, building long-term relationships with your brand throughout the individual's career.
- Longer-term thought leadership research programmes – these can take a lot of time and investment if multi-year, multi-geo and industry.
- Research and development programmes – investing in the future of your product by understanding the changing needs and future requirements of your buyer across the product itself, distribution channels and pricing.
- Customer experience (CX) research programmes – understanding the experience your customers receive, often targeted through online platforms, both your own and any distributors or aggregators.
- Restructuring and increased investment in your marketing technology – this includes customer relationship management (CRM) capabilities to enable a smoother sales cycle as you focus on removing the friction for both customers and your sales teams.

Long-term initiatives generally need multi-year investment, so must be agreed at a senior level and should not be defunded until they have had the chance to take hold or until the programme is complete. Measurement should be aligned to the ongoing outputs and measured over a meaningful timeframe to give them a chance to succeed.

Overall, the balance of short-, medium- and long-term initiatives needs to be considered in line with your business objectives and the success and maturity of the business. These latter two – success and maturity – will influence how quickly you need to bring in revenue. If your relatively young business needs to unlock revenue immediately, you will likely be asked to divert all attention to short-term objectives, whereas a more mature business with deeper pockets might invest in both long- and short-term in a downturn. In each time frame – short, medium or long – you should think about the impact you are aiming for across the four factors: brand, reputation, relationships and revenue. The spread across these factors will likely differ across time but thinking through the impact you are looking for and what your plan will enable gives you greater opportunity for success as you look towards execution.

Allocating budget

The core component to your plan is the budget. You might be one of the lucky few allocated an annual budget aligned to the previous year's performance or as a percentage of revenue. Looking at industry benchmarks and your direct competitors, you can gauge if you are in a similar state of investment or punching above or below your weight. This is always useful to know as it will change the attitude for investment and planning. For instance, if you receive significantly less funding than the rest of your category competitors, you will need to ensure you stand out as a challenger brand and prioritization will be key to drive focus. Conversely, if you have significantly more investment, you have capacity to also invest in the long-term infrastructure changes that will position you well for the future.

To work through what you need to achieve with your funding, you need to understand the holistic business objectives, the full product portfolio you need to support, the geographic footprint you need to cover and the size of your total addressable market. Working through what your business is trying to achieve, their detailed success measures and any inter-related functional or personal objectives and then, importantly, converting them into marketing objectives, is key. The business case you will likely need to build to access and justify funding should show that you have considered the full requirements, they are aligned with the business needs and have support from across the leadership team.

An example of aligning business, marketing and personal objectives is depicted in Table 3.3 with a tactical recommendation that addresses the collective needs.

TABLE 3.3   Example of objectives connected through a tactical recommendation

Business	Increase sales of your cybersecurity product in the next 12 months.
Marketing	Drive consideration of your product for those buyers currently in the market.
Personal	Global cybersecurity leader is looking to increase their personal brand in the industry.
Recommendation	*Build out a programme that increases the credentials of your brand in this space and includes a talking-head case study with a client who uses your product featuring the cybersecurity leader as the interviewer. Create assets to fit the bottom of funnel (BOFU) requirements of your buyers to drive conversion. More details on requirements are covered in Chapters 2 and 7.*

With clarity on your business objectives, your marketing objectives and an understanding of the interconnected personal objectives of your leadership, you will have a full understanding of the needs you are responding to and can then define the functional objectives and key results (OKRs) and key performance indicators (KPIs).

Ensuring that your internal stakeholders are aligned to your plan means it will need to be fully socialized. Investing time to take each inter-related team through the thinking, hitting on the mutual objectives and ensuring engagement and alignment will make further leadership conversations more likely to be successful. Not everyone will agree with you which is why all stakeholder conversations should occur ahead of any leadership presentations. You need to both understand and manage any objections ahead of time and elicit support from across the table to get to a successful outcome and, ultimately, budget approval. Knowing all opinions around the boardroom table will help when it comes to your ask. Remember to talk the language of your business – do not fall into the trap of marketing jargon. You need to be clear on the benefits of the investment in marketing and how you will add value and unlock growth.

Once you have succeeded in accessing funds for the marketing plan, it is then down to you and your marketing team to define the tactics and deliver on the goals you have agreed, aligned to the needs of your target audience.

SUMMARY

- Focus on understanding your industry
  - Who are your current and potential customers – what need are you satisfying?
  - Who are your competitors in the eyes of your customers?
  - How big is your market – what is the TAM?
- Think about how your business is set up and the broad market context in which it operates
  - Understand the macroeconomic dynamics that might impact your business so you can build this understanding into your plan.
  - Understand the microenvironment and potential new entrants into your market, plus other potential disruptions.
  - Look to define the white space you might be able to expand to enable your business to thrive.
- Start to build your marketing plan
  - Define your short-term, medium-term and long-term objectives.
  - Balance the aligned initiatives in line with your objectives.
  - Build in measurement – both OKRs and KPIs.
  - Socialize with all stakeholders to drive agreement and support.
- Understand your budget
  - Do you need to pitch to claim your allocation?
  - Understand your industry benchmarks and align your ask.

Coming up next:

Defining your audiences, thinking through their needs and starting to build out targeted plans.

AN EXTERNAL PERSPECTIVE
The delicate balance of short-term revenue targets and long-term brand building

Throughout my career I have worked in B2B, from large-scale organizations like BNY Mellon, EY and the NYSE through to today, where in recent years I have been working with private equity (PE)-backed high-growth SaaS companies who are focused on driving more immediate returns. The latter has brought the balance of short-term and long-term planning to the fore.

As a CMO in a PE-backed business, I have a seat at the table. I work closely with the CEO, CFO, CRO and across the C-Suite. I report into the CEO aligned to their agenda, but also need to deliver on the needs of our board and our investors. This is a balancing act as a marketer. I am on the hook for real dollars in terms of short-term contribution to pipeline and closed/won revenue, but from experience I also know the financial upside of long-term brand investment. The latter can take a leap of faith as results are not immediately obvious and require time to pay back.

In a larger enterprise, there is more room to test, more space to fail. This luxury is removed within a more agile business. Plans will shift and change at pace. There's an extra layer of complexity with a focus on EBITDA (earnings before interest, tax, depreciation and amortizations) – where the business will likely need to clamp down on expenses throughout the year, removing investment dollars to ensure they are on track to hit the financials, without changing the revenue targets. So, the ask can often shift to meeting previously assigned marketing contribution targets but with significantly less investment.

I am in the throes of planning for next fiscal. We have modelled out the returns we are expecting in terms of revenue. In my current role I am marketing to three separate markets which have different sales cycles and different products – with different efficiencies. For instance, in one market I get $30 back for every $1 spent, in another $60 return and another might be $5. I need to balance the spend to reach my demand target, but then what do we need to spend on retention and upsell? What do we need to spend on brand? We all know as marketers that the investment in brand is going to lift the investment in the other areas significantly, but there isn't the time to wait for this to prove itself. Plus, it is difficult to measure – and we can't predict when the brand investment will start to pay off. Compare that to the short-term where I can model based on past performance and have clear levers to pull to bring in the return we expect. As such, brand is a leap-of-faith investment, and I've yet to see a private equity investor operate on faith.

Most B2B high-growth businesses hire for demand experience, which means their marketing teams are lacking skills in the broader brand space. The B2B firms hiring therefore don't see or understand the power of brand – it is discounted or overlooked compared to the short-term performance. So, it is a virtuous circle.

To combat this, we need to go back to basics to drive stakeholder alignment. You need to figure out what your stakeholders care about and build credibility there. This will buy you more time, enable more of the right conversations and build more trust, giving you the potential to experiment and make investments in brand. You need the credibility on the demand side to show that you can contribute real results while you are having the right long-term investment conversations.

Building the sales and marketing partnership is key. Looking at the sales motions across the business – 'net new' versus 'client upsell and retention' and then also activating the partner channel – all are co-owned initiatives. Driving the handshake is fundamental – you need to have rigour and understanding on both sides, optimizing and improving lead scoring across the whole demand organization, which combines both sales and marketing teams.

My biggest piece of advice is to make sure you understand the language of your business. Is success about double-digit growth? Is it about EBITDA? Are they looking at specific metrics? And if so, through which lens are they looking at them? Dig in with both your C-suite and your board to really figure out what motivates them – what angle are they having in these conversations? Know the business metrics and statistics, not just the marketing ones, and understand how the marketing ones fit into the bigger picture. But more than speaking their language, really understand what their individual drivers are, both personally and professionally.

Lorelei Lenzen

CMO, RethinkFirst

An accomplished and passionate B2B CMO with over 25 years' experience building and transforming brands, developing successful marketing, demand and communication programmes and engaging employees. Lorelei is recognised for her ability to partner with global business and sales heads to develop tailored strategies to position products, generate demand and achieve targeted sales growth across regions and segments.

References

1 Aguilar, F (1967) *Scanning the Business Environment*, Macmillan, New York
2 Porter, ME (1979) How competitive forces shape strategy, *Harvard Business Review*, 57(2) 137–145. hbr.org/1979/03/how-competitive-forces-shape-strategy (archived at https://perma.cc/ZVX7-6VNM)

4

B2B audience targeting

Gaining a detailed understanding of your current and future buyers is an absolute imperative. You should know the size and scale of the total address-able market (TAM) in your industry or sector, and then you need to drill down into the detail of who your specific buyers are. As I noted at the beginning of this book, there has been a shift in thinking over the last decade, recognising that buyers, while individual people, work in buyer groups who decide on the outcomes of potential purchases and appoint suppliers together. The current thinking is to look at the buying group in its totality, including those who are influential to the purchase. This is the group of people on the client side who work together to decide supplier appointments. When this thinking is combined with Antonia Wade's approach to the attitudinal movement through a buying cycle detailed in her book *Transforming the B2B Buyer Journey*, it is necessary to drive a connected view across both their role and thought process as an individual buyer but also within the broader buying group.[1]

To know the scale of your audience and understand their needs, the first step is to think about the users of your products and services – the primary, secondary and potentially tertiary buyers – alongside your buying influencers. I have built the following approach to summarize who you need to think through as you define your target audience (see also Figure 4.1).

Enterprise level sales are a lot more complicated than smaller- or mid-scale sales and a lot more difficult to move groups of prospects through the buying process. This same theory can be applied to simpler sales, but you will not need to get to quite the same level of detail as those who are selling larger scale products and services.

FIGURE 4.1 The audience circle

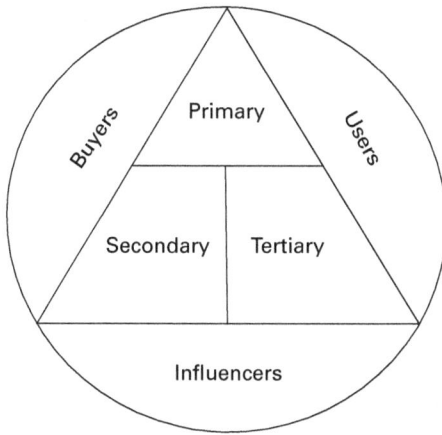

Primary

The main buyer of your products and services can be seen as the primary buyer. They are likely to lead the team that are also the primary users. For instance, if you sell accounting software you will probably deal with the finance function as the buyer and will have to think through how you appeal to and deliver for the CFO and their team (with the CFO as the primary individual buyer with the power to sign off). This group needs to feel confident that you are the right choice for them personally and professionally. The CFO, for instance, will need to believe that you are the company able to deliver their requirements. In some cases, the success of this decision will make or break their career. This is where the old adage 'no one gets fired for buying IBM' plays out. There is a fear of blame within B2B, compared to a lower-level fear of regret in B2C. It is much more difficult for a new entrant to play in a high-value space for this very reason. In order to convince a buyer that you are able to deliver, you will need to jump through more hoops. This leads to certain players being seen as the most trusted, partly due to the collective belief that they are known to all the decision makers around the table. Looking at LinkedIn Financial Services' Payment Buyer Services research, released in 2024, 74 per cent of those surveyed said that it was important for the buying group to be aware of a provider before the buying cycle begins.[2] They also note that buying committees are increasing in size with an average of seven members, so it is increasingly important to build trust and credibility with all individuals who might be in the buying or influencing group.

For a smaller scale sale, you are likely to only deal with the primary buyer, who is key to the decision to purchase from you and your business. You will need to ensure that they have both mental and physical availability to buy from you. Are you considered by your prospects in this space and are you easy to buy from?

Secondary

A secondary buyer could be someone in a role that is an integral part of the buying group but is not necessarily one of the primary users or in the same function as the primary buyer. Thinking through the accounting software example, this could be the next layer of users of the product. For instance, those who are looking for information from the CFO or finance function, including those who work in operations or are looking after ordering aligned components to fulfil manufacturing requirements. This group includes those whose roles and responsibilities are directly impacted by the insights and information coming out of the software. This group will have direct input into the requirements for a product or service, are likely to be able to drive scope or likely to be involved in the decision-making process itself. You will need to drive both broad-scale awareness but also a deeper understanding of your value proposition – the 'why you' versus the competition in this category.

Tertiary

This third level of buyers will probably only be part of a larger enterprise level sale. They can comprise another set of users. For instance, using the accounting software example, they could be those individuals inputting their timesheet or customer data into the software. They will drive functional demands for a product or influence the adoption of a new service within a business, so you will need to think about driving broad awareness of your business and value proposition with tertiary buyers.

Buying influencers

There are many influencers of a B2B purchase, significantly more so than B2C, and with huge influence on the decision itself due to the size and scale of the spend and potential personal impact to the buying group themselves. Making the wrong decision when buying insignificant products, like toothpaste, is unlikely to produce an adverse outcome for the individual.

These influencers exist internally and externally and are often overlooked. There are formal and informal influencers, those that influence as part of their roles and those that influence solely on purchases that relate to them.

Internal

Internally, these include all of those involved in a sale.

For example:

- The procurement department, who will be involved in the process and contracting.
- Legal for contracting sign-off on significant purchases and to ensure adherence to data regulation.
- IT departments, both in information security and cybersecurity teams where needed.
- Quality assurance for physical product purchases.
- Supply chain management when integral to onward manufacturing.

You should look at the full scale of those involved in influencing the purchase of your products or services, making sure you know who they all are and mapping them out as you work through your plan. Ensuring that you include internal influencers in your marketing plan will ensure that sales are less likely to get blocked by an influencer such as procurement – an increasing player and decider in the end result as noted in the external perspective from Ian Ewart at the end of this chapter.

External

Externally these can include trade bodies, media and industry analysts.

Trade bodies will influence buyers who are looking for suppliers who are members of groups that convey trust to their members through adherence to standardized processes or regulations. This can range from manufacturing kitemarks to process sign off, e.g. ISO certification to financial regulation, the UK's FCA or US's SEC.

Being a member of an industry's key trade body can also help with getting early notification of those businesses bringing contracts to market. For example, for creative agencies who advise and build marketing assets, being involved with the Advertising Agency Roster (AAR) in the UK or the Association of National Advertisers (ANA) in the US can mean being alerted to more new business pitches or being proposed by a third party as a potential long/shortlist supplier. Entering or judging industry awards means that you can both gain recognition and get involved in defining what is deemed to be the 'best' in the awards categories that are most relevant to your business.

Media influence is derived from both proactive and reactive media relationships. Ensure that you use PR as a strategy to directly influence journalists, bloggers and vloggers to deliver your message in earned media channels where you do not pay for placement, but where coverage is based on the journalist or influencer's knowledge of your brand, products and services. Earned media delivers your message into the hands of potential buyers when they are open to receiving messages. As 'news' is consumed by buyers on their own terms, this coverage is hard earned but incredibly well received and influential. You will need to ensure that PR is a key part of your strategy if you have particularly senior buying groups who are hard to reach with 'paid for' advertising. It is also important to ensure that you are continuously publishing to the media and individual influencers so that your prospects are aware of you, even when they are not ready to buy. It is also good to think through how you might solve or respond to negative stories. Is there anything that you can get ahead of through background briefings? Can you manage the message around anything that might hit outside of the planned campaigns or at least be prepared to deal with anything difficult that might arise? Trust and integrity are key to most buyers, and while this is built over prolonged periods of time, it can be lost very quickly. Associations with specific stories in the press can also have long standing influence (see the external perspective from Elliot Moss in Chapter 1 for an example of how this has been used to drive growth for the Mishcon de Reya brand).

Industry analysts are key to large-scale enterprise decisions and the analyst firms are highly valuable as direct influencers of sales. If a company is reviewed and rated as a top provider of a specific solution or service, this creates greater credibility. Many procurement teams start a request for proposal (RFP) process with a review of the industry analyst reports in the space they are looking to buy. Companies, therefore, court analyst teams to ensure that they are fully briefed on all innovations, areas of investment and the strategic direction the company is taking so that they can be seen in the best possible light. They are also highly valuable sources of research as analyst teams have specialists aligned to, and fully aware of, details across an industry. They speak regularly to your customers and prospects and can give you greater insight into potential trends and disruptors in your space.

If you consider large language models (LLM) and how they are trained and consume data, it is clear that technology is an external influencer. You need to ensure that the right information about your company is available to those using AI and GenAI models like ChatGPT to curate information for them. This will only become more of a need moving forward and is something you need to build into your digital plans by ensuring you have web content that is both right for prospective customers and for web crawlers feeding the models. One hypothesis that exists is that more buyers across B2B and B2C will rely on their AI assistant in their mobile to share the most relevant information to them based on their needs. When we also look at a cookie-less future and the need for content that exists behind a login or paywall to enable a true value exchange for registered users, both prospects and customers, this poses more interesting questions. Will websites only exist in the future for commerce and crawlers and if so, how do we balance the different content needs for both?

Functional buying drivers

As you start to build an understanding of your specific buyers, users and influencers, you will be more aware of who you need to include in your audience planning, which will be built into your tactical marketing execution plan. Understanding the drivers for each of the members of the buying group will help you think through the messaging and value propositions you will need for your products and services.

There will be commonalities by function as well as those that are driven by both personal and professional preferences.

Legal and compliance will need to see that you comply with the relevant geographic requirements and regulations. While these may not be what you want to emphasize in your messaging, there needs to be content within your product descriptors, handbooks etc. that can be referenced as required. If you are working in a regulated environment, it is essential that these have all the detail available for prospective clients and customers.

If targeting a specific company with *procurement* involvement, you should ensure you are aware of any policies and procedures that they follow. Do they base their buying decisions on a maximum level of exposure per supplier. For example, is there a maximum that they will enable any one player in the market to sell to them (e.g. 25 per cent of their spend with any one player) or a percentage of your sales that they wish to spread the risk of buying from you (e.g. no more than 49 per cent of your sales can be reliant on them as a single supplier).

By demonstrating your previous work through use cases and impact stories that cover the geographies you operate in (including how you have executed and implemented your products and services), it will enable those broader functional influencers to see that you have both credibility and experience in these areas.

There are many foundational tactics that you can build in across your annual plan to ensure you have your baseline influencer audiences covered, but it will ultimately be a case of prioritizing and targeting where you are most likely to realize the revenue you need, aligned to your agreed priorities.

Segmentation

As marketers we need to segment the market to work out where to target our messaging efficiently. The size and scale of our industries and categories mean that we need to work out who the most valuable people and companies are to focus our efforts.

With the 2021 research from the Ehrenberg-Bass Institute showing that 95 per cent of businesses are not in the market for most products and services at any one time, we need to build our plans to drive immediate sales for the 5 per cent that are primed to buy while also building the mental availability for those not yet in that position.[3]

Building your segmentation

With a broad understanding of your industry, the size of the market, the typical buyers in the buying group and the influencers who play in your space, you can start to think about how you target the most lucrative segments for your business. Segmentation of the audience you are looking at will enable you to think about groups of businesses you might be interested in. These segments can be driven by any number of distinctive features. There used to be a focus on driving clearly distinct segments where individual accounts had to be in one segment or another, all delineated on behavioural or sociodemographic differences which had been validated through research with the aim of building a clear list of target accounts to work through. Now, with the B2C-thinking around category entry points (CEPs) starting to become more prevalent, I think the crossover application for B2B should be considered.

CATEGORY ENTRY POINT

The different needs a customer might satisfy with your product. The prevalent thoughts that a buyer in your category has when moving towards the point of purchase.

In B2B purchases this could mean different functional needs that are met by the same integrated solution or service.

The points at which a business needs your products or services should be the starting point for your thinking. Ask yourself:

• Why does a business need what we do?

• What are the products/services used to meet the requirements?

• What are the drivers behind a buyer starting to research the category?

• What are the ways into the sale?

• Are we able to predict the drivers that nudge buyers?

Looking at your customer base, speaking to them and understanding their answers to these questions will help you gain a greater insight into what they use and why they buy your services. Using this will help you work out what it is you actually help your customers and clients do. I think about this as 'unravelling spaghetti'. The first answer will never be the end use. Really getting to the underlying need is key – what are people buying your product or service for? It might seem really obvious, but it can be a difficult task.

For example, the house building company needs more materials. They need them to build more houses. *Why?* They have a new contract with a local government scheme. *Why?* They pitched and won their contract partly based on the sustainable policies they built into their plan, so they need your FSCS-certified materials to be able to validate their delivery. The underlying driver for purchasing your materials is the sustainable nature of them and the entry point to the purchase is underpinned by this. In this example, there will be a segment of buyers that are driven by this factor, with others delivering to completely different drivers.

Knowing why companies are choosing products and services gives you the insights you can build into your plans and highlight in your messaging to target the specific segment of buyers. It might be that your size and scale mean that by focusing on one entry point you are able to deliver the business objectives, or you may be large enough to support multiple buying segments. Each segment will need its own plan aligned to the needs of the specific buyers, and this will not only define the promotional plan, but will influence all 4Ps: pricing, the place for distribution and your detailed product thinking.

For large-scale enterprise level sales, you must understand the needs of the full buying group and may well need to segment and target them differently. This is both due to their needs but also due to the driver behind them being able to buy. An example I often use is selling large-scale technology implementations using a CRM system.

- The *CIO/CTO* will need to know you are able to deliver in this space.
- *The finance function and CFO* will need to ensure that you will deliver the value you promise.
- *Procurement* will both need to balance the share of basket and ensure you are fit for the job.
- *Information security* and *cybersecurity* will be interested in the technical detail.
- The primary buyer, probably a *functional leader in sales and marketing*, will be driving the decision based on your functional delivery and previous credentials.

Each of these members of the buying group has different drivers, different needs and will need different proof points in the messaging. The potential opportunity could also be triggered by any member of the team, not just the primary buyer, which is another factor you should build into your segmentation as well as onwards into your execution plans.

Segmentation based on buying behaviour – recency, frequency and regularity of purchase – can also add a layer of understanding when looking at building profitable segments. Looking at how you can increase the frequency or scale of purchases within your current customers should be one of the first strategies you investigate. Driving a more frequent or larger scale purchase within a loyal customer base through incentivized retention or loyalty programmes is often more cost effective than looking to acquire entirely new customers. A loyal customer base can also be used to drive advocacy through case studies or co-marketing to the broader potential prospect population.

Individual segmentation

Alongside the business segmentation – where you might be looking to target specific companies or deliver within a specific account base for your business – you will need to think about the individuals within those buying groups. These individuals are all obviously people, but they are often referred to by title or by groups of titles and targeted as such. For instance, focusing on CxOs (e.g. CEO, CIO, CFO) is something often discussed when selling enterprise-level services. Grouping people together by role is certainly a starting point, but you need to think about the overlay of a number of other factors – industry, geography, tenure in role – all of which is available as public data. This will then need to be combined with more attitudinal details – their personal objectives, social styles and buying drivers. These are much harder to glean. As part of your plan, you might look to drive awareness at the role level, with a programme that targets CIOs, for instance, at a broad level, through targeted advertising driving to useful insight and thought leadership that can be self-selected by your audience. This element of self-selection enables you to understand your prospects better – what are they interested in and what you can therefore deliver for them through a targeted nurture programme that is built on a value exchange. We refer to a value exchange here because the individual needs to see enough value in what you are delivering in exchange for them to share their data, and hopefully sign up for further updates. This then enables you to build a relationship between your brand and your audience at an individual level, which can be operationalized through marketing technology and automated based on steps in a pre-planned journey.

INDIVIDUAL PREFERENCES

Preferences that are selected by an individual through an online subscription process for their communications, often referred to as a preference centre, should be combined with the behaviour individuals display by using your online platforms. There is a tendency for people to be incredibly rational when selecting preferences via a tick box process, but they are often curious about unrelated options. When building your segmentation, the category entry point approach allows you to be more inclusive with both stated and behavioural preferences as it is less delineated on these rational grounds than the main driver of the segmentation. There also needs to be room for serendipitous stumbling, where an individual can be shown a range of other areas that might pique interest alongside the obvious topics.

This starts to build a bigger picture of the individual as a person with interests, which will in turn help the sales teams or key account teams build an offline relationship.

The use of AI and GenAI is driving the ability to hyper-personalize at scale so campaigns that were previously built on broad brush segments are now able to be driven to individual needs with progressive profiling (the understanding of your buyer through small ongoing asks), built at greater speed than ever before. This takes away a huge amount of time that marketing departments previously spent building aligned assets and planning campaigns across different industries, geographies and buyers. Unlocking the value AI can bring relies on your data being AI ready – with a clear data dictionary, unique individual profile IDs across the business and a customer data platform that brings both the individual- and account-level data together. A focus on these fundamentals will set you up for the future. You must ensure that your business has a clear and clean data strategy, aligned to, and a core part of, your marketing function to stand you in good stead for the future.

CORPORATE BUYER PERSONAS

Buyer personas are an incredibly useful way of bringing potential buyers to life and are often used in B2C companies to enable teams to think about the people they are selling to, their motivations and what the optimal messaging might be for that specific buyer.

The use of personas within B2B marketing is often reserved for user experience design for customer journeys across online platforms, enabling digital marketing teams to think through how the platform should be designed to optimize the next best action the audience should be driven towards. Personas should be built to reflect your ideal buyers from across your segments and can be used across the broad business to align teams around their needs. By putting your target buyers at the heart of your business, you are more likely to deliver an outstanding experience that will ultimately increase revenues.

ACCOUNT-BASED TARGETING

At scale, segmenting your approach to your audience will involve building out an account-based segmentation that looks at tiering the accounts based on the growth potential you are looking to realize. Aligning marketing support focused on the account tiers enables you to drive maximum potential from marketing campaigns with a clear understanding of the needs of individual accounts.

FIGURE 4.2 Account-based targeting tiers

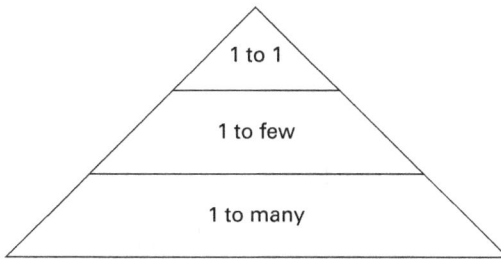

As Figure 4.2 shows, this support can be divided into three tiers.

1 to 1: account-based marketing (ABM) focused on a single account, treating each like a market in its own right. Individual campaigns focused on supporting the growth potential of a single account, with marketing focused on driving experiences that enable deeper relationships that can land and expand your business' footprint within the client landscape. Campaigns that focus on a single account will be clearly focused on driving quality relationships that specifically target the individual and business needs.

1 to few: focusing on a small group of accounts normally driven around specific themes or topics that are common to the group. There might be obvious triggers that enable you to build a target group, for instance a regulatory change, or other external force. There could also be more attitudinal shifts or potentially emerging trends or themes that might bring potential new opportunities to the fore, including new technology like the focus on AI.

1 to many: focusing on broad swathes of accounts which have common attributes that enable you to target them as a holistic group, for instance selling SaaS products to the CIO and CMO across a number of manufacturing companies would need you to target both buyers with messaging that resonates for those roles within the industry they operate in.

Across all account-based targeting, the key approach is to look to drive upsell and cross-sell potential within accounts that know and trust you through a focus on enabling the optimal customer experience. This increases the understanding of the full portfolio available, bringing the account as a holistic buying group closer to the point of purchase.

Research

Research is often used to evaluate products and services, marketing assets and messaging directly with potential customers. They can be assessed against multiple audience segments to understand the interest and resonance of various products and services with different business segments and individuals within the buying groups.

To find out the rational and emotional drivers that can be used as relevant attributes built into a segmentation, both primary and secondary research methodologies are implemented.

Primary research methodologies

Quantitative research methodologies include surveys and questionnaires that are focused on understanding populations as a whole, providing statistically relevant findings that can be used as an approximation to the holistic audience in question.

Qualitative research includes deep, focused research that gets into the detailed attitudes and drivers that might exist behind broader thinking. This will include verbatim quotes and opinions that will give depth to the data uncovered through a quantitative approach. This type of research includes focus groups and 1-to-1 interviews.

Secondary research methodologies

Primary research involves the creation of new data and insights, whereas *secondary research* collates data sources that can include primary research sources and pulls together the available data. It includes desk research methods, which include reviewing newspaper articles, journals, publications and other published sources.

A new source or method of data or insight collection includes the use of *AI tools* as a provider of basic understanding and initial draft thinking. An LLM that has been trained on data sources, e.g. ChatGPT, which is built on the GPT AI model, can answer prompts and, along with other similar apps, be a useful source of secondary research.

Synthetic audience research

There are a number of companies that are combining leading-edge research methodologies and new marketing methods with innovative AI approaches.[4]

Synthetic research can generate samples at scale, enabling you to build simulated segments that you can interrogate through quantitative and qualitative methodologies, allowing you to test messages, creative ideas, add creative assets, email copy and also conduct large-scale surveys. There are very positive outcomes of testing synthetic research versus traditional research methodologies, with an increasing accuracy in outcomes and insights, which is likely to solidify over time as the technology learns to emulate your customer base.

Customer lifetime value

Once you have established your segmentation, the next step is to determine the most valuable accounts or businesses to target. This value can be calculated only if you understand the longer-term value that an individual buyer and account is able to deliver. Looking at the total value of all sales at the account level and the annualized revenue by year over the life of their time as a customer or client will give you their total customer lifetime value (CLV).

With an established understanding of your current most-valuable clients, you will be able to build look-a-like segments. These segments would be based on those that have been seen to be valuable, using similar demographics, behaviours and industry information to pull out and target those companies or clients that look like they should behave in the same way as your current most-valuable segments. Machine learning techniques used to build these models can be updated over time as your acquisition programmes come to fruition. The consistent goal for you and your marketing team should be to minimize the customer acquisition costs (CAC), bringing in the highest value clients at the lowest possible price (ahead of them leaving you). Customer churn – when a client leaves you – is an element to build into your retention model, looking for likely blockers to that churn. Lead generation techniques optimized against your look-a-like segments are the ideal strategies to follow to maximize value from your acquisition budget.

Positioning

The positioning of your product and services should be built on the deep understanding of the segmentation you have built and the needs of each segment, the human need that your product or service can help overcome and the unique position your product or service takes in the mind of the buyer. We will go on to work through value proposition development in Chapter 5, however the steps to segment and understand the needs of your buyers is key to achieving a successful brand position.

Measurement and optimization

Measuring the success of your segmentation should be built into your ongoing performance and impact understanding.

For instance, if you know the share of each segment that you currently service, or the volume of customers that buy your products, one target would be to increase that share, therefore increasing revenues. You are also likely to know what each segment buys from you, what adjacent products they might buy from you and be looking to drive the upsell or cross-sell accordingly. This should be built into your ongoing measurement frameworks so that you can see the overall change in revenue impact but can also drill down into the performance of each segment.

Segments are not static, so will change over time, with individuals and accounts cycling through different segments as they evolve. This in itself is something to understand and get under the skin of. What is driving movement? Is it driven through exposure to your brand and marketing messages? What are your competitors doing that might be impacting your segments? Does your pricing hold up against the needs and demands of your customers and clients? You must ensure you understand your competition, who will also have identified their target segments and be positioning themselves to target them. An ongoing review of the macro context will keep you focused on both the external customer and the external market holistically, so that you will be able to pivot if market dynamics shift or external changes nudge you or your customers in a different direction (think about your PESTLE from Chapter 3). Looking at the value of your segments, across both the short and long term will also help you identify where you need to invest your efforts, alongside both financial and human resources.

Driving a detailed understanding of how your clients, accounts and segments value the delivery of your products and services will also enable you to optimize your brand experience, setting you up for the long-term. As we have seen previously, both physical and mental availability are key to driving long-term growth. There are multiple methods to understand how your customers and clients value the experience you deliver, which we will discuss in coming chapters, across four areas of focus: **brand, reputation, relationships** and **revenue**.

SUMMARY

- You have defined your audiences

    o   Primary, secondary and tertiary buyers

    o   Internal and external influencers

    And you have thought through the functional buying drivers

- You have begun to build your segmentation, with an understanding of

    o   Your category entry points

    o   Individual segmentation and preferences

    o   Corporate buyer personas

    o   The potential of account-based targeting

    o   Where you might need further information and research methodologies
        that might apply

Coming up next:

The importance of your brand, developing aligned value propositions and
driving a connected brand experience.

AN EXTERNAL PERSPECTIVE

*Taken from a conversation with Ian Ewart, Adviser, Board Member Non-Executive
Director FinTech and Financial Services.*

The rise in the purchasing power of procurement and hidden influencers

As a young executive, part of my brief was to be on the lookout for good ideas;
disruptive thinking that would help the organization grow. And, importantly, I
had approval to move forwards at pace – often referred to as 'fail fast'. I think it
is essential that organizations have the flexibility to test and learn and evolve
thinking as the market shifts around you. Innovation should be a core principle
of the function's delivery approach.

Today, it frequently seems that teams do not have permission to pivot
without jumping through numerous and ever more complex internal hoops.
They will likely have to review an amended scope of work with their internal
governance teams, which includes both legal and procurement. These two
functions have increasing power in driving the direction of a business, which
means growth could be restricted by their appetite for risk.

The biggest difference I have seen between my time in both B2B and B2C roles is how people buy; consumers make their own buying decisions (other than the large communal family purchases). All B2B sales are about unlocking value for the business to sustain growth – be that through cost efficiencies, transformation or revenue enhancements – but B2B is now driven by procurement, and the influence of these hidden buyers is increasing. Procurement has become all powerful in corporate terms, budgets are approved in line with the business strategy and then managed by their team. No approved budget equates to no engagement. And if there is no engagement there is never going to be a purchase at the end of it.

As a buyer of business services in multiple previous roles, I know that a successful purchase is increasingly like docking a spaceship with the space station. You need a planned course, led by procurement, with a pitch process for potential providers. Agreed budgets, specification and the mechanistic process itself stifles the innovation in the initial conversation. The project sold then must deliver to the timing and specifications agreed upfront, aligned to success factors and impact measures. The suppliers' brand, capabilities and reference material will play a part, but it is a part in a heavily controlled procurement process. The process often includes both a request for information (RFI) and the completion of a long reference procurement document, ahead of the request for a proposal (RFP). Once you have answered the hundreds of questions around the alignment of your values and internal policies, there is little room for innovative good ideas.

For the supplier, the sale process then becomes a question of resilience. How much do you value the sale? Can you afford to sell to your largest potential customers? If you have 16 months of runway and their buying process takes 18 months, then there is going to be an issue. What are you prepared to do, how many meetings, how much time will you invest in the relationship ahead of the sale? Is the long-term relationship worth the resources to get to the starting point?

There is an efficiency driven through procurement which takes much of the human aspect out of this initial stage of the relationship. Once you are an approved supplier and on the approved supplier list, with a Master Service Agreement (MSA), then you are in. And that is when it becomes more interesting as you can start to work in a consultative way with your clients and can be involved in writing the next RFP, giving you a step ahead of the competition. But the slog to get there can take out the smaller, more entrepreneurial types, as the resources for these lengthy business development processes can be too much for those without deep pockets.

My advice is to understand procurement as a buyer, understand what drives them, what their objectives are and work with them. In the future the procurement team and their process will be seen as a value differentiator. If businesses get better at buying and make the process simpler, the economy would move at greater pace with more innovation and higher growth. As the purchase of new strategies and ideas becomes more efficient, we could see a more fruitful, innovative business environment.

Ian Ewart

Formerly CMO Barclays Wealth, and previously held senior marketing roles at Bank of America Merrill Lynch, Coutts and HSBC. Currently board member and strategic adviser to multiple start-ups and early stage fintech and financial service providers.

References

1 Wade, A (2023) *Transforming the B2B Buyer Journey: Maximize brand value, improve conversion rates and build loyalty*, Kogan Page, London
2 LinkedIn (2024) It always pays to stand out: How financial services marketers grab buyers' attention, B2B Institute Financial Services Research business. linkedin.com/marketing-solutions/financial-services-marketing-back-up/ it-always-pays-to-stand-out (archived at https://perma.cc/Q6HL-CE7Q)
3 Dawes, J (2021) 'Advertising effectiveness and the 95–5 rule: Most B2B buyers are not in the market right now, LinkedIn – The B2B Institute. business.linkedin.com/content/dam/me/business/en-us/marketing-solutions/ resources/pdfs/advertising-effectiveness-and-the-95-5-rule.pdf (archived at https://perma.cc/6V8F-UUKR)
4 WARC (2024) 'The WARC Podcast. *How Synthetic Data Is Transforming Market Research*, 11 June 2024. podcasts.apple.com/gb/podcast/the-warc-podcast/ id1563243327?i=1000658586289 (archived at https://perma.cc/7C6Z-3F7L)

5

B2B brand: Why it matters more than you think

Marketing folk know the power of building a brand for consumers and customers but what does it mean in the world of B2B?

Taking a step back and looking at the basics and working through the foundations, we're going to first look to understand what a brand is and then recognize the value of a brand itself. We will look at how we can build a strong and consistent brand in the market through all elements of the marketing mix.

What is a brand?

A brand is the name used to publicly identify you in the market, aligned with the values and promises you deliver through your products and services. The brand consists of all elements of your business, both the tangible and intangible, that drive the perception of your business in your audience's mind. Jeff Bezos famously suggested that a brand can be defined by what is said about you or your company when you are not in the room. This is also known as reputation – and is only one of the intangibles that align to the brand in its entirety. Your brand is how you, your business, your products and services are thought about. It is the lasting impression left by the experience that your clients and customers have and, even more importantly, what they anticipate the experience will be.

WHAT IS A BRAND?

A brand is the sum of all expressions by which an entity (person, organization, company, business unit, city, nation, etc.) intends to be recognized.[1]

There are many facets of a brand – tangible and intangible – each of which play together in unison and create the experience of the brand. This entire holistic experience defines how a brand resonates with its audience and, importantly, how it builds value through trust.

Building trust

Trust is built consistently over time by delivering a brand's promise in every touchpoint the audience experiences. It takes years to build a trusted association with a brand, and it can disappear in an instant with one negative experience. Trust is built on an expectation that is delivered steadily over time. In the early parts of this book, I referred to finding the brand truth and connecting that to the human need. The brand truth is the distinctive value proposition that is only delivered by you and your brand. To truly drive trust, this value proposition needs to be embedded into everything that you do. Using this as the lens with which you define and judge how you deliver across all elements of your business will help you drive a consistent brand experience.

Brand value

The value of your brand is difficult to quantify. As an intangible asset, it is hard to understand and ascribe an attributable worth to the brand and its surrounding assets. Building the brand is seen as a cost partly because the brand itself is not seen as a valued asset on the balance sheet. However, we know that brands have immense value, as is often demonstrated when companies divest themselves of branded businesses. We also understand brand equity and know that the added value a brand delivers against a non-branded item is considerable enough to enable differential pricing within the same category. Brand equity is driven by the perception of the brand, which in the mind of the buyer justifies the additional costs charged for a branded version of the same product or service.

Evaluating the total monetary value of a brand is not something that B2B marketers do on a day-to-day basis. B2C brand managers, however, are trained to maximize the value of the brand. Understanding brand management is a B2C speciality and something that we as B2B marketers can learn from. We need to hold each other to account and ensure that marketing teams understand and evaluate the brands that they manage. Building brand value into the KPIs for your marketing team will ensure that this is a priority.

An interesting piece of research, quoted by the American Marketing Association, looking at marketing asset accountability shows that it 'has the potential to bring about fundamental change in firms by documenting the economic value of marketing assets. Managers usually aim to optimize results reported to external investors. Without marketing asset accountability, the focus tends to be on short-term results, sometimes at the expense of long-term marketing investment and outcomes.'[2] If marketers were able to show the long-term growth of the value of branded assets in a financial context, rather than being seen as a cost on the balance sheet, the conversation would pivot to viewing marketing as a growth driver rather than a cost centre.

The strength of a brand can be measured through several methods. Brand Finance, the world's leading independent branded business valuation and strategy consultancy, has several published methodologies. These methodologies, and the resulting rankings, are often used in this space to bridge the gap between finance and marketing. The annual Brand Finance rankings evaluate the brand strength of more than 5,000 brands globally across both B2B and B2C.

BRAND VALUATION: TWO DIFFERENT APPROACHES

Brand finance

Financial accounting and reporting standards need a clear definition of what intellectual property is included in the definition of 'brand'. Brand Finance defines a brand as a 'bundle of trademarks and associated IP which can be used to take advantage of the perceptions of stakeholders to provide a variety of economic benefits to the entity'.

Brand Finance calculates brand value using the Royalty Relief methodology which determines the value a company would be willing to pay to license its brand as if it did not own it. This approach involves estimating the future revenue attributable to a brand and calculating a royalty rate that would be charged for the use of the brand.[3]

Interbrand

The Interbrand Brand Valuation Framework was the first to be certified as compliant with ISO 10668 (requirements for monetary brand valuation).

The three components of the framework include an analysis of the financial performance of the brand, the weight of the role that the brand plays in purchase decisions and the strength of the brand itself.[4]

The Global Intangible Finance Tracker (GIFT) reported annually by Brand Finance, found that global intangible value increased by 8 per cent from $57.3 trillion in Nov 2022 to $61.9 trillion in 2023, with the 6 brands at the top of the heap being Meta, Apple, Microsoft, Amazon and Alphabet (MAMAA – the top 5 global tech companies) and Aramco.[5] All of these brands deliver across both B2B and B2C.

Looking back at the EPIC report mentioned at the beginning of this book, we can also see that the value of a brand is key to driving the four types of stakeholder value, which aim to extend beyond short-term shareholder value.[6]

Financial value

Sales and revenue growth – driven by brand equity with value added through improved margins and support of sustainable business models that enable brand extensions and adjacencies, as described in detail in Chapter 3.

Consumer value

Brand trust and brand perception – maintaining brand value through consistent and responsible marketing messaging, enabling the voice of the customer at the core of the product design to build competitive advantage and drive increased customer retention.

Human value

Purpose and culture – embodying the brand throughout the company to ensure that the brand is at the heart of the business, delivered through all touchpoints employees have with the end customer; increased employee retention and productivity due to cultural alignment.

Societal value

Purpose, society and community engagement – limiting environmental impact, enabling brand advocacy across aligned community areas of focus.

We can also look at the influence and impact of brand viewed through the lens of the 4Ps:

- **Price:** The greater the brand equity the higher the pricing power that can justify an increase versus the competition or other unbranded, but similar, products and services.

- **Product:** A branded product can use brand power as a competitive advantage, consistently innovating at the core to ensure they are aligned with their buyers' evolving needs.

- **Place:** A strong brand will enable you to drive differential distribution power, ensuring you are stocked in relevant retailers, recommended by intermediaries or drive credible search engine results and client advocacy.
- **Promotion:** Perhaps the most obvious, promotions that surround your brand will drive awareness, consideration and ultimately sales when they authentically communicate the value proposition.

Looking at these elements, both the mental and physical availability are equally important. The power of your brand comes down to both the emotional triggers and connection to the brand alongside the distribution access and ability to purchase your products and services. According to BCG's 2021 report 'Why B2B Brand Marketing Matters', those organizations that focus on driving a clear and consistent approach to their brand marketing 'show a 74% higher return on their brand marketing investment and hold a 46% larger market share than weaker brands'.[7] It is therefore an absolute imperative to build your brand and ensure the right level of focus within your investment mix.

Elements of a brand

Building a consistent brand is increasingly important in B2B. With so few buyers in the market at any one time, plus a growing number of people in the buying group, you need to build memorable brand signals that can be a shortcut in your buyer's memory to what it is that makes you distinct. This individual brand story will then be associated in their minds with your branded assets, freeing up space in communications for you to share deeper messages, e.g. specific product and service details. It all starts with defining your brand story. What is it that makes you distinct? This then needs to carry through all marketing communications bringing your brand to life.

Purpose

The purpose of a company is its reason for being: what it is that it does every day and what it aims to do across all stakeholder groups it serves. It should be a statement that resonates with all employees and is the focus of how you deliver your products and services. It is a key part of the culture of the business and needs to be reflected in your brand, marketing and communications. It is also at the core of how you drive relevancy to the communities you operate within. A business or brand purpose that resonates with your employees can be built into their own personal purpose. This alignment gives an even greater sense of belonging to those that work for the business.

There is a traditional Japanese concept, thought to have been first coined in the 7th century, called *Ikigai* that is a framework used to enable individuals to find and build a sense of purpose. It can also be translated to businesses, firms and organizations, helping you fathom your north star. Working this through will enable you to think about what it is that drives you and your audiences, aligns to your profession and makes you money. The overlap between passion, mission, profession and vocation is where you need to focus as you develop your own unique purpose that gets to the heart of your own unique value proposition (see Figure 5.1).

FIGURE 5.1 Ikigai map

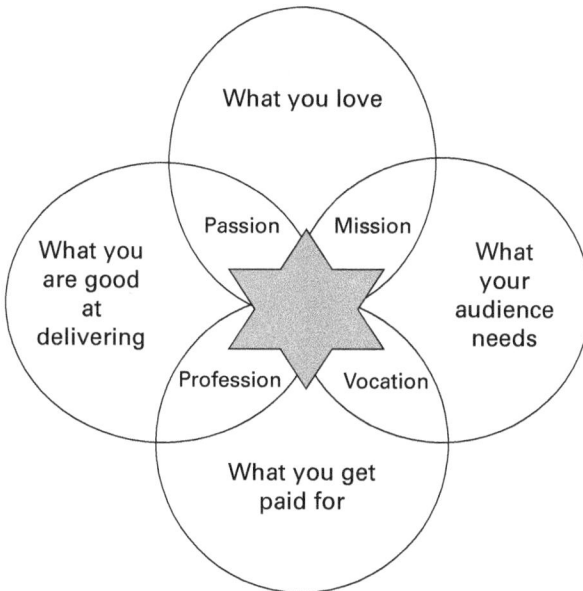

Brand positioning

The positioning of your brand in the minds of your audience should reflect how your brand sits alongside your *competitors*, how and what it delivers for your *customer* alongside how it operates as a *company*.

It should be built on what your customers know about you, your products and services, and what they feel when they use or consume them. An understanding of your position against your competitors is key. Looking at the variables relevant to your company, you can plot your position against your competitors by using an established 2x2 block model (Figure 5.2). Plotting out variables that are relevant to your business will help you understand the competition and how they position themselves. Variables might include price plotted against quality as a starting point – this will help you see the perception of you against your competitors as either low or high quality against low or high price. You will be able to see if there are any gaps in the market you might be able to own – either through an extension of your product or service portfolio – or the development of new offerings for the market.

You need to ensure that your positioning is true to what you actually deliver as a company. Overclaiming or overpromising will only end up with a mismatched customer experience which can undermine any trust you might have built.

FIGURE 5.2 Competitor positioning 2x2 block model

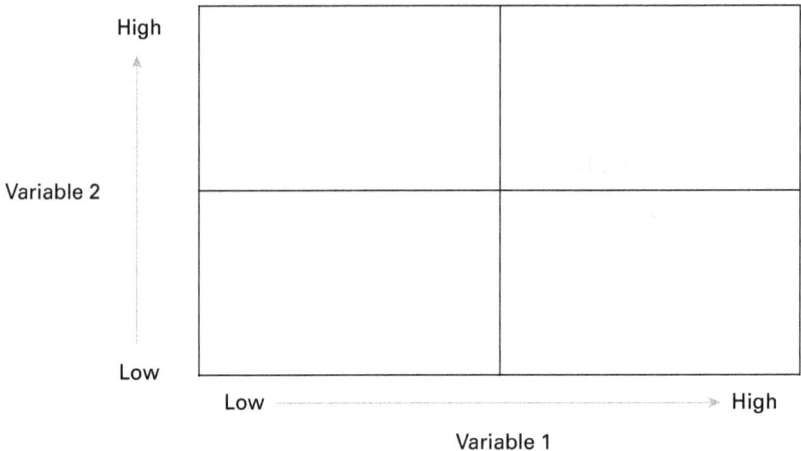

Brand promise

The brand promise is key to developing the value proposition. It is the promise to the buyer or customer that is realized when they purchase your products or services. It is your distinctive differentiator that details your brand position in terms that are relevant to the market, specifically your target audience, and is a key step in developing your messaging and narrative.

Value proposition development

There are lots of methods and frameworks that take you through the steps to develop a value proposition which are fundamentally the same four steps:

1 **What is the client's issue or challenge?** What is not working? What are the clients trying to solve?

2 **What does your brand, product or service do to overcome this issue?** What value can you add to your client? What elements of your product resolve these challenges? What are the proof points – what gives your client reasons to believe you can help them?

3 **Outcomes and impacts – What impact does the product or service have on your client's business?** How have you helped others like them? What stories and credentials can you tell them about the impact you have had?

4 **What is the fundamental promise of your brand in overcoming the pain points?** What is the truth that your brand conveys – and only you can promise? What is your unique differentiator that helps you stand out against the competition?

As you work through the development of your brand value proposition you will start to build your assets. By working through the detail of your target audience and your positioning, you can define the following.

Messaging and narrative

The messaging you develop around your brand needs to communicate the value proposition, the reasons to believe the detail and any insights that can help you solidify your position. This messaging and longer form narrative – the full prose around your positioning, which you might include on your 'About Us' page of a website or pitch proposal – needs to reflect the totality of your brand. Working through the inputs to your purpose development (using the Ikigai framework in Figure 5.1) will also help you think through the 'Why you' questions. Why choose you over the competition? What do you deliver that others can't? How do buyers feel when they buy or consume your products and services? Does this differ by role in the buying group? Have you considered all potential influencers in the messaging framework?

Elevator pitch

The elevator pitch is used as a shorthand for your messaging. It originates from the thinking that if you have the time it takes to go up in the lift with a potential buyer or investor, how would you convince them to either buy from you, or invest in your business? What would you say to them in the small, concentrated amount of time you have with the target audience?

Unique selling point (one liner)

Sum up your position in one simple line. What is your unique selling point (USP)? The one thing that should be remembered by the audience and stick in their mind. The association of the USP with brand assets will ensure recall of the message when the brand is seen.

Brand identity

A distinctive brand sets you apart, influencing audience choices and driving long-term value. The identity of a brand is vital to driving recognition. To stand out against your competition across all facets of your business, you will need to focus on driving a consistent brand construct across all aspects of its identity. Consistent delivery of a memorable identity anchors the brand in the part of the memory that enables recall, and the use of brand signals provides a shortcut to the associated messaging.

The first step in understanding your current brand identity is to conduct a brand audit. What is the current identity? How does it come to life across your portfolio and what assets are available? Looking at all of your messaging and campaigns will help you understand how consistently your existing brand identity is used across the full spectrum of your marketing mix. Ensuring greater alignment across all elements will help drive familiarity with your brand, business and products as you build out your market presence.

The second step would be to consider tonal alignment. Is your tone of voice telling the same brand story? Do the channels you choose for media or PR work together to substantiate who you are? Do you have a culture that enables your audiences to experience the brand from all touchpoints?

It is essential to revisit and refresh the brand identity, if needed, to fit your business strategy.

The identity, brand signals and assets are often summarized in a brand essence document which brings together all elements of your brand that make up its inherent personality or fundamental essence. These often include the overarching approach and guidelines for a number of brand elements.

LOGO, MARQUE AND ICON

Your logo embodies everything about your business and is often a combination of typography and an image. It is the stamp on a product that transfers the purpose, experience and credibility you have built through the delivery of your products and services. It is often the memory link needed to trigger familiarity.

Marque is originally a French word and translates to 'brand' in English. It is often used in reference to luxury brands in the automotive space.

An icon is the image aligned to a logo that can make up the logo as a whole when combined with the typography.

VALUES

Your brand values should reflect what you stand for. They should reflect how you operate your business and be key to your offering versus the competition in your category.

These will need to be actionable, applicable to and resonate at all levels of your teams. Simon Sinek, bestselling author and inspirational speaker, talks about values saying, 'Values are verbs, not nouns. In order to build the culture we envision, we have to enact our values in how we show up every single day. On both the positive and the negative side, ultimately what you value is what you will have.'[8]

We know that most of a brand experience is driven through the individual's specific experience of the products, services and associated aftercare, so culture is key to enabling a consistent brand identity.

TONE OF VOICE AND PERSONALITY

The tone of voice that your brand embodies will bring to life the personality traits you are looking to express.

As you think about your personality, it is useful to picture the individual who might be your brand. Are they formal or informal, a peer or an adviser, focused on value or luxury?

Once you have established the tone and personality these should be, use as a filter to all assets. Would your brand, as you have defined it, act in this way?

VISUAL IDENTITY AND BRAND ASSETS

These powerful, recognizable elements of your brand are at the core of your brand identity and can include assets that align to your look and feel across physical assets, such as the packaging or employee uniforms, but also covers digital imagery used across online channels. The questions you need to work through are:

- What does your brand look and feel like?
- What are the colours associated with your brand?
- What imagery or photography style do you follow?
- What is the iconography that fits with your brand essence?
- What visual identity aligns to your brand personality?

MNEMONICS/AUDIO BRAND

A great example of an audio brand is the Intel inside sound logo, which plays a simple five-note mnemonic and is uniquely linked to the Intel brand. Finding an audio logo that aligns to your brand is a useful step to take, particularly when using high-impact advertising channels that will drive audio awareness, and can behave like a catchy piece of music you can't get out of your head.

GUIDELINES AND TOOLKITS

Your entire brand identity should be documented so that all employees in your business understand what it means to be part of your brand and how it comes to life. You should show what 'good' looks like and also demonstrate what shouldn't be done (the brand guidelines you don't cross).

Keeping your guidelines up to date and providing toolkits aligned to the channels you use will also enable your teams to adhere to these rules and collectively you can protect and build your brand as a key growth lever for your business.

Brand versus marketing campaign messaging

The messaging you create should be aligned to all elements of your brand and able to be used across brand marketing, but it should also be able to be applied to products or services and used as part of campaign assets. These written assets should include credible reasons to believe your claims and your position.

'Reasons to believe' can be a combination of case studies, use cases, data-led intelligence and other proof points that add credence to the position you are taking in the market. These insights should be built into your campaigns to back up the execution of the value proposition and should be fundamental to the content used to drive further consideration and purchase of your products and services.

Your brand, product and campaign messaging should nest like Russian dolls and all align to each other, building throughout to a clear understanding of what each element means to the audience. The brand messaging should be built for the long term and have durability, whereas your products and services will change more quickly with client and customer feedback. As noted in Table 5.1, the messaging and assets for your products and services should therefore be reviewed annually, adding in any new features, benefits or additional proof points. Campaign messaging is driven by the current macro context and will likely be themed around short-term delivery targets, so should be reviewed more regularly.

This gives you a useful review time frame that should be built into your impact studies with an ongoing understanding of performance against the targets set for the brand, product or individual campaign metrics.

TABLE 5.1 Messaging review timeline

Timeline	5 years+	Brand messaging and narrative	Aligned to long-term brand positioning and value creation	Long-term targets, e.g. messaging resonance, brand awareness and recall metrics
	12M+	Products and services value proposition	Should be reviewed and refreshed annually to ensure continued relevance to audience needs	Increased consideration, client feedback and experience scores
	0-12M	Campaign messaging	Aligned to specific campaigns with short-term strategic goals	Short-term targets, e.g. lead generation, influenced revenue and direct sales

Brand management

Managing a single brand or multiple brands across your business has slightly different nuances that need to be managed intentionally depending on whether you are a branded house, a house of brands or somewhere in between. The decision that you take in this space will be driven by the needs of the market and the power and potential transference of the overall corporate brand.

A branded house

A branded house is one that leverages the main corporate brand for all products and services. GE, prior to a strategic shift in the late 2000s, was a great B2B example of this. GE Corporate, GE Capital, GE Healthcare, GE Aviation etc. were all built as a conglomerate and as an extension of the main corporate brand across all categories, building on the trust and heritage of the master GE brand. Its shift to sell off business units as separate companies meant a retraction to its core sectors and, in 2021, it announced it would divide into three public companies, which were later named as GE Aerospace, GE HealthCare and GE Vernova.

For B2B, the creative consistency experienced across a portfolio of brands is a positive outcome of the branded house. This is felt both internally – driving a combined culture, enabling combined talent strategies and aligned growth strategies – and externally, for enterprise clients who can avail themselves of solutions that cross the portfolio. However, at scale it can be difficult to manage, particularly if you have a strong acquisition strategy. There is also a potential downside of all brands being seen in the same light if something less positive happens, which could in turn taint the overall corporate brand and have far-reaching impact. Due to the smaller budgets spent in B2B compared to consumer-focused brands, we are more likely to see the branded house in the majority of B2B companies. B2C brands, with greater budgets and investment in marketing, are often able to support greater growth across multiple brands with different target audiences.

The trust conveyed by a master brand should not be underestimated for B2B buying groups. When dealing with enterprise-level sales or large-scale technology purchases, the credibility of a trusted brand will help the conversation at all levels, particularly with those outside the sphere of technical understanding. There is also a lower risk associated with the purchase of a larger, well-known brand in B2B, which removes some of the potential personal impact if something goes wrong. The power of a master brand can also simplify what might otherwise be complex messaging to the market – enabling an elevated conversation with your target audience.

House of brands

A house of brands is one that facilitates a different brand for differing groups of products and services. This allows for a differential focus on specific target audiences and enables a business to deliver distinct brand promises to each discrete audience. New, innovative opportunities often require an approach that can stand alone so that the value of the opportunity can be understood and then optimized, potentially through a divestiture of the branded business. Conversely, a house of brands is often a result of acquisitions where the purchased brand value is significant enough to be retained. Microsoft is an example of this. In the last few years, some significant purchases have been made and brought into the fold, including the purchase of LinkedIn in 2016, GitHub in 2018, ZeniMax Media in 2021 and Activision Blizzard in 2023, all retaining their own brands and sub-brands.

A house of brands enables you to build adjacencies in your own portfolio that might target a similar audience but differentiate on price – for instance, a higher value consultancy strand housed within a larger professional service organization. The maintenance of multiple brands is often only tenable when you have niche products targeting specific buyer groups or where your brands are at such a large scale that they operate as separate business units with capacity to invest and grow independently.

Portfolio management

Looking at both strategies, alongside any combined hybrid approach, it is imperative to define your brand architecture, ensuring you manage your brand identity across your products and services in line with your approach to the brand strategy of your portfolio.

Looking across the potential portfolio of your business, you can identify opportunities to expand your offering through potential acquisitions, product extensions or new products and services. An optimal portfolio will deliver brands that have minimal overlap but are able to drive maximum value from the audiences they collectively target. Understanding your brand's top- and bottom-line performance, both sales and margin, will help you determine those brands that are needed for long-term growth. When this is overlaid with market sizing, share of market and potential market growth, it becomes even more useful when you are looking to determine where you might want to prioritize the investment of your resources.

An ongoing review of your portfolio should be built into your performance and impact report. Are you growing ahead of competitors or just in line with overall market growth? The former is a successful result, whereas the latter is standing still against your competition. As you review your portfolio there may be some brands or products and services that are more valuable to you as an asset, so a sale or spin-off could be the right approach. There are others that might need to be closed and removed from your portfolio and there will be the golden nuggets – those that, with the right investment, could unlock much larger value than previously anticipated. When a brand is underperforming, it is worth investigating any crossover usage that may not be the core product category entry point upon which you focus. The adjacent usage for the product could prove to be a positive space for future targeting and should be investigated more thoroughly.

The performance of your brands can be measured throughout your business. With a single brand it will be more straightforward to measure the awareness and perception of your brand against the competition while understanding the macro context for your market. As you look at measuring brand performance through the impact on sales, pipeline and revenue, this becomes a much more detailed exploration, especially so when you start to look at the contribution from your planned initiatives across multiple brands. However, it is essential to test, learn and optimize as you invest in the marketing mix.

Knowing what is foundational to maintain as you build your plan, what messaging and channels contribute, and which successful tests should be rolled into business-as-usual is crucial. Measuring the long-term impact of your brand via brand value metrics and understanding the positive impact you can deliver through a strong position will help to continue justifying the investments needed.

Your business leadership, specifically the CFO, will be interested in understanding the detailed financial contribution the brand makes to drive sales. It is therefore imperative that you are able to isolate the impact of brand marketing – one method of doing this is through A:B testing, where your brand is supported (A) versus not supported (B) in your market. You can isolate any growth driven through the external marketing to show the uplift you help to influence. It is also useful to ensure you build the voice of the customer into any feedback so as to understand the resonance of your brand as the market continues to evolve and grow. This is an area where data scientists excel – with the combined curiosity, skills and technology to sift through the detail and find the nuggets that you can act upon. Bringing all available data points together and scrutinizing the numbers across your territories will give you powerful insight into where you should place your future bets.

Asset management

In a world where we are all consistently asked to do more with less, we need to ensure that we 'sweat the assets'. This means extracting every bit of value out of the investment in the assets you create. This is not something anyone can disagree with, but something we as marketers often neglect as we move onto the next thing on our ever-increasing to-do lists. The rise of both AI and GenAI helps with this challenge and using technology to store, tag and manage assets will enable this to work for you across an entire enterprise and brand ecosystem, both internally and externally.

DIGITAL ASSET MANAGEMENT (DAM) AND ENTERPRISE DIGITAL ASSET MANAGEMENT (eDAM)

Digital asset management enables you to store all your assets in one place, in digitized formats, enabled for easy multi-market access, storage and searchability. These assets include white papers, thought leadership, videos, advertising executions, sales brochures etc. They should be well tagged to facilitate search of the assets and enabled by keywords related to the content they contain. The imagery should also be tagged for licensing renewals and ease of removal. There should be a layer of governance to understand usage and links into the relevant workflows and interfaces where the assets might be used.

However, to get the ultimate value from your DAM and ensure it is highly useful, usable and efficient, the initial step should be to understand your content supply chain. Where and how are assets used? Which assets are most valuable to your company? Who needs to be able to access them and how are they built? Then you should look to standardize the library of branded assets you house. The inventory of all needed formats should be analysed from a component basis to standardize them across all outputs. This will help you use the same content across multiple formats. An eDAM enables the same efficiency across the totality of the enterprise and is the single source of truth for all content.

FIGURE 5.3 Creating a component-based asset

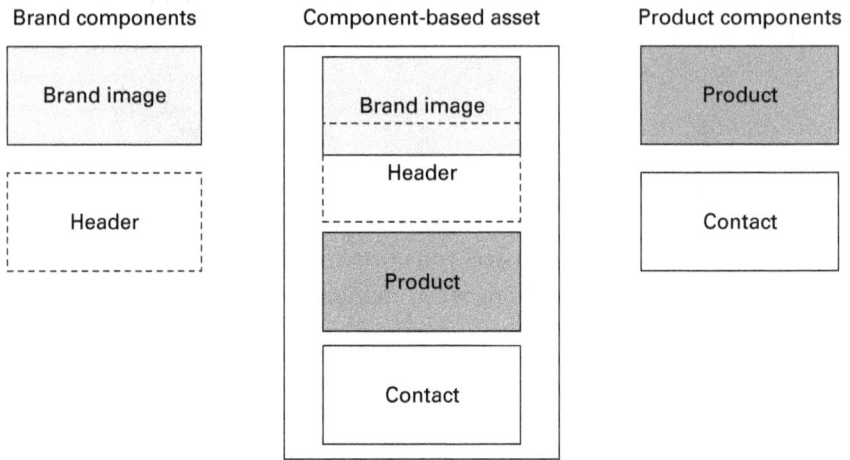

Brand components	Component-based asset	Product components
Brand image	Brand image	Product
Header	Header	Contact
	Product	
	Contact	

For instance, looking at Figure 5.3, the *brand image* component and *header* component will likely have several consistent outputs, sized and scaled to a standardized set of online and offline formats. A *component-based asset* for a particular product will have several components within it, including the related *brand image* and *header* components. It will also include the *product* component that describes its features and benefits and a *contact* component for the relevant sales team within your company. Now, if you imagine that all of these are consistent across your entire portfolio, built in a standardized approach for the needs of the component-based assets, you can start to see, as shown in Figure 5.4, how components can be used across all of your business' sales and marketing outputs, driving efficiencies and enabling testing at scale alongside simplifying the build of combined multi-product assets.

Layer in the use of GenAI to be able to deliver standardized templated assets from a master at the push of a button and you have an extremely powerful tool to enable you to service all of your markets and territories with a standardized and simplified approach. Translation can be built in but transcreation – where the content of the execution is changed to resonate in a different market but the tone, style and brand is maintained – is more difficult. An eDAM can be used to store any additional versions created, which can also be tagged for geographic usage so that cultural differences are understood, and you can conform to market driven norms that might impact the imagery, fonts, colours and other variants you use as appropriate.

FIGURE 5.4 Building multi-variate component-based assets

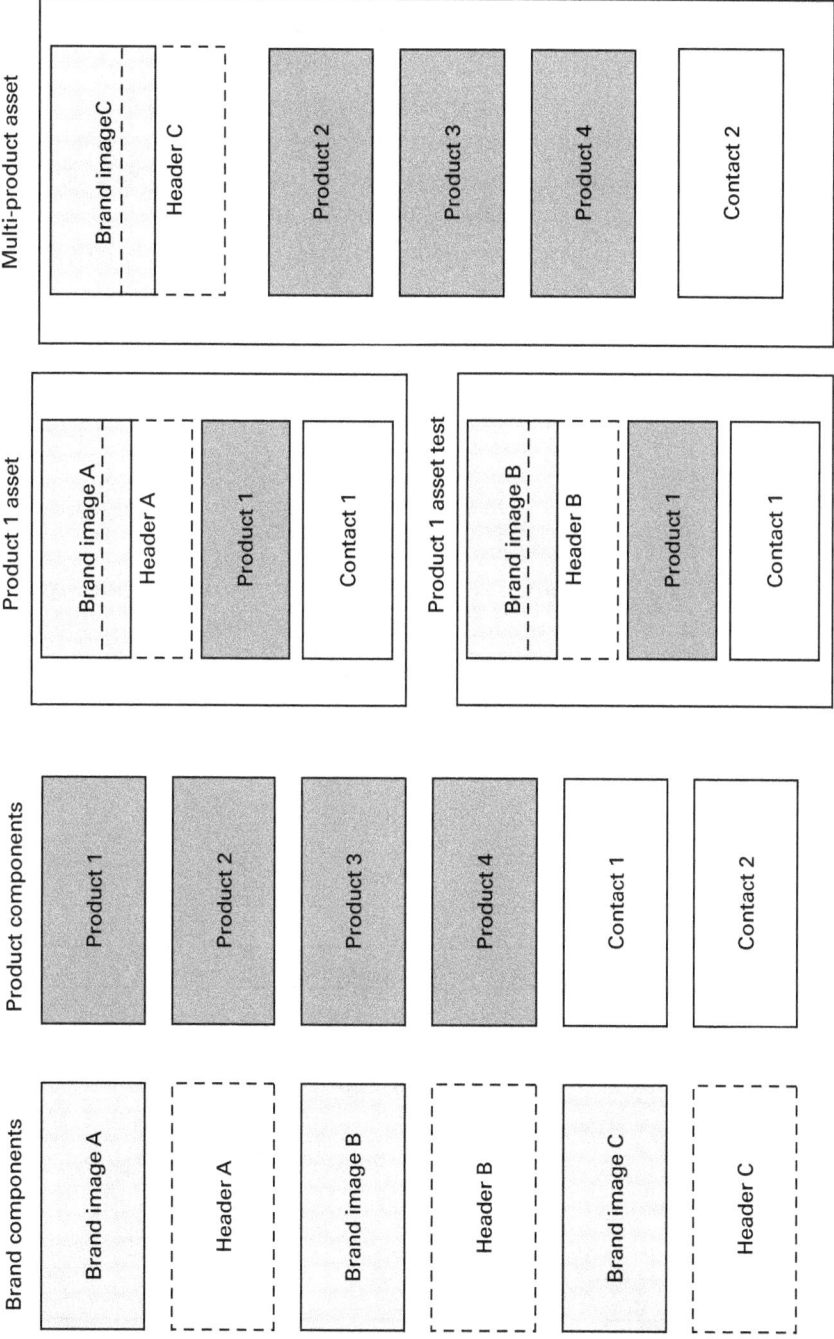

The key to any DAM solution, and there are many on the market, is to approach it like an online library for all your assets. You need to have the same rigour as an offline library within your metadata and tagging so that you can maximize the value of any originally created assets. It also provides you with a powerful tool to understand usage and performance of formats, particularly if linked into your analytics engine. Where image rights run out or product details (for instance) change, you may need to update or remove a particular asset; the governance built into an enterprise level DAM enables you to see where this might be used and therefore make these changes more easily than through manual search methods.

A DAM can also be used to house your brand guidelines, style guides and mandatory training, which can be set up as a registration requirement to drive completion.

Brand communication

The fourth P – promotion – is perhaps the most obvious one for marketers but has nuances within the B2B context. It is incredibly important that you tell your brand story across all channels, with an aligned messaging hierarchy that enables you to flex from brand to lead generation. A simple way of looking at this, aligned with the messaging work we have walked through to date, is seen in Figure 5.5.

FIGURE 5.5 Brand message house

Brand promise		
Brand positioning (elevator pitch)		
Brand campaign messaging (USP)		
Product/service value proposition	Product/service value proposition	Product/service value proposition
Campaign message	Campaign message	Campaign message
Proof points 1 2 3	Proof points 1 2 3	Proof points 1 2 3
Call to action	Call to action	Call to action

This helps you to see all messaging and proof points in one place and can be expanded or decreased to fit the scale of your business. You might have multiple campaigns per product or service, but they all need to nest together so that your overall messaging is cohesive and tells one brand story.

Bringing your messaging to life

We have discussed the power of emotional resonance in B2B, which becomes even more important when you are looking at landing your brand story. Communication across your full portfolio needs to be built around the brand promise, which hits at the heart of your business and is aligned to your purpose. This will give you the best springboard for delivering authentic, creative executions that resonate with your audiences.

The power of creativity should not be underestimated. Marketers talking to their business leaders often feel like they should discount the power of a creative idea, particularly when talking to highly rational individuals. Creativity is both an art and a science – it melds the right- and left-brain thinkers together. We can try to measure the performance of creative executions, but ultimately the spark of creativity comes from an insight that is given to a creative team via a simple creative brief (as mentioned in Chapter 2) and crafted into an idea. There is an intangible innovation that cannot be quantified. Some of the best creative ideas are the simplest but can take longer to develop than the more complex. This is because the client need should be understood by getting to the absolute core of why they will purchase the product.

As marketers we need to tell the story, weaving the proof points and case studies into a narrative that drives a desire to buy the products and services, even if the buyers are not in the market now. This ensures that you continue to build and drive a connected memory for when the buyers are ready to buy and at the category entry point. Storytelling is recognized as an important facet of the creative skillset – using stories and allegories to engage audiences, build connection, inspire different types of memory and build links from how you feel to an association with your brand.

Storytelling

Stories resonate so well that a huge proportion of advertising – in both B2C and B2B – follows the pathway of the 'three act structure' (Table 5.2). This is a structure used by playwrights and is often attributed to Aristotle but made popular by Syd Field in his 1979 book *Screenplay: The Foundations of Screenwriting.*[9]

TABLE 5.2 Three act structure

Act 1	The set up	An inciting incident or question
Act 2	The confrontation	The protagonist attempts to answer the question
Act 3	The resolution	The climax of the scene that brings it all to a head and ultimately answers the initial question

Think through any adverts you can remember as it is an often-used concept from B2C e.g. chewing gum... (Table 5.3)

...to much more complex B2B sales (Table 5.4).

TABLE 5.3 Three act structure applied to B2C advertising

Act 1	The set up	I don't have minty fresh breath...
Act 2	The confrontation	How do I get the girl or boy?
Act 3	The resolution	Chewing gum.

TABLE 5.4 Three act structure applied to B2B advertising

Act 1	The set up	Humanity is under threat from deepfakes and misinformation...
Act 2	The confrontation	How do I know and trust who is a real person in online content?
Act 3	The resolution	Intel Certified Human: The world's first technology to detect AI-generated deepfakes in real time.

There are more similarities between B2C and B2B than we acknowledge. Storytelling crosses over and is common to the needs of all audiences. Brands are as powerful, if not more so, in B2B as your audience is making what often feels like a bigger decision. If you buy the wrong B2C product you aren't putting your livelihood on the line when you make your buying decision. That is why a strong B2B brand will win every time as it takes an incredibly confident buyer to look outside the most well-known providers, whose reputations have been built on years of delivery and execution in their specialist fields.

SUMMARY

The key areas we have covered in this chapter are:

- Brand definition
    - o What is a brand and what does it mean
    - o Measuring the value of your brand

- Elements of a brand that make up your toolkit
    - o Purpose
    - o Brand positioning
    - o Brand promise
    - o Messaging
    - o Brand identity
    - o Logo, marque and icon
    - o Values
    - o Tone of voice and personality
    - o Brand assets
- Brand management
    - o The application of a branded house versus house of brands
    - o How to think about portfolio management
    - o Managing your brand assets
- Brand communication
    - o Bringing your brand to life
    - o Using storytelling to communicate your brand

Coming up next:
    How to build and manage your reputation through PR and social media, alongside influencing by using success stories

AN EXTERNAL PERSPECTIVE
The role of the marketer as creative translator

Creativity is a mindset. At our core we are all inherently creative beings – whether you are a hard-core, right-brained, crackpot scatty, out-of-the-box and beautifully out-on-a-limb problem solver or a dyed-in-the-wool, left-brained, rational, programmatically mechanical problem solver. That we all solve problems, albeit different types of problems, shows that we are all, in fact, creative.

But why then is creative so hard for much of business to really understand? The answer often lies in the environment and the day-to-day tasks that people are involved with. If you discuss creative ideas day in day out, you learn the language of creativity. If you discuss spreadsheets, regulation or finance day in day out, that becomes your language.

As a marketer, your currency within an organization is creative – this is fundamentally what's at the heart of the value that you add. But when you are talking 'creative' you must remember that your role is to translate for the other languages of the organization.

How? In the same way that you think about your brand's audience, think about your organizational audience. What do they need to see, hear or experience to help them open up to your language? Don't hide creativity away to 'get it approved' (something we often see in B2B scenarios in particular), embrace it and embrace other organizational languages within it. If you're talking with finance teams, talk about your expected impact and return, as well as the creative benefits of spending more on a shoot location or brand ambassador. If you're talking to product or service leads, link their drivers of growth to the insights or language used in your assets. Don't just reveal a print ad with an empty 'ta dah' and expect a positive response. If you're developing a creative proposition, don't hide it away as a marketing team process, do the work in a collaborate *creative* workshop, bringing in people from all over the organization to build it together.

As the marketer, it is your responsibility to demonstrate the power that brand and marketing can deliver. To do this you will need to be an effective translator for creativity. Don't dumb it down. Dial it up. But, do it while making sure that you are helping others within the organization understand the opportunity from their points of view.

Roo Mackie / VILFRED

VILFRED is a boutique strategy and ideas agency dedicated to using creativity (not just creative) for business transformation

References

1   Hertioga, C and Christensen, J (2024) Interbrand thinking: What is a brand? Interbrand. interbrand.com/london/thinking/what-is-a-brand/ (archived at https://perma.cc/W34Q-5NK4)

2 Guenther, P, Guenther, M, Lukas, B and Homburg, C (2024) Consequences of Marketing Asset Accountability – A Natural Experiment. *Journal of Marketing*, 88(5), 24–45. doi.org/10.1177/00222429241236142 (archived at https://perma.cc/4W5M-CYRS)

3 Brand Finance (2024) Brand Valuation Methodology. brandirectory.com/methodology (archived at https://perma.cc/GH38-L9Y7)

4 Interbrand. Best global brands methodology, 2024. interbrand.com/thinking/best-global-brands-methodology/ (archived at https://perma.cc/DYA5-X5DM)

5 Erricker, P (2023) Value of global intangible assets regains some ground after sharp decline, Brand Finance, 2 November. brandfinance.com/press-releases/value-of-global-intangible-assets-regains-some-ground-after-sharp-decline (archived at https://perma.cc/Z6RJ-NZT5)

6 Coalition for Inclusive Capitalism (2024) The Embankment Project for Inclusive Capitalism. coalitionforinclusivecapitalism.com/epic/ (archived at https://perma.cc/TDT5-QXXW)

7 Sheerin, A, Dewey, P, Ratajczak, D, Katerman, M and Rice, T (2021) Why B2B brand marketing matters, BCG. www.bcg.com/publications/2021/why-brand-marketing-matters (archived at https://perma.cc/9MQD-MC9V)

8 Sinek, S (2019) How should a company share its values? YouTube, 16 September 2019. www.youtube.com/watch?v=5yE541BY-1c (archived at https://perma.cc/A282-UG86)

9 Field, S (1979, Revised Edition 2005) *Screenplay: The foundations of screenwriting*, Random House Publishing Group, US

6

Reputation: Built through loyalty, advocacy and success stories

Your reputation is closely entwined with being seen as a trusted brand. Reputation is an incredibly important asset that spans the full gamut of experience. Within the B2B business model, most large-scale purchases occur so irregularly that your company is generally only known by reputation; whereas if you are a provider of smaller, more regularly purchased goods and services, you can build your reputation through consistent delivery. As a B2B marketer it is important to understand how you can build and manage the reputation of your business.

What do we mean by reputation?

The reputation you have is the general opinion that is held in the minds of your audiences about you, your company and the products and services you provide to the market. It can be driven solely from a corporate perspective or built in balance between the corporate reputation and the internal individual's reputation (often the subject matter expert or technical specialist). In a professional service where your people are your product or where the research and development process around your products relies on individual scientists – their scientific breakthroughs and patents – the latter is extremely important.

If you are a corporate-listed company or one looking for investment, your reputation is key to unlocking funding. Investors rely on the reputation of a business to understand its trustworthiness and to determine whether to invest. There is a philosophical debate around the fact that a company that doesn't have a reputation to protect doesn't have anything to lose and is therefore not reliable. Reputation alongside brand and goodwill is an intangible asset on the balance sheet – not something that can be easily assessed and yet is often cited as the number-one reason for investment in a business.

There is a confluence of forces at play; with decreasing trust in governments, non-governmental organizations and the media, businesses are seen as the most trusted institutions according to Edelman's Trust Barometer Report 2024.[1] This report shows that governments are seen as far less competent and ethical than previously, which means it is the right time for businesses to step up and lead for the future of all stakeholders.

Reputation, like trust, needs to be built over time and driven through the experience delivered against the promised expectation. In much the same way as any messaging, it can be viewed through multiple channels aligned to the position in the buying journey and the individual needs of the buyer.

Online reputation

Building your reputation should be seen as a key component to your marketing plan. Looking at your reputation through the lens of online channels and analysing the unprompted discussion of your brand, products and services will give you a greater understanding of how you are perceived by different audiences. Some of the most important information and commentary includes customer reviews that cover the experience they have had of your brand and their after-sales experience.

Share of voice is a measure of the volume of mentions about you in the media which can be viewed as a percentage of the total mentions of you and your competitors in the category. The sentiment of your mentions can be good or bad, as well as everything in between – and often all at the same time.

You should aim to build a deeper understanding of the reputation you have, the sentiment surrounding you and that of your competition and the industry context you operate in. If you are in a low-trust category but the sentiment around you is neutral, this is very positive. The context is key to understanding what 'good' looks like.

Online sentiment analysis is also the 'canary in the coal mine' when it comes to early warning signs of any risks or challenges you might encounter. Due to the immediacy of social media, comments and discussions might surface before you are aware of the detail through other channels.

Media categories

Looking at media across paid, owned and earned categories, there are different ways to use the media and specific channels to build your reputation, cementing your position in the market.

Paid channels

Paid channels are those that you 'pay-to-play' for placement of your message to target the audience you hope to convert to your brand. Placing your messages in channels and titles that align with your values can add native credentials to your positioning.

Alignment with top tier press or trade titles can position you at the right level for your potential buyers. Targeting is key to ensure that you optimize your investment and minimize your wastage. All media titles – both on and offline – have detailed research as to who their readership is, the behaviour exhibited on their platforms and the audience information you need to make an investment decision.

Media agencies are the experts in this field. Most large-scale brand advertisers will have aligned agency relationships, many with coverage at a global level who may also be local to you. The brief to media buyers is to determine the right media owners to target for inclusion in their platforms. This can be a version of your creative brief but focused on the consumption habits of the audience you are targeting. Include what you know about them from previous campaigns and any performance results from previous digital campaigns. It is important that your agencies are fully aware of previous campaign results and can understand what channels and creative assets drove the optimal outcomes and delivered against the agreed objectives.

Owned channels

Owned channels and content are those that are specifically owned and managed by your brand and teams. The creative assets, content and information you share across your channels need to be in line with the holistic position you are looking to convey to the market. This links back to your brand messaging house, with campaigns and proof points taking prospects and customers on the right journey for them – driving to the next best action as you aim to move the individual closer to the point of purchase. These channels include your own website, corporate social media accounts, any direct marketing, publications, event experience and any other channels where you control how and what can be consumed by your audiences.

Earned channels

Earned channels are where media relations and PR kicks in and where you need to earn your coverage. Building the right relationships with the right journalists, influencers, associations and even your own employees are key to driving your reputation through these channels. These channels are generally more trusted as your coverage is not controlled by you. This is not to say you can't manage your messaging, your commentary and your reputation, but this is a highly skilled approach which we will examine in more detail throughout the rest of this chapter as we look at how you can oversee your reputation.

Building and managing your reputation

The first step is to understand where you currently sit: understanding your current share of voice and sentiment around your brand, the products and services you sell and the after-sales care or account management that your buyers receive. The conversations around your recruitment processes and experience, alongside the way you work with alumni or ex-employees is a consideration. You must also understand how those who influence purchasing in your industry, e.g. analysts or intermediaries, and how those who influence your potential buyers, e.g. CXO networks, position you in their communication.

You should conduct research among your current and prospective customers to understand their perception of you. Aligned with your brand survey you can add in questions that look at how you rank against specific statements or brand values. Understand the association between your customers and, importantly, those not buying from you. This will help you build out the messaging you need to affirm decisions and drive new consideration with prospective customers in new businesses.

LinkedIn's recent B2B buyer research – conducted across three industries, shows high levels of reliance on reputation before the buying cycle even begins.

- Financial services: 74 per cent of those interviewed stated that it was important for the buying group to be aware of a provider before the buying cycle begins.[2]
- SaaS (sold as a service) providers: 82 per cent agree it is important that a SaaS provider creates a positive impression on the buying group before the procurement process begins.[3]
- Professional services: 90 per cent of buyers agree it is important for the buying group to have a positive view of a management consultancy before entering the procurement cycle.[4]

It is therefore critical for you, as a marketer, to build the reputation of your brand with potential buyers before they start to consider their next purchase.

The same LinkedIn research also showed that across all three industries buyers use a variety of channels to build their shortlists. Alongside your owned website and published insights, often known as thought leadership, the assets that your prospects use to conduct detailed research about your business and reputation include:

- business press
- social media
- analyst reports
- client testimonials
- search engine / digital channels
- Generative AI

You should assess how valuable these channels are to you and understand your buyer's relationship with them.

Managing your reputation

Once you understand the position you have across the relevant channels, and depending on the appetite your company has for being in the news, you will need to build and manage your reputation. Organizations that subscribe to the adage 'no news is good news' will err away from being in the press at all and will focus more on the loyalty and advocacy you are able to build through these channels, whereas those who are more of a 'challenger brand' with perhaps a more entrepreneurial mindset or in a more competitive market will be comfortable with as much coverage as possible. Knowing where you are on the spectrum will help with how you position yourself and what you will need to build into your annual plan.

CHALLENGER BRAND

A challenger brand is one who must punch above their marketing investments to outweigh their larger established competitors; often seen as more entrepreneurial than the current industry leaders.

Business media

No matter your appetite for coverage you will need relationships with the relevant business media and journalists that cover your industry to either increase the interest in positive stories or manage the coverage of more difficult topics.

Forming relationships with journalists will mean that you have insight into the type of story they are interested in covering, how it might align to their editorial calendar and the lead time that they need to secure coverage.

Consumer media

If you operate with a B2B2C model or produce goods and services that are sold via an intermediary to consumers, you may also need to consider consumer targeted channels to drive your reputation. There may also be interest in these media channels for recruitment that you can leverage if applicable.

Some common terms that you will need to know are as follows:

Press release – a press release is the controlled statement that you and your company share with chosen media outlets, featuring quotes from your key spokespeople and referring to methods of contact.

Boilerplate – a press release contains a boilerplate which is a summary of who you are and what you do, included as general information for the journalist.

Embargo – a release might be shared in advance of an announcement but with an embargo that will only lift at a certain date and time when it can then be published. Journalists will generally respect the request for the information to be embargoed.

Exclusive – you might try and gain an exclusive, where you work with an individual media title and give them the exclusive right to share the information first.

Pitch – you can pitch an exclusive to a title – this is not as formal as a press release but is where you try to share enough information to whet the appetite of the journalist and persuade them to agree to the exclusive or other format of coverage you are asking for.

Press kit – messaging statement, proof points, detailed background information if needed (particularly regarding product releases), case studies or client testimonials.

Spokesperson – the person who will speak to the journalist and be quoted as the source with full attribution.

Subject matter expert – can be someone different to the spokesperson, brought into the conversation to give the next level of detail on a technical topic. Will often be used to authenticate more complex information.

ON BACKGROUND VERSUS OFF THE RECORD

There are a few commonly used terms you may have heard referenced when it comes to media sources:

On the record is directly attributable to the individual source and can be quoted word for word. Journalists aim for as much information as possible to be on the record as it drives greater trust in their reporting.

On background is used when you do not want to be quoted individually but are comfortable being referred to as a company source, e.g. 'a person close to the matter' or 'a member of X company shared'.

Off the record is exactly that – if you agree upfront with a journalist that you are talking to them off the record, it means that you cannot be quoted and your story should not be published or used in their coverage.

All of these need to be agreed upfront with the journalist you are speaking to and should be used with journalists you have a relationship with, as there is no guarantee that the ask will be followed. There is always the chance that you may still be quoted or the information you share may still be attributed to you. Your company will have a PR/media relations policy you should follow and if you need additional support, make sure you are working with your PR specialist or liaising with a PR agency.

There is a lot of jargon used when it comes to press and PR formats. The list below is by no means exhaustive:

Byline – the attributed author of an article written from the individual's point of view.

Blog/vlog – generally a more relaxed form of content, and more frequently updated with points of view which can be both professional and personal. Vlog refers to a blog in video format.

The wire (e.g. Businesswire and PR Newswire) – you can pay for your press release to be released 'over the wire' to maximize your reach and gain a greater distribution to many global and local news outlets.

Syndication – content is reused across a network of media outlets and is republished on multiple channels.

Sponsored content – content that you have written and place into the content stream of a media platform, tagged as sponsored so your audience know you have placed it there.

Advertorial – content that is pay to play but is written in the house style of the media platform and purposefully looks like native content.

MAT release – paid content inserted into a printed publication, as a guaranteed media placement.

Online reputation management (ORM) – managing your digital footprint to elevate positive content and mitigate negative reviews or content.

Social media

Consumer brands can be more heavily embedded with social media than traditional media – they have reviewed where their audience spends its time and have taken their messaging to the prospect. This is something that we B2B marketers are also embracing, especially when we look at LinkedIn's research which showed that over 80 per cent of B2B buyers across the three industries use social media throughout their professional lives.[5] According to HubSpot's Social Trends Report 2024, 'last year 78% of B2B marketers felt that social media marketing was effective for their brand, compared to 84% of B2C marketers', so B2B is not far behind.[6]

Some useful terms and areas of focus in the social media space include:

Social media PR – an extension of traditional PR skills into the social media space working across networks and platforms to drive both broad reach and deeper engagement depending on your objectives.

Social media selling – selling via social media channels has become part of the core functionality of the platforms. This may align with the products and services that you sell and should be considered as part of your distribution strategy.

Social media management – the immediacy of response expected on social platforms aligns with the expectations derived from personal use of similar platforms. Brands need to manage how they show up, how they respond and how they engage with their followers. The management of social channels requires PR skills and community management understanding. Depending on the markets that you operate in you will need to think about how you manage in multiple languages.

Social media management tools (e.g. Hootsuite, Sprinklr) – platforms that bring scheduling content creation, analytics and listening across multiple social networks and accounts into one place.

Influencers (macro versus micro) – macro influencers are generally celebrities who might endorse your brand gaining you wide reach whereas micro influencers can be closer to the audience you are targeting and drive increased engagement. Micro influencers often feel more accessible thereby credentializing the use of your products and services in a more authentic way. Followers are likely to range from 1k–100k for micro and 100k+ for macro.

Forums – there are multiple forums that might be of interest, those where your industry or your products and services are reviewed and discussed. There are also employee specific forums that review compensation and your broader approach to your employees. All of these should be part of your social listening so you can get a fully rounded understanding of where you sit reputationally across all target audiences.

And, with the increasing number of channels that your audiences could be across, you will need to balance PR and social media to ensure you are managing your messaging and your reputation across all channels using technology tools to drive effective communications as efficiently as possible.

Analyst relations

Analyst relations (AR) differs from public relations (PR) but needs to be considered as part of your holistic media relations strategy. It focuses on building and managing two-way relationships with key analysts in your industry or sector. They are increasingly important in the technology, business consulting and manufacturing spaces and enable your customers to have a clear understanding of how you stack up against the competition. Analysts are an important part of the buying process and are often used to either build or prioritize longlists ahead of final request for proposals (RFPs) being solicited.

Analysts produce reports that summarize their view of the market. They include analysis of your corporate strategy, vision and business objectives alongside your specific products and services. Many reports are confined to specific products or services and really dig into the detail of the offerings at play in a space.

Analyst research is incredibly useful to understand your competition, clients' and customers' view of your business. Analysts spend most of their time in the market talking to your competition and customers and are therefore extremely well placed to advise. Most analysts will also work with you as paid research partners to help you understand the needs of your customers and where you might build products and services that serve them better.

As part of their review of the market, all competitors will be included in their research and reports. However, if you have a paid relationship where you are using the analyst's research services, an analyst is more likely to understand you better and be able to represent you appropriately. Like relationships with journalists, your relationship with the relevant analysts in your market should be cultivated to drive the best impact for you and your corporate reputation.

One example of a highly influential analyst approach is produced by Gartner and referred to as a Magic Quadrant.[7] It uses a 2 by 2 matrix, plotting the position of all providers, driven by their review of the whole market and enables your potential customers to understand where you sit against the competition. It looks to position the ability to execute against the completeness of a company's vision. As a buyer you are likely to want to work with those companies who make it into the 'leader' quadrant.

Many prospective clients closely align with their preferred analysts during the search for a new provider. Alongside the reports themselves, analysts offer guidance in the selection process, offer consultations with senior leaders who used to work in your industry and have a series of events, roundtables and ongoing thought leadership that your prospective clients will likely attend and review. It is important to remember that analysts are often used by procurement departments to verify shortlists, and many RFPs include a section around your market position where positive analysts' positions will elevate your proposal.

Client testimonials

As prospective clients and customers review the market and conduct their research, an important element that has considerable weight are previous client testimonials. Your prospective clients want to see that you have done this before, solved this problem or implemented this product or service and driven substantial impact to your current client portfolio. It is important that you encourage your current clients to advocate on your behalf through case studies and success stories that show how you have delivered and demonstrated considerable, successful experiences in this space.

You must optimize the customer journey as you look at the research pathways audiences can take through your channels. You need to build out your plans, looking at how you drive top-of-funnel awareness. This should include client testimonials that lead into mid-funnel content to drive further consideration of your products and services through credentials, case studies and expert thought leadership with a view to nurturing and converting prospects to customers when the time is right. We will go into further detail about planning full-funnel content in the coming chapters.

Once a prospect becomes a client, your after-sales team should be targeted with driving further loyalty through ongoing renewal programmes while also looking to drive additional sales through upsell and cross-sell strategies – a large part of these strategies include building relationships with clients and customers so that you are seen as the go-to provider in your market. The most impactful relationships are where you are true partners in building a future vision together, with your products and services enabling mutual growth.

In many organizations with enterprise-level sales, it is a complex task coordinating case studies and success stories across your customers. Often the sticking point is internal, and you must first convince the key account team that it is advantageous for your relationship, so thinking about the value exchange for your client is key. What is in it for them to be an advocate for your business? Can you offer them inclusion in advertising that is beneficial for their business objectives? Can you invite them to meet with other clients in a client advisory board programme or can you align with the personal objectives of the key buyer to drive mutual impact? Always consider that you are unlikely to be the only provider asking these questions. What can differentiate you and make it an easy choice for your buyers?

Search/digital

While the trend towards search is starting to move away from search engines and towards in-app search, e.g. through TikTok and YouTube, search engines remain a core channel at the research stage for a prospect. There is also an increasing focus on using an AI assistant for a curated answer, which we will cover next in this chapter.

You need to understand what your prospects are seeing when they search for your business, products and services. Understanding what appears when your audiences search will help you consider where you need to focus. Search is something you need to have an ongoing understanding of so you should implement alerts across the different engines to ensure you are aware of any new content or forum feedback that appears.

You are looking to build a positive digital footprint so that anyone searching for you will receive the information that you feel represents your business in the best light. This is influenced through a combination of search engine optimization (SEO) and online reputation management (ORM).

SEO focuses on driving your organic rankings on search engine results pages (SERPs) so that you appear when potential buyers search for keywords related to your business, products and services. You can impact your position on the SERP by optimizing your onsite content, keywords, structure and user experience alongside increasing the credibility of your site through inward links from other well-regarded sites. There are many free tools that will help you understand where you sit and why. Using these as a first step ahead of engaging outside help will give you clarity on where you might focus. Media agencies, digital and SEO specialists can all help with your site content and structure. This needs to be factored in as an ongoing need as the search engines regularly update their algorithms to put greater emphasis on different types of content, reviews or technical structures depending on what they are seeing resonate for their users. They are ultimately competing for attention with their users and need to serve the most useful results as quickly as possible, so your SEO team must stay on top of these changes.

Online reputation management is related to SEO but is focused on ensuring your reputation is optimized across your digital footprint, including social media. Once you are aware of your current position, you can then work through what you might need to do to build greater positivity. This might include looking at all relevant review sites and taking ownership of your relevant profiles, including LinkedIn, Google and any of the sites specific to your industry, both from a buyer and an employee perspective.

Responding to negative coverage on review sites or social media can help show that you take concerns seriously, showing how you manage issues as they arise and solving them as quickly as possible so that you look to turn any negative coverage into neutral or positive where you can.

> **GOOGLE BUSINESS PROFILE**
>
> This profile is specific to Google but is something that you can influence. It is a free tool that enables you to bring the relevant topline information together into one place and is accessible through Google search and Google maps. You can link your social media profiles, and it will pull all of your Google reviews into one place so that your prospective customers can find them.

Generative AI

The impact of Generative AI on reputation management is not yet fully understood. With the rise of large language models (LLMs) and the launch of SearchGPT as a prototype from OpenAI (which will eventually be combined with future ChatGPT releases),[8] there is convergence between search and Generative AI tools.

If we begin to rely on personalized Generative AI assistants, we are likely to move further away from traditional search engines, and SERPs will become unnecessary in their current form. We will become reliant on curated outputs from a trusted assistant that we have trained on our own needs based on the relevance of previous results. You will be looking for an authenticated, summarized, singular 'best' answer to your prompt, rather than a current list of potential answers to your search. The conversational nature of AI means that you are likely to refine your search as you go. This makes the training content for LLMs important – something that your website and digital presence will play a meaningful role in as we move forward. It is therefore necessary that you start to establish what information you are comfortable being crawled for AI learning purposes, and what is your own intellectual property (IP) that you wish to keep for clients and customers. For instance, you may not wish to share all insights, research reports and other thought leadership on an open site, instead you might want to increase the value exchange for clients by keeping the detail for those who log in or have registered to do so.

Corporate reputation versus internal individual reputation

Corporate reputation is a key part of building awareness of who you are and what you do. Your reputation in the market is often directly attributable to the experiences your clients and customers receive before, during and after they have purchased from you. This reputation can also be aided by awards and associations. Joining the trade bodies and accrediting associations relevant to your industry helps you to be seen in the right context. Entering and winning awards also helps bring attention to the success of your business, particularly if client case studies which include the financial impact of your products and services can be evidenced.

There is a balance to be struck between the corporate reputation of your business and that of the internal individuals who work with you. Most companies have a distinct PR and social media policy which includes the approach that individuals must follow on their own channels. 'Views all my own' is a statement often seen on an individual's social handles to distance themselves from their employer. Harnessing the power of your employees' social media is a channel in and of itself. If you have specific individuals in leadership positions who are seen as influential in their space, they will add to the reputation of your business, particularly if you sell services where you deploy your people into client's businesses. These individuals could be those in positions of leadership or technical specialists.

Leadership

You will want to review your list of spokespeople and understand who you will be supporting as part of the reputational build of your company. It is widely accepted that the executive positioning of individuals at the top of your company will be leveraged as advocates of the brand and your business.

You should work with your leaders to align their messaging platforms with their roles and their professional and personal interests to ensure that they have a fully rounded messaging house that enables them to be authentic as they build their leadership reputation. The reputation of an individual is built in much the same way as a business. Start with a current assessment and work through what you might need to do to elevate them, what associations or organizations they should be part of and where they should align their influence.

Technical experts

Subject matter and technical experts can give great depth to your brand. As mentioned previously, in professional services or anywhere that thought leadership, scientific research and insights are key, the individual specialist can be nearly as important as your brand. Ensuring that these experts can showcase their thinking at events, roundtables and across media channels will aid the build out of your corporate reputation.

Employees

Enabling your people to help build your reputation will also drive a positive view of you as an employer, which could in turn lead to lower recruitment costs over time as you also become more attractive to the talent market.

It is important that you understand the internal sentiment of your employees if you are looking to them to share their thoughts on external platforms and give guidance and training so that your people know what they should and should not share. Many companies use employee engagement systems, e.g. Haiilo, to help share internal content with employees who wish to safely share information externally.

With a broad spectrum of voices in play, you need to have a grasp on your messaging framework for the business and how each of your internal groups plays to that. You will want to ensure that there is a distinct space for each voice, otherwise you could end up with overlapping coverage which could reduce the overall impact.

There is always the human risk of working with individuals in any capacity when linked to your corporate reputation. There are myriad issues that can arise personally that could dent the broader image of your business and not all are in the control of your employees. For anyone in a leadership position that you are going to rely on, you need to understand where there might be potential issues, building potential mitigants from the start.

Messaging

Your PR plan and messaging should align with your overall brand messaging, corporate values and business objectives. You will need to understand your internal schedule – when product releases, service upgrades, thought leadership releases, event attendance and other time-sensitive activities are due to take place.

From there you can start to build out the themes, topics and thinking that you can align to both the corporate and individual message plans, looking at the balance of business versus individual and technical versus industry trends and start to get your spokespeople in shape. Specialist topics can be led by functional leadership and business/performance-led topics might sit with your CEO. It is all about planning your messaging across the team by topics – who aligns where and with what message.

If you are a multinational with a global footprint, you will need to work out how you will cover your full geographic spread, dividing up both messaging and media to those most relevant. In-house teams can build strong relationships on the ground and be connected through global oversight or augmented with agency support as needed.

When it comes to training your spokespeople, it is all about practice. How do they react under pressure? How can they bridge out of difficult questions back to the topics they are comfortable with? Ensure that you build in adequate time for training and continue to drill them ahead of any important appearances. It is your responsibility as a marketer to protect the reputation of your business and only field the individuals ready for prime-time. There are easier assignments that can help people gain comfort before hitting live TV. Pre-recorded fireside chats or panel interviews can help your spokespeople get exposure in a lower-risk environment.

Investor relations

If you are a listed company, investor relations (IR) is a mandatory part of managing the reputation of your business. The IR team work closely with the CFO and finance team and lead on the communications between the executive leadership team and the financial community. The information shared by investor relations helps potential investors make decisions about whether the company is worth investing in.

Managing investor relations is a very specific skillset and something that has a crossover between finance and PR. You need a deep understanding of the financial drivers of investment in your industry and your business, a thorough knowledge of the strategy and the workings of your company, and should be able to communicate across your full spectrum of products and services. You need to be conversant on the regulatory and reporting requirements of your industry and be thoroughly familiar with the financial metrics so you can translate the company story into a clear pitch to investors.

PR agencies

There are a plethora of PR agencies and individual consultants that can help you from start to finish or pick up elements that might be out of your comfort zone. For instance, media training your spokespeople is often done by an external party – a journalist who can put them through their paces without having to also be mindful of maintaining a positive day-to-day relationship.

It is important that any agency you engage with has relevant industry experience and expertise as they will be acting on your behalf to pitch to journalists and need to understand the topics you cover. It is also worth understanding their current roster – are you comfortable with competitors being represented? How have they delivered against similar briefs? What is their retention rate? What are their standout PR campaigns where they have driven similar impact to your requirements? Chemistry is also important – do you get each other? Who will you and your stakeholders be facing off to, both at the leadership level but also day-to-day management?

You should make sure that whoever you appoint is aware of your messaging, social, PR and ongoing business plans. They will then have a holistic view of their requirements but can be mindful of the complete overview.

Crisis communications

In many cases 'no news is good news'; however, it often takes a lot of work to ensure that negative stories stay out of the press. In a previous life, I spent over six months building relationships and navigating historic stories so that on launch day for a new product there was absolutely no negative coverage and some positive reporting.

Not all negative coverage can be anticipated so it is important that you have a plan B you can implement as needed. PR agencies can help with crisis communications either in anticipation of or during a crisis, but you should also build a playbook that you can lean on at speed in case of an emergency, with predefined, approved options for potential issues that might arise.

Business continuity planning (BCP) and disaster recovery (DR) processes are likely to be run as part of your company's approach to risk. During times of crisis, it is imperative to manage your PR and social in a way that protects your reputation as much as possible by communicating with impacted teams and customers in an open and transparent manner.

When I worked for a regulated bank, this was absolutely built into our core. We had a risk log, key risk indicators (KRIs) and aligned mitigants. We also ran DR drills and ran through potentially negative scenarios to ensure we knew how to handle them across all relevant functions.

Even if you work in a totally different environment, I suggest looking at what might have a negative impact on your reputation if managed incorrectly. Reviewing the types of crises that might affect you, ensuring you know how to react and building out any pre-prepared messaging as part of the playbook will help you move swiftly if anything were to occur. Consider your reliance on specific technologies, any disruption to your supply chains, your manufacturing process and how your customers might be impacted if your utilities were interrupted. It is also worth reviewing where individual impacts might need attention, for example a negligent data breach or reputational damage aligned to a spokesperson.

As much of this is in case of an emergency, the minimum requirements I would suggest are that you make sure you have the starting points documented, you know who you would need to pull together for simplified decision making and you are able to access and update all owned channels.

SUMMARY

In this chapter we have considered

- What your reputation means and how you might build and manage it.
  - What you can build across paid, owned and earned channels.
  - What formats you might want to think of.
  - How to build your messaging to balance both corporate and individual reputations.
- How you can rely on the experts, and understand if you should engage with a PR agency.
  - The purpose of an inhouse investor relations team.
  - What you might do to work with external influencers like business analysts.
  - How you might plan for any potential crisis communication.

Coming up next:

Understanding individual and client objectives to strengthen and deepen your relationships.

AN EXTERNAL PERSPECTIVE
Corporate communications: Own and shape the narrative,
or fall by the wayside

Working in B2B corporate communications is an incredibly interesting and rewarding role. It is very different to B2C, where consumers interact with your brand every day. Building brand awareness in the B2B space takes much longer and can therefore be more challenging than for consumer-facing brands. To succeed, B2B communicators need to think creatively about strategies to elevate their brand and stay relevant in a competitive but often sparsely covered market. B2B is also a great place to learn strategic and commercial skills to elevate your role as a communicator and leader.

In my current role, I work closely with leadership to drive corporate positioning, manage and build the company's reputation and grow engagement with our company stakeholders. I believe that to be effective, communication strategies should always be aligned to the strategic growth and revenue drivers of the business. If there is a disconnect between the two, impact will be lessened and credibility can be damaged. Communicators *must* be connected to – and have an understanding of – their company's underlying financial narrative in order to succeed.

An ever-present challenge for communicators in the B2B sector is the ongoing struggle for column inches in earned media. Companies in the engineering and industrial technology spaces, for example, are in many ways the lifeblood of the economies in which they operate, contributing hugely to economic growth, employment and GDP, and largely making the world a better place with the products and services that they create and sell. However, these companies often fly under the radar in the media – with many people being totally unaware of them or the value that they create.

At the macro level, this is challenging because we can only start to build much-needed public confidence back into the UK economy and celebrate the merits of the UK stock market (and private sector companies also) if we acknowledge and recognize the companies that are driving growth. It's also a frustration for communicators who strive to share the progress they are making and the positive impact that their companies have!

Some of this stems from the way that traditional media is being squeezed. Largely speaking, gone are the days when industry sectors were served by a healthy and empowered national press in addition to trade and regional newspapers. Media budgets are always under pressure and sector specialists are gradually becoming generalists who are forced to cover a range of sectors.

For instance, UK national newspapers can now only count a couple of dedicated industrial reporters, and the direction of travel means this trend is becoming ever more pronounced.

Another factor is the changing nature of the news cycle. Looking back just a few years ago, the corporate and financial calendar (company results: full year, half year or trading updates) drove much of the corporate news cycle. As a B2B company, you knew that this would be the moment when the eyes of the business world would be on your company, for better or worse.

However, in today's news cycle, with the advent of 'always on' news, most UK nationals have stopped reporting on straightforward financial results stories – with the newswires and automated AI crawlers picking the headlines up first thing in the morning it is quickly old news.

This external communications evolution creates a vacuum and, to fill the void, it's no surprise that the move towards 'owned' content strategies continues apace. Many corporates are now focused on creating their own 'content machines' with the goal of generating high quality content to drive engagement with key company stakeholders. Social channels, such as LinkedIn, become ever more important in this environment, to connect with employees (past, present and future), analysts, regulators, customers and even journalists. New social platforms are also increasingly required, particularly from a careers perspective, to appeal to – and be relevant for – younger, diverse talent.

Building high quality content that works right across your digital ecosystem is critical. This includes website hosting as well as sharing on internal communications platforms and on social channels. To get cut through now requires a significant increase in the use of video content to become more visually appealing and compelling, and investing in a paid social budget behind this content to increase engagement and maintain relevance with stakeholders. It also requires telling more human-interest stories, breaking down impenetrable industry jargon and, again, always aligning the owned-content plan with the key drivers of the company's business strategy.

This approach reduces reliance on earned media and ensures that you tell the stories that matter most to your business in the way *you* want to tell them, and when *you* want to do it. It also creates a platform to celebrate the achievements of great people across your organization and can be an incredibly powerful tool to create and build engagement.

> B2B communications is evolving faster than ever amidst a changing media landscape and technological backdrop. Creating an owned content machine is a big part of this evolution.
>
> Tom Steiner
> FTSE 100 communications leader
>
> Tom is an experienced corporate communications leader with more than two decades experience spanning in-house and agency roles. He has held senior roles at a range of large, iconic companies in the finance, media and publishing, and engineering sectors.

References

1 Edelman Trust Institute (2024) 2024 Edelman Trust Barometer: Global Report. www.edelman.com/sites/g/files/aatuss191/files/2024-02/2024%20Edelman%20 Trust%20Barometer%20Global%20Report_FINAL.pdf (archived at https:// perma.cc/FYM6-UMKL)

2 LinkedIn (2024) It always pays to stand out: How financial services marketers grab buyers' attention, B2B Institute Financial Services Research business. linkedin.com/marketing-solutions/financial-services-marketing-back-up/ it-always-pays-to-stand-out (archived at https://perma.cc/9MAZ-R8G3)

3 LinkedIn (2024) Breaking out from the crowd: How businesses buy SaaS now and what it means for marketers, LinkedIn SaaS Buyer Survey 2024. business. linkedin.com/marketing-solutions/success/breaking-out-from-the-crowd (archived at https://perma.cc/2SHB-GQT6)

4 LinkedIn (2024) Stand out from the crowd: How management consulting marketers can influence buyers at ever stage of the decision journey, LinkedIn Management Consulting Buyer Survey 2024. business.linkedin. com/marketing-solutions/success/stand-out-from-the-crowd (archived at https://perma.cc/6VZG-JR7N)

5 LinkedIn (2024) Stand out from the crowd: How management consulting marketers can influence buyers at ever stage of the decision journey, LinkedIn Management Consulting Buyer Survey 2024. business.linkedin. com/marketing-solutions/success/stand-out-from-the-crowd (archived at https://perma.cc/6VZG-JR7N)

6 Hubspot (2024) 2024 Social Media Trends Report. offers.hubspot.com/ social-media-trends-report (archived at https://perma.cc/3TQX-QY9E)

7 Gartner (2024) 'Magic Quadrant: Positioning technology players within a specific market. www.gartner.com/en/research/methodologies/magic-quadrants-research (archived at https://perma.cc/72YK-S45F)

8 Open AI (2024) Prototype release 25 July. openai.com/index/searchgpt-prototype/ (archived at https://perma.cc/EXC9-EDTT)

7

Relationships: Maximizing your most valuable asset

Relationships can vary from transactional buyers to strategic partners. The role you play will depend on the size, scale and importance of the purchase. If you are selling widgets – unless you are selling them at scale as part of a broader supply chain – the buyer relationship could be driven by a straightforward functional need. The right features and benefits of the widget are likely to be more important than the buyer's relationship with you as the brand owner. Where the relationship needs to be deeper – perhaps with a larger, enterprise-level or more impactful purchase – the relationship has a greater level of importance. Key tenets that apply to relationships at both ends of the spectrum – transactional buyer to strategic relationship – are transparency, respect and a growth mindset. These need to be built into the approach to drive mutually beneficial collaboration and drive an ongoing trusted relationship.

Defining the depth of relationship you are looking to build with your buyers will affect how you think about enabling an optimal experience across your internal and external relationships. In B2B sales, people buy from people. As we've touched on previously, when a purchase is of such a scale that it has the power to influence your own personal income, trust is increasingly important. You must understand how to harness this influence and build trust at each stage of the buying process across the full buyer group.

Relationship types

The spectrum of relationships is broad, and the type of foundational connection needs to be understood to enable you to then build depth. Fundamentally recognising what the individual requires from you will enable you to understand what you might need to build as a value exchange to engender further trust and ensure mutual benefit.

External relationships include your prospects, buyers and all strategic partners who might interact with you in the sales process either directly as an introducer or indirectly as an influencer.

Prospects

Much of your target audience are likely to be prospective new buyers, but current buyers could also be considered prospects for new products and services. We have seen in Chapter 2 that 95 per cent of B2B enterprise buyers are out of the buying cycle at any one point so there will only ever be a minority of active prospects who you are aiming to move from awareness of your brand to consideration of your products and services or trial of new products and directly towards an immediate sale.

Prospects should be nurtured through a programme that focuses on warming up interested but inactive individuals as they start to show buying signals. Nurture programmes will be discussed in detail later in this chapter.

Buyers

The type of buyer can range from a one-off functional purchase to an ongoing year-on-year annuity enterprise-level relationship. Understanding the dynamic of the buyers' relationship with you will help you define how best to land and expand into new adjacent opportunities.

By understanding the full customer lifetime value of your buyers, you can drive the right investment in the relationship. This comes back to the potential you built into your initial segmentation and the opportunity for each of your segments to grow and mature.

Enterprise level client and accounts

Individual buyers can act as enterprise level clients that roll up to an account relationship. If you are selling multiple products and services to a specific company, you will want to understand the holistic relationship needs as well as the individual client buyer needs to ensure you are optimizing the potential of the account as a whole. There is also the additional potential of greater revenue driven through upsell and cross-sell opportunities that might exist if you can deepen multiple relationships to become a trusted adviser across the boardroom.

Strategic relationships

Sales can be driven both directly through an introduction and influenced indirectly through strategic relationships.

INTRODUCERS

Those that drive direct sales will most likely benefit from the sales themselves, through direct compensation, co-marketing initiatives, shared resources or by leveraging the reputation of the partner brand.

- Co-sell or alliance relationships have a deep heritage in the technology sector with vendors, consultants and systems integrators working together to build greater value for their collective clients as they foster their own revenue.

- Intermediaries play an introducer role in many industries with affiliates, agents, brokers and wholesalers enabling direct onward sales. The intermediary lists your products and services and, with each recommendation that turns into a sale, it provides a mutual revenue source.

- Online aggregators take a small percentage of the sales made through their online channels, enabling dramatic reach for a limited cost to the seller. These channels are highly price sensitive so you can test slight changes to ensure optimal pricing of your products.

INFLUENCERS

Indirect influencers are valued for their opinion as subject matter experts, opinion shapers and content creators. The value exchange with an indirect influencer is an information trade that enables the influencer to be seen as 'in the know' with greater levels of information to share with their audiences. There are a variety of types of influencers that may be relevant to your business and target buyers.

- Media/journalists – we have covered media and journalists within the chapter on reputation. Transparent relationships are fundamental to building trusted media networks that can help amplify your message or protect your reputation as needed.

- Subject matter experts exist in numerous guises from associations and awards judges to business influencers and, where relevant, celebrities. Relationships with these individuals can help you add credentials to your products and services, with brand transference from the influential individual. Recommendations from subject matter experts can be used as part of your marketing strategy to enable greater reach.

- Analysts such as Gartner, who we have previously referred to, have a key role to play in larger more complex sales, where the independent scoring nature of their reviews are built to help buyers navigate to the right supplier.

Internal relationships

Where the internal team is a channel to the buyer, they are the first audience you will need to gain traction with. This could be an account team, a sales team or a client adviser. As the marketer of your business's products and services, you need to understand the level of appetite for the adoption of new products and services by those who hold the key client relationship or lead the account. Internal engagement and marketing will likely be needed to ensure that the experience of the product or service translates for the internal audience.

As you look to understand the potential for your products and services, I find it useful to think through the internal stakeholders and build out a map of how each individual or function aligns to your ask. This helps you understand who you can rely on for support, who you might need to further engage with and to understand any objections that might be raised. Stakeholder maps are useful when thinking through any task which has a high degree of change across multiple individuals and are used with great effect when seeking to understand the full breadth of opinion around a particular topic (Table 7.1).

Managing your supplier relationships should be seen as an imperative for protecting your reputation and be aligned with your brand equity. You need to have trust in the provenance of your materials and know that you can rely on your suppliers to align to your purpose and sustainability ambitions and metrics. Cultivating suppliers like clients will help you build these deep, trusted relationships that can be leveraged for greater sales impact.

TABLE 7.1 Stakeholder map

Name	Title	Function	Power	Influence	Priority	Comms
John Smith	IT project manager	Operations	Medium	Medium	Medium	Detailed regular
Ruchi Patel	CIO	Technology	High	High	High	Strategic regular

Understanding relationships

B2C companies have finely tuned programmes that enable a brand to understand the ongoing relationships and loyalty of their customers. Voice of the customer research is at the heart of decision making and seen as an expansive tool that impacts all areas of the business. We as consumers are used to sharing our feedback, whether that is staying on a call after your banking query has been resolved to answer questions or responding in real time in e-commerce. B2B companies are not, yet, as mature. Understanding your customers' experiences is known to be useful but there are still learnings from our B2C peers that we can draw on to leverage the real power at scale.

Depending on your exact business model, you are likely to have a patchwork of understanding, with greater detail being sought from introducers, influencers and internal teams than your actual customers themselves. This is driven by the transactional nature of these relationships – with you in a buyer role. You want to know you are getting value for money for the channels you are choosing to implement. While these are hugely important relationships, the fundamental asset to your business is your current customer base.

Harvard Business Review notes that the cost of acquiring new customers can be anything from 5 to 25 times that of retaining an existing one, so it is imperative that you understand and treat your customers as the asset they are.[1] The benefits to your business of focusing on maximizing the relationships of your current customers are across four distinct areas.

Increased loyalty and retention

With the consensus that buying cycles are taking longer than ever before and are more likely to include self-navigated steps, you must keep customers loyal to your brand throughout an often arm's-length process.

Loyal customers are the bedrock of your revenue. They will tend to repeat purchase, buying more over time. A loyal relationship is often a mutually beneficial relationship that can be expanded into adjacent services more easily. Cementing the relationship with your loyal customers will help you identify and manage potential upsell and cross-sell opportunities. Loyal buyers can also be leveraged as advocates for your business and brand, which in turn can attract new customers at a lower cost.

Segmenting your customer base to understand the type of customers that are loyal to you, and why they are loyal, will help you define strategies to bring in a greater number of a similar customer segment. Building in price sensitivity to this segmentation will also help you see their reaction to price changes, which in turn will aid your pricing approach.

Loyalty programmes within B2B are more expansive than those in B2C – if you are selling to a wholesaler or part of a value chain it might be about economies of scope and scale akin to more of a traditional B2C loyalty programme, whereas at an enterprise level it is less about collecting points and more about co-developing preferred relationships that are mutually beneficial.

Reduced attrition and churn

Attrition and churn metrics show you how many of your customers leave you. This is often reviewed monthly, referred to as monthly churn or monthly attrition, and is a key metric for you to understand in marketing. Each time a customer leaves, you need to fill the leaky bucket, which incurs the associated customer acquisition costs. The attrition could be down to a timebound position like the end of contracts or licensing. It could be driven by a bad experience and result in the shift to a competitor product. There may also be an unprofitable segment – you might be trying to reduce your exposure to these customers and clients – where attrition is the positive outcome. Customer churn happens for many reasons, but you need to understand why your customers are choosing to leave you and then build plans to plug the holes.

It is important to look at every step in the end-to-end buyer journey. You should focus on the pain points and remove the friction, making the journey as seamless as possible while also looking for those moments where you can drive distinctive differentiation, making the user experience positive for your customers and clients.

Keeping your attrition rates as low, or as targeted as possible, reduces the overall customer acquisition costs and enables you to invest in your loyal, more beneficial, relationships.

Reduced customer acquisition costs (CAC)

If you maximize the value you are able to drive from your current customer base, you can minimize the additive costs to acquire new customers. You should be looking to continually fill up the funnel with potential new customers with cost-effective programmes that ultimately deliver ROI and nurture the prospect to a sale. Enabling this ongoing lifecycle should be the foundation of your marketing plan.

If your business need for customers increases significantly your CAC will also increase significantly. Looking at the return on investment (ROI) of all marketing programmes, initiatives and channels will ensure that you are using the optimal mix to acquire new customers, but in times of stress you will end up paying over the odds. It is therefore important to maintain a steady stream of cost-effective customer acquisition, with marketing levers built to drive growth as needed by your business.

New customers are likely to exist within your current accounts – if you can expand your footprint to bring in new buyers, building on the loyalty and advocacy of the deep relationships you have, you can maximize your sales within the account as a whole and keep your CAC down.

Increased customer lifetime value (CLV)

You need to interrogate the full value of a buyer at both an individual and account level over the lifetime of their relationship with you. If looked at across your entire portfolio, you can spot the relationships that are driving the greatest value and build plans to emulate the best practices you have built with those buyers.

Within B2B, people still buy from people so the strength of a personal relationship is the key to enabling a strong business relationship which in turn will be mutually beneficial.

Concentrating on the full value of a client will mean that a customer who is out of a current buying cycle this year, but a previously high-value buyer, would still be treated as an important client. These customers can be used to drive advocacy within their business to enable you to find and define the next high-value opportunity that might be in your sweet spot and used externally as a proof point or case study for similar customers who might be looking to solve comparable issues. They might be flagged as high value within a waning sales segment of your audience, but you should concentrate on reactivating the value within the account, with marketing keeping the individuals interested.

Retaining and reactivating previously high value clients is more cost effective than finding new clients.

Listening to your customers

You need to set up a process with which to understand the needs and objectives of your customers in their own words. Ongoing listening programmes should be built into all channels of communication so that you are engaging with your customers on their preferred channels and encouraging a response to your questions. Using research gained at the point of sale can test the experience of your customer service or e-commerce channels enabling you to immediately gain insightful feedback and amend your programmes to be more effective.

Feedback routes also exist for purchases on forums where customers are seeking the provider that can solve their problem or deliver the specific services they require. You should monitor these forums and respond as needed.

An ongoing brand survey, as mentioned previously, can measure the relevance and association of brand values and the overall experience of your brand at all touchpoints. This should be built to cover all aspects of your business, across business units and geographies, so you can deep dive and understand where specific challenges may need to be overcome or where there are significant best practices being developed.

Many of the larger enterprise-focused technology, finance and professional services firms appoint customer advisory boards (CAB) that are aligned to particular functional buyers or product lines and have a say in the direction of travel of the technologies that the business delivers. These are often a great way to let your most valuable customers into the inner workings of your business, driving even greater loyalty within their buying groups. They are also valuable to your customers as they get to network with their peers and prioritize the functional requirements that are built into the technology products that they use.

Businesses that build out an ongoing customer research programme, sometimes known as a Voice of the Customer programme, often use Net Promoter Score (NPS) as the measure of the relationship. This was developed in 2003 by Fred Reichheld, a partner at Bain & Co.[2] It measures how likely you would be to recommend the business and is a specific question, 'On a scale of 0 to 10, how likely are you to recommend this product or brand?'. By using the same question at different points in the buyer journey it enables you to understand the points that drive real advocacy and customer loyalty. Figure 7.1 shows the three NPS categories.

When calculating an overall NPS, you subtract the Detractors from the Promoters and ignore the Passives; you are looking for a score that is greater than 50, where your promoters outweigh your detractors. The closer to 100 the better.

FIGURE 7.1 NPS categories

0	1	2	3	4	5	6	7	8	9	10
Detractors							Passives		Promoters	
Those who would not recommend you and may negatively impact your future prospects							Those who are not impartial to you		Those who would actively promote you	

You can use an NPS score to compare and contrast across your business – understanding the loyalty of different customers in different regions buying different products and work out what improvements might need to be made and what best practices can be emulated.

There are many different approaches to measuring and listening to the voice of your customer. The best place to start is with your own customer base. Build your segmentation, understand the value of each segment, then run focus groups within your segments to find out why they buy from you, what they value and what you might be able to do differently to encourage them to buy more, more often.

Day-to-day relationships are incredibly important to customers. The people they must deal with every day will make or break the relationship. We often lean into a new client when we are in the throes of initiating a relationship, but it is key, just like a normal relationship, to be there when times get tough. Client service and account management teams are tasked with managing specific accounts and when a client's role or objective changes you might end up moving with them if you have built the right strength of relationship.

My first roles were all in account management in the advertising industry. Account management sits between marketing functions and business development, focusing on the execution and delivery of day-to-day initiatives, while also spotting those opportunities to deliver the next project. I learnt from extremely experienced professional account management leadership that the best way to drive loyalty was through the little moments of surprise and delight that made the life of your client easier (and often more fun!).

Client service is a skill that translates across industries; it is not purely about doing the bidding of the client or customer, it is about really knowing what drives them, what they need to succeed in their corporate world and what they need personally, then helping them get there. This can sometimes mean having incredibly difficult conversations. You might turn down work as you know you're not the right company to deliver to the ask or you might have to deal with under delivering to the ask you were given. You might need to be their business coach and help them grow into a new role. You will almost certainly have to talk to them about the value you and the team deliver, often justifying the time spent or team utilization and price increases. The strength of the partnership is often tried and tested through the challenging times – with the aim to get out the other side with the relationship intact and able to thrive.

Expectation management in B2B

You are no longer competing against other B2B businesses for awareness, you are competing for your audience's attention. Back in 2002, the estimated number of messages being bombarded at people was 3,000 per day.[3] Since then, with the advent of digital and social media at scale, this number is estimated to be anywhere up to 10,000 marketing messages per day being put in front of your potential customer. Even if these numbers are exaggerated, we are all living in a time of immediate gratification with likes and engagement on our social media posts leading us to seek immediate responses from the brands we interact with. They look at the best experience that they receive and presume all brands should be able to match it. People now expect a consumer grade experience at all touchpoints.

As a new generation of digitally native buyers rises through the ranks, Gartner predicts that 80 per cent of B2B sales interactions between suppliers and buyers will occur in digital channels.[4] It is therefore hugely important that the value exchange for a prospective client's data is pitched at the right level. In order to deepen the online relationship, you need to turn the unknown visitor to a known user and then nurture them towards a sale. In 2023, Forrester reported that Millennials and Gen Z-ers had become the majority of B2B buyers at 71 per cent.[5] The expectations of these buyers go beyond the digital experience. According to Forrester they:

- expect a seamless experience pre- and post-sale
- think beyond economic value
- make participatory buying decisions consulting with a larger buying group than previous generations
- want to co-create the solution.

The above elements need to be built into the overall approach to optimize your buyer relationships.

Customer relationship management (CRM)

CRM is a strategy that includes the process of managing customer relationships using the relevant data, tools and technology to enable you to track an unknown visitor to your website, retail store or contact centre through to attributable revenue. There are multiple functions involved with CRM across your business including marketing, sales, account management, customer service and finance.

Direct marketing has been a bedrock of B2C for years – particularly in e-commerce, fast moving consumer goods (FMCG) and retail – and is now often combined with performance marketing, maximizing delivery at the bottom of the funnel to optimize sales. Learnings absolutely overlap into B2B – more directly with similar e-commerce and retail models – but with the maturing of B2B marketers' approach to MarTech, there are now useful platforms that align both individual and account data so that you can see the interactions rolled up to an enterprise level.

If possible, your B2B CRM should include a customer data platform (CDP) which is directly integrated into your data capture forms and can effectively populate any new data straight into your databases. The data can then be used in real time by all functions involved with the client, e.g. customer service representatives should be able to view the latest information from the individual in case there is direct outreach.

There are many enterprise scale tools that are sold to enable your CRM strategy, which can track and attribute revenue through to the source of the enquiry and link through into your broader technology. If this is the way you are going, reviewing the detail of each product against your specific needs will help you get to a shortlist, where you can then act as the buyer within your own purchase process.

The key benefits of an effective CRM strategy are:

- A seamless experience for your clients and customers through the definition of a unified data strategy across all functions. Better service as all purchase data is in one place, with a more anticipatory journey towards a sale.

- Opportunity identification across the buying group through the unification of individual buyer data at an account level. Multiple buying signals can flag as an account opportunity.

- Effective pipeline management and predictive forecasting on performance and demand for your products and services.

- Better collaboration across siloed functions, e.g. sales, marketing and finance by putting customer needs, underpinned by customer data, at the heart of the process. There is a common goal and objective to coalesce around.

- A greater understanding of the objectives of your buyer through the behaviours and buying signals displayed throughout the customer journey.

- Working with built-in AI technologies, most CRM systems include the potential to automate triggered campaigns and, with Generative AI, can create highly customized content delivered to your customers at the optimal point in the buying process.

These are some foundational types of CRM initiatives.

Customer acquisition

The act of acquiring new customers to build closer relationships can be through multiple channels, e.g. search, social, digital, text outreach and email, with all leading to a hosted form that the individual fills in. The ask needs to be of high enough value for the individual to feel compelled to share their details. Your systems should be set up to both track channels and the offers that have brought the individual to the form so that you can optimize your campaign.

Nurture programme

A successful nurture programme keeps leads interested until they are ready to buy, moving individuals from awareness to consideration through a process of defined interactions with mid-funnel content, see Chapter 2 for definition. You need to build a plan that reflects your buying process, anticipating the needs of the prospect through the journey based on what they are engaging with on a predetermined path to a sale – are they looking for webinar details to hear from the experts? If so, share the next available webinar in their region about the product they have most recently been researching.

Nurturing leads gains greater importance if the opportunity is of a larger size and there is a significant buying group. Once collective signals are seen in your customer data platform (CDP) at both an individual and account level, the details of any interested leads should be shared with the sales teams for follow up.

Two types of nurture programmes are:

DRIP CAMPAIGN

A drip campaign is an automated series of communications across multiple channels based on an individual taking specific actions or based on specific timings or a change in the status of the audience member, e.g. becoming a marketing qualified lead due to actions they have taken on your website that means they move segments or hit a threshold.

NUDGE CAMPAIGN

A nudge campaign is a series of communications that try to entice the individual to take action. Nudges can be overt – like a time-bound offer, e.g. specific access to an expert, a price discount or trial period – or inferred – appealing psychologically to the individual, e.g. showing the prospective buyer the upside of buying – through case studies, impact stories and specific solution success.

Preference centre

You should build out a single online space for your customers to manage their preferences. For each newly acquired name, as part of their registration process for a webinar or piece of content, you could ask them to fill in their full preferences. However, it has been shown that asking for a large amount of data can be a turn off, increasing bounce rates at this point. Instead, a more palatable approach is to progressively profile the individual – asking for and adding small amounts of data to their individual profile at each interaction so that you are building a clearer, more fulsome picture over time. This will enable you to personalize and target the right communications towards them, and, because you are collecting small amounts of data each time, it does not overwhelm the individual.

Building your CRM strategy

Once you have all the elements in place, these are the steps I would advise you take to build your CRM strategy:

1 Ensure you have a robust customer and prospect segmentation.
2 Map out each segment's current journey in detail.

3   Understand what each segment is looking for and what their objectives are for each pathway through ongoing listening programmes.

4   Analyse the current journey to understand if you have optimized it for the needs of your audience. It will not be a straight line and there are likely to be multiple branches, so this will be an ongoing iterative approach.

5   Look at the optimal journey – ask yourself how you might build automated triggers into these journeys so that when high-value points in the journey are reached, the relevant CRM campaigns start to nudge the potential buyer closer to the sale. This will include online and offline communication and, in many cases, will need to involve the account team to follow up when the audience needs deeper verification or a personal touch.

6   Keep going... build out your full suite of journeys, with automated pathways that feed directly into your MarTech stack and into your pipeline management tools.

7   Optimize all channels as you go, it is likely you will be looking at a basic measurement to begin with, but as you build your understanding make sure you look at the full journey. It is the aggregated journey, not the last channel or asset that tipped the prospect to a buyer so make sure you build that into your measurement as you mature your reporting.

8   Test and learn with content, subject lines, timing, channels and use your audiences to help you build the journey they need from you. Ask questions. Listen.

Customer relationships through the funnel

While there are many builds on the traditional funnel, it is a useful overlay to the behaviours, journeys and relationships you can observe, measure and influence, which will enable you to understand the needs and objectives of an individual and also the account as a whole. Looking at the diagram from Chapter 2, we will take each section in turn and cover some of the detail you will see at each stage as you are building and nurturing your client relationships, looking for indicators that show they might be moving to the next stage and ultimately towards a purchase. Different formats of content are more relevant at different stages of the journey. Keep these in mind as you build out the next phase of your CRM process through the funnel.

Content marketing is key to furthering your relationships online. The right content helps bring audiences to your website through improved ranking on search engine results pages, with better keyword targeting for a broader and more relevant range of keywords. It also allows you to demonstrate your thinking and share a greater number of impact stories in context. The ideal is that you create content that resonates and engages your audience but is also worth sharing. This is key when thinking about social media – your content needs to have social currency.

Awareness:

- *Behaviour:* Likely to be searching around the topic, need or issue that they think they have. You need to insert your branded content into this space and drive awareness of your products and services communicating the value of your brand. The audience may be reading about broad thematic topics that align to the issues in their industry that your products and services might be able to solve.

- *Content Types:* Top of funnel – Keeping the content focused on the high-level topic but including your voice and brand as an authoritative expert: case studies and video explainers, webinars, search engine marketing, social media, high-level white papers and thought leadership that includes infographics, benchmarking and calculators.

- *Data indicator:* Continued engagement spending time with your brand, leading to an initial value exchange. Asking for further information.

Consideration:

- *Behaviour:* Will be searching for and considering potential solutions. Is likely to be in the process of creating a longlist of providers who might be able to help. They will not be ready to buy yet and will be weighing up the features and benefits of the potential solutions available.

- *Content Types:* Middle of funnel – Concentrate on content that positions you in the market against the competition. Why should the buyer pick you for their short list? Taking the next level of benchmarking into features and benefits, backed up with both case studies, reviews and user-generated content (UGC). This could include researching at trade fairs and attending smaller roundtables.

- *Data indicator:* Deeper engagement, signing up for newsletters and engaging with them. Asking questions within customer webinars. Sales/account team should be notified to ensure that the prospective customer has all they need.

Preference:

- *Behaviour:* Will now be moving from long list to short list consideration. Will likely be at a request for proposal (RFP) stage for larger engagements and will be searching for detailed examples of the work you have done. May well be researching the team they might work with and reaching out to influencers and advocates for validation.

- *Content Types:* Bottom of funnel – Driving shortlist consideration. You are preferred over other brands and providers; you might be down to the last two, so there will be detailed research being done. Run books and 'how to' guides, social media content around the team or experts involved. Conversations with indirect sales influencers to ensure they have the most relevant content for the prospective buyer. Direct mail plays a role in this space with confirmation over email or post of the potential impact they might be looking for.

- *Data indicator:* This is the final dance, so engagement should be high; you should be aware that the prospect is showing definite buying signals. Sales outreach should be in place with referrals from indirect sales influencers adding to the mix.

Purchase:

- *Behaviour:* Will be about to commit to a purchase, so will be looking for validation of their decision. Might be talking to current customers for references to understand what impact you have delivered and how easy it is to work with you.

- *Content Types:* This is now the stage for final action, so new buyers may enter the buying group, with procurement and legal aligned to validate the purchase decision. Ensure that all content you have supplied is available on your website. Your supply chain ethics, purpose and any value-add you have committed to should be present.

- *Data indicator:* Invitation to proceed with face-to-face pitch meetings and validation of written submissions. Meetings should be taking place with broader leadership. Depending on the rules in your industry ensure the correct position is taken on inviting the prospect to events, for example in some regulated industries you cannot overtly court the potential purchaser during the pitch process.

Loyalty and Advocacy:

- *Behaviour:* The prospect is now a client and should be feeling that they have made the right decision. They should be receiving the experience they expected and should be treated as a new asset to your business, with the relevant care in place. They should continue to be invited to webcasts and events that cement their choices and start to show additive opportunities adjacent to their purchase. You should continue to share thought leadership and relevant content. Once you have delivered the agreed impact you should try and feature their story in case studies, invite them to speak at events and advocate on your behalf.

- *Content Types:* This content needs to validate their decisions and link them to other clients of yours. As you move towards completing the agreed scope of work, you should be looking at what might come next – co-developing future opportunities with your customers as the macro context shifts around them. Content should include invite-only social media community groups, exclusive customer-only events, webinars, loyalty programmes, client surveys and customer advisory boards, customer offers and client zero-technology programmes.

- *Data indicator:* The Net Promoter Score of a loyal customer who is moving to advocacy will be 9 or 10, ensure you know where the individual customer sits and where the account does. At this point you should be aware if you have missed, met or succeeded expectations and be dealing with this as relevant to your business. You might be looking to the next sale and starting back at the top of the funnel with awareness of new products and services.

OMNICHANNEL JOURNEYS

We previously defined omnichannel marketing as being 'focused on holistic customer experiences, deepening the relationship across all on and offline channels – moving to the next level of communication at each customer touchpoint'.

This definition applies throughout the funnel as the journey should be building in a seamless, yet considered, way across all potential channels your customer and their influencers might use. Assets and content do not need to be matching and mirroring each other exactly (this would be known as more of a multi-channel marketing tactic) but the overall story should be consistent, tailored to the channel and bring in the relevant face-to-face and digital interactions as navigated by the buyer.

Both in-person and digital interactions need to feed the information you hold about the individual and the account, keeping note of outcomes and preferences from all stages of the journey. A unified customer data platform (CDP) that feeds your CRM is key to ensuring that the same information is held, and accessible across all customer-facing functions, about the prospective buyer if they individually interact with you or if a new member of the buying group contacts you. As a buyer myself, I know I should really be aware of all the interactions the business I represent has with a supplier or external partner, however it is never the case at scale. Buyers often rely on trusted external partners to connect the dots and make them aware of additional conversations happening across their business.

Unified data enables you to see your customers and clients furthering one connected holistic conversation across the buying group. This moves towards a new anticipatory approach to intelligent buying groups. As buyer demand signals are seen across the known members of a group, there are now technologies that have built-in sensing so that you can see disparate buying signals earlier in the process through an understanding of look-a-like groups in the buyer's industry.

Creative assets

The huge volume of personalized anticipatory journeys that this form of marketing contains, if you are building a full-coverage model mapped against all potential needs of your prospect and customer base, can only be delivered efficiently at scale using AI.

Historically, AI has been built into data engines to understand the audience needs, to predict look-a-like buying groups within an industry and to elevate multiple buying signals across an industry segment with a predictive understanding of potential revenue, but delivering aligned assets was a monumental task.

What Generative AI brings to the table is the ability to produce the assets needed for a full CRM map of journeys in minimal time, solving this challenge. If set up correctly, this is one of the biggest gamechangers in marketing. Marketers need to build the rules and guardrails for the journeys, combine them with the master asset and context for segmentation and enable a model to drive the delivery of multiple personalized assets within an entire customer journey, at scale and with built-in test and learn opportunities. We are at the point where this is seen as foundational within B2C campaigns. It is no longer a vision of the future, it is a strategic imperative for B2B to embrace the opportunities Generative AI brings to foster deeper personalized relationships.

SUMMARY

In this chapter we have

- Built an understanding of relationship types

    o Prospects

    o Buyers

    o Enterprise level accounts.

- Thought through who your strategic relationships include

    o Introducers

    o Influencers

- Looked at your internal relationships and how you might need to think about managing them and communicating with them

- Understood that with current customers as your biggest asset, the benefits of maximizing these relationships should be embraced

    o Increased loyalty and retention

    o Reduced attrition and churn

    o Reduced customer acquisition costs

    o Increased customer lifetime value

- CRM has been considered with benefits and programme types defined. We have looked at the customer relationships through the funnel

    o What type of content should you use at each stage?

    o How can you define buying signals?

Coming up next:

How to drive lead generation, unlock marketing-influenced revenue and work with your sales teams to drive growth.

AN EXTERNAL PERSPECTIVE
Embrace Technology as the Relationship Transformation Catalyst

There is a fine line between marketing and the technology that drives it. By embracing the right tools based on value, scalability and usability, marketing teams can generate insights and build programmes that directly connect to revenue, demonstrating value and driving growth.

Marketing technology, often called MarTech, has become essential for B2B teams looking to achieve sustainable revenue growth. Simply put, MarTech is a set of connected tools, platforms and data-driven approaches that help businesses understand, engage with and retain clients effectively.

We're entering a period where advancements in machine learning, cloud capabilities and Generative AI are pushing marketers to become tech-savvy strategists. With over 14,000 products available in 2024, and growing nearly 28 per cent year-over-year, the MarTech landscape shows no signs of slowing.[6] With marketing often seen as a cost centre, it's more important than ever to prove how each activity contributes to revenue. Given how much B2B engagements rely on relationships, time and trust, it can seem challenging – even impossible – to quantify the value of marketing programmes. This is where the technology we choose can make all the difference.

MarTech harnesses vast amounts of customer and market data, enabling marketers to understand client behaviour, personalize interactions and guide potential clients towards marketing-qualified opportunities (MQOs). From automating lead nurturing to measuring precise revenue attribution for campaigns, MarTech makes it possible to track the impact of each initiative on revenue. Platforms like content management systems (CMS), CRM systems and CDPs work together to create a unified experience across channels, fostering deeper relationships and increasing conversion potential. Furthermore, MarTech aligns sales and marketing through shared data and streamlined communication, enabling both teams to work seamlessly and pursue leads with confidence. In a world where marketing budgets are scrutinized, value-driven MarTech initiatives bring the clarity, consistency and effectiveness needed to prove marketing's impact.

Where should we start to unlock the 'secret sauce' that proves the revenue-driven value of marketing efforts? Understanding what technology to use and where to deploy it is essential, though challenging, given the growing MarTech landscape. It's easy to feel the urge to procure tools from sales teams vying for attention in a crowded marketplace, but hasty adoption often fails to meet expectations. Large technology firms can provide integrated solutions across marketing and sales, or a mix of specialized solutions may deliver the same result. Success lies in choosing scalable, measurable solutions that fit the business's maturity and focusing on specific needs rather than rushing to adopt new tools. Sometimes, the best approach is blending large-scale systems with specialized, off-the-shelf solutions to tackle tactical areas – always with a focus on usability for marketers who themselves can make or break adoption success.

The real power of MarTech lies not just in having the right tools, but in deploying them with purpose and precision. By carefully selecting scalable, measurable solutions aligned with business goals, marketing teams can transcend the cost-centre mindset, demonstrating clear revenue impact. MarTech isn't just about technology – it's a strategic catalyst for transformation, directly linking marketing efforts to business outcomes and building sustainable growth on a foundation of data, trust and value-driven engagement.

Kathryn Williams Macdonald
Global Technology Transformation Leader

Kat has driven multiple digital transformation programmes for professional services and IT consultancies, including PwC, EY and IBM. She is passionate about telling stories and bringing connected teams, processes and client experiences together to drive business-focused outcomes. She is driven by a purpose for problem solving and building high-performing, virtual teams across the globe in ambiguous and fast-moving environments.

References

1 Gallo, A (2014) 'The value of keeping the right customers, *Harvard Business Review.* hbr.org/2014/10/the-value-of-keeping-the-right-customers (archived at https://perma.cc/9NU2-BCUK)

2 Reichheld, F (2003) 'Net Promoter Score, Bain &Co, 2023. www.netpromotersystem.com/about/ (archived at https://perma.cc/KEB3-WRBP)

3 Cracknell, A (2002) The Campaign essay: Drowning in ads, Campaign / Haymarket 15 March 2002. campaignlive.co.uk/article/campaign-essay-drowning-ads-andrew-cracknell-fears-consumers-bombarded-ads-first-piece-new-series-prominent-writers-will-air-issues-polarise-business/139271 (archived at https://perma.cc/D6NQ-MRPQ)

4 Blum, K (2020) 'Gartner says 80% of B2B sales interactions between suppliers and buyers will occur in digital channels by 2025, Gartner Press Release, 15 September 2020. gartner.com/en/newsroom/press-releases/2020-09-15-gartner-says-80--of-b2b-sales-interactions-between-su (archived at https://perma.cc/5FDY-7KXM)

5 Hayes, A (2024) 'Younger generations are shaking up B2B. Are you prepared? Forrester, 25 March 2024. www.forrester.com/blogs/younger-b2b-buyers/#:~:text=Forrester's%20Buyers'%20Journey%20Survey%2C%202022,B2B%20buyers%2C%20at%2064%25 (archived at https://perma.cc/C6AT-VNDG)

6 Brinker, S (2024) 2024 Marketing Technology Landscape Supergraphic, ChiefMartec. chiefmartec.com/2024/05/2024-marketing-technology-landscape-supergraphic-14106-martech-products-27-8-growth-yoy/ (archived at https://perma.cc/3QU9-ZAF5)

8

Revenue: Unlocking marketing influenced sales

In accounting terms revenue is the money generated from normal business operations. It is sometimes known as the topline or gross income. Revenue or sales keeps your business running. Your business stakeholders are likely to think that this is the most important impact measure across brand, reputation, relationships and revenue but also the one least likely to be driven by marketing. We know that brand, reputation and relationships all help drive revenue and that focusing on the short-term – tomorrow's – revenue is less likely to lead to long-term success than a balanced approach to the long and the short. As noted at the beginning of Chapter 2, we need to approach 'the long and the short of it' together. Les Binet and Peter Field's seminal paper for the IPA (Institute of Practitioners in Advertising) back in 2013 analysed successful companies looking at both the effectiveness and efficiency of focusing on short-term metrics versus the long-term profitability of brands.[1] This research has been well challenged over the years, but still stands and has become increasingly relevant as marketing departments have more data and digital channels to play with.

A few of their key findings have been pulled out for this chapter.

- Data suggests that the optimum balance of brand and activation expenditure is on average around 60:40.

- The most successful, rounded approach is to develop highly creative campaigns supported by powerful activation to drive short-term sales while the long-term brand impact gains momentum.

- Strategies that maximize short-term volume growth are different from those that minimize price elasticity over the longer term. To achieve both, a balance of brand (long-term) and activation (short-term) elements are needed.

Taking these three as our guiding principles, you should apply them to how you build your marketing plans, align campaigns and teams to deliver both the short- and long-term revenue required to keep your business a success far into the future. The key is to work through what is right for your audience, your industry and your business, layering in this context to focus on your buyers.

Thinking about the budget will depend on what is aligned to marketing; bringing all spend into one place is probably the first task to ensure you have a transparent understanding of what you have available. Remove the infrastructure budgets that support the function and business from your total budget. The remainder can then be allocated with these foundational costs removed. In some cases, customer service budgets will be in marketing and in others, running your digital infrastructure will be in the foundational costs. Forrester reports that the technology investment for 2025 for B2B budgets is predicted to be 23 per cent of the budget.[2] This investment should be optimized for both brand and revenue marketing. In B2B, marketing is often a catch-all bucket for 'client entertainment'. This reflects a lack of understanding of what marketing can deliver, but with education it could be a useful budget to repurpose.

I would argue that this is not about finding executions that you feel can play both a short- and long-term role, combining the two needs together. Instead, they should be clearly delineated but connected. Think 'omnichannel' – create the right role for each channel, format and target so that your audience can connect emotionally with the brand and are receptive to the products and services when relevant but through different campaigns. The brand campaign is at the top of the funnel and is more akin to mass targeting across all elements of your business, whereas the activation or short-term elements come into play at the bottom of the funnel. There needs to be appreciation for both, so this is not about dividing teams according to focus on either brand or revenue, instead they must understand the interconnected roles they play and appreciate both the similarities and the differences.

Marketing mix modelling is one method of understanding the effectiveness across your portfolio of your full channel mix. It includes data from throughout the funnel, including brand tracking data, share of search and return on investment (ROI), so it can build a full picture of the levers at play for your brand.

Long-term brand equity

As noted in Chapter 5, the value of your brand can be quantified and is a huge asset to your business. Kantar Brand Z analysis looks at brand valuation in the world's largest study devoted to brand equity – research involving 4.3 million consumers covering 21,000 brands across 525 categories in 54 markets.[3] The data shows that 'brand' accounts for roughly 30 per cent of business value, rising to 50 per cent for the highest performing brands. Their findings show that 'Brands grow by being meaningfully different to more people.' Kantar breaks this down into three sub-points:

- Predispose more people
- Be more present
- Find more space

This again boils down to both mental and physical availability. Customers that are predisposed to your brand through an emotional or meaningful connection will, we know, buy more over time.

Your media and activation spend is key. According to System 1, which has developed a Creative Effectiveness Platform that uses a specific methodology to harness the power of emotion to drive profitable growth for the world's leading brands, 'your share of voice relative to your market share is a strong predictor of your brand's growth the following year. Spend above your market size (ESOV – Extra share of voice) and you will grow. Spend below your market size and you will lose market share.'[4]

Differentiation or meaningful difference is seen to be equally as important in consumer brands as it is for B2B brands. Making the meaningful connection with your brand and your buyers is fundamental no matter what you sell. The power of emotional connection is proven to drive growth. Strong differentiation also enables strong *pricing power*. It means that your customers value you for who you are as much as for what you sell. Making your brand more present equates to increased physical availability. You need to determine more usage occasions or appropriate portfolio expansion within your brand to find more space.

PRICING POWER

Strong brands are a source of pricing power. It is an attribute that enables you to maintain your prices and your revenue even when the economy that you sit in contracts. If you have strong pricing power, you should also be able to raise your prices without seeing a drop off in market demand.

Investment fund managers look at pricing power and continued steady revenues as a predictor for growth. Brand and marketing contribute to both attributes. Make sure you read up on these as they are key to your conversations with the finance function and will help you justify further marketing investment.

Revenue and performance marketing

Moving from the long to the short-term (the subject of this chapter), there is a school of thought in marketing that looks to focus on 'revenue marketing'. This is where the marketing and sales teams are fully aligned around the sales objectives they can collectively deliver. It includes a focus on driving predictive growth with the ROI of programmes fully understood and marketing seen as the lever to generate leads and help drive growth. This has greater success where the sale is more straightforward but can be applied to larger enterprise sales in a comparable way to customer relationship management (CRM). Where CRM optimizes relationships and experience to move closer to a sale, revenue marketing has a similar focus on ROI.

Revenue marketing is not to be confused with performance marketing – the latter focuses on digital channels and is where companies only pay the media owner based on the performance of the channel. This is useful within extremely specific bottom of funnel (BOFU) strategies, like search or keyword campaigns, but should not be the sole focus; neither should it creep up the funnel. If you were to measure brand campaigns in this way, they would increasingly morph into sales promotions as long-term brand building metrics are not as easily optimized for short-term growth. A revenue play without brand is likely to become a commodity, which means your products and services become interchangeable with others of the same type. It is then a pure price play and hard to justify premium or value-add pricing.

There are a number of different measures that you can include in revenue marketing. Two of the most widely used are marketing-influenced revenue (MIR) and marketing-attributed revenue (MAR). The former, MIR, considers the journey through all interactions with the brand and looks at the combined influence of all touchpoints whereas the latter, MAR, looks to identify the sole source of the revenue.

Marketing-influenced revenue (MIR) – Once a sale is closed, you attribute revenue across all elements of the journey. You can play with the percentage allocation to each channel if you have seen greater influence or efficacy of individual elements or spread evenly. My preference is to look at influence as marketing contributes throughout a journey, particularly when we look at the indirect impact the brand has on a sale itself, but also pricing power and business value.

Marketing-attributed revenue (MAR) – You need to decide on your attribution model. Are you looking at initial source, so the first touchpoint, or the closing source and therefore the last touchpoint? Attribution is always going to be tricky – not everything that influences a sale can be measured, so know that this is a best guess rather than concrete evidence and be willing to change your model as you understand more about your buying journey. Attribution is fundamentally a case of real-time optimization.

If working with business development and account teams where the sale is often face to face, attribution is an even more difficult measure to agree on as there is often a push for 'last conversation attribution'. This position discounts all the work it took across your business to get the buyer warmed up for the closing conversation. While there should absolutely be recognition for the team that closes the sale, this does not give you the opportunity to understand what got the buyer to that point in their buying cycle and what impact the investment ahead of the sale had. I believe that the power of MIR is key to building out an understanding of the optimal channels you need to enable your sales teams to cross the line from opportunity to revenue – the true cost of sale – and it should be your optimum BOFU measure.

Working with sales teams

Marketing and sales teams' roles interlock throughout each stage in the funnel and across the full buyer journey, working together to drive your go-to-market (GTM) strategy. This GTM strategy should determine how you take your portfolio to market, what the unique value proposition is for your customers and how you can achieve a distinctive position in the market against your competitors.

Here are the topline roles each team plays across the traditional funnel. As always there are nuances, but understanding the interlock at each point will help you determine the combined GTM strategy. Thinking this through to determine the roles and responsibilities that each team covers will stand you in good stead for a successful ongoing relationship.

Awareness

- *Marketing*: Initial lead generation and data capture through targeted campaigns.
- *Sales:* Qualification of marketing leads, based on viability for a sale.

Consideration

- *Marketing*: Content marketing, nurture campaigns and lead scoring based on buying signals at an individual and account level.
- *Sales:* Lead prioritization – which leads should be followed up as warm.

Preference

- *Marketing:* Communicating the value proposition and building confidence in your offers.
- *Sales:* Converting qualified leads into potential customers, running the request for proposal (RFP) and ensuring that the customer has everything they need to make their choice.

Purchase

- *Marketing:* Adding credentials to the decision through case studies and impact stories.
- *Sales:* Converting the lead to a customer, enabling a frictionless onboarding process.

Loyalty and Advocacy

- *Marketing:* Nurturing relationships until the next potential purchase, sharing potential adjacent offers.
- *Sales:* Upsell and cross-sell strategies, looking to increase the customer lifetime value and drive repeat annuity business.

Aligning to the sales team and your specific sales approach will help you determine the role you need to play at each level and the impact you can have. There is often tension between sales and marketing as sales is seen as the direct driver of revenue and marketing as an indirect driver. This can create a difficult relationship between the two, so it is useful to create boundaries and understand the importance of each, with metrics aligned that optimize the power of each team. Building and agreeing the GTM strategy with aligned goals and agreed initiatives will elevate the combined performance, enhancing the sales process and driving increased revenue. It will also address the efficiency question.

If sales and marketing teams are misaligned, the marketing team could be warming up segments that the sales team see as low value, or the marketing campaigns could be targeting potential buyers where the sales teams are unable to deliver, which is potentially damaging as they warm up the market for the competition. To drive efficiency and do more with less, all parts of the business should be aligned to the same GTM strategy, decreasing wastage and overlaps across all teams.

Field and inside sales and marketing

Two nuanced approaches to sales and marketing are worth covering to ensure you are fully aware of the opportunities to work together.

Field sales and marketing is a traditional sales approach and is where marketing and salespeople are present at in-person touchpoints, such as events, trade shows and conferences. Field marketers enable field sales to sell face-to-face to prospects through demonstrations and targeted promotions.

Inside sales and marketing is where sales and marketing teams rely on selling over the phone, through digital channels and direct email marketing. This tactic is part of the overall customer journey and is triggered through behaviours and buying signals communicated through your CRM. It includes hosting webinars and responding to asks for more detailed information to drive interest in a product or solution that aligns to the needs of the prospect. This team can also be used to follow up once a lead has been qualified as one to pursue. The goal is to move prospects to buyers as efficiently as possible. Inside sales is not cold calling – it is communicating with those who have already been identified as potential buyers.

Aligning brand with demand

In an article written by Peter Weinberg and Jon Lombardo for the LinkedIn B2B Institute and featured in Marketing Week, they noted that the average alignment between B2B marketing and B2B sales is just 16 per cent.[5] The article also noted the following.

- Most B2B businesses do not adequately invest in brand marketing so the targeting of future buyers is extremely limited, despite there being a relatively small and finite number of businesses. Marketing needs to target broadly to enable increased alignment.

- Within the marketing department itself there is even less overlap, with brand and demand having even less alignment with only a 5 per cent overlap, where demand reaches current buyers and brand reaches current and future. A total misalignment between the top (TOFU) and bottom funnel (BOFU) strategies.

- It is a problem worth fixing as it was found that when there is high alignment, marketing generated revenue can increase by 208 per cent, customer retention by 36 per cent and significant efficiencies can be driven in both sales and marketing expenses.

Sales and marketing alignment starts with aligned objectives. What are you trying to achieve, what are you trying to sell and to whom? Agreeing on the minutiae of individual roles, industries and target accounts within the sales plan will enable the TOFU targeting to the whole of the market and will encompass the audiences you are trying to sell to within your BOFU campaigns. The ideal plan is that you spend your 60 per cent, the long-term brand budget, on an umbrella brand campaign able to run throughout the year that can resonate across all audiences and be pulled through the funnel into the 40 per cent spent on interlocked sales and GTM initiatives. These latter campaigns should maximize the marketing contribution to short-term sales targets. Depending on the business model, up to 50 per cent of sourced pipeline could be attributed to marketing campaigns. This is higher for more direct sales models and lower for more consultative selling. The key takeaway is that you absolutely have huge influence over revenue and need to grasp this and manage it appropriately.

Lead generation

Lead generation is the process of attracting and converting unknown prospects into known individuals who have shown interest in your products and services and could ultimately end up being a customer. As mentioned in Chapter 7, it is essential that you use the initial marketing touchpoints to deepen your understanding of the individual, ensuring that you understand the individual's role and buying potential. By progressively profiling unknown individuals, you can make this a straightforward process with limited friction. You are looking to build a number of points of value exchange within the customer journey so that you are able to find out more about the individual as simply as possible. This might be through a variety of channels that drive customers to complete web forms on the internet.

Search engines

- Build out your understanding of keywords in your market. Use the most competitive to optimize your onsite web content and select smaller, less popular but more unique keywords for your pay per click (PPC) campaigns that are used in MOFU (middle of funnel) and BOFU conversations around your products and services.

- Align your content to enable a visitor to find what they need and then jump into content marketing tactics.

Social media

- Social selling – using the information an individual shares on social media to understand their needs and how your products and services might align. Then build authentic engagement with those individuals, sharing targeted content that they are likely to be interested in.

- LinkedIn sales – building out your company page with content that will resonate with your known buyers and the segments of prospects you are targeting. Ensure that you are sharing content across the customer journey with different formats and messages aligned to specific outcomes. For instance, if you are launching a new product, build awareness through in-feed advertising that links to a sign up for a LinkedIn live webcast with your product specialist to answer questions. The value exchange of the webcast sign up should attempt to find out who the individuals are, where they sit in the buying group and when they are looking to buy. Sales Navigator is a subscription-based technology tool provided by LinkedIn that helps with on-platform lead generation.

- Consider the potential of each platform through its native content type, for instance, Facebook is for community building, Instagram to see behind the scenes and TikTok to share the latest thoughts. Using a fitting message and format will make you more credible on the relevant platform.

Content marketing

- Webinars – this is the most useful format for lead generation with content marketing. Although time consuming, you can find out a lot about your prospects if you include live chat, in line surveys and feedback question-naires. You can showcase your products and solutions, introducing your subject matter experts as hosts who can evidence and add credibility to the impact your work has with other customers.

- Content downloads – templates, guides and white papers all give the prospect value for their data. 'Gated content' is a form of content that the individual must register for, enticing the individual with some initial statistics or advice and then asking for data at the point of download.

- Benchmarking and interactive calculators – by encouraging your pros-pect to fill in the relevant information, you can share where they sit against their competition in their industry and geography while also building out your own understanding of their needs and adding addi-tional data to the underlying benchmarking model.

Event marketing

- Collecting leads from those who approach you at trade shows and events, using offline to online data capture and through on-stand technology to enable efficient follow-up.

An issue with allocating your marketing team lead generation targets is that it can lead to a quantity-over-quality approach, so any lead targets need to include a focus on sales acceptance. (See Figure 8.1.)

FIGURE 8.1 The sales and marketing lead generation journey

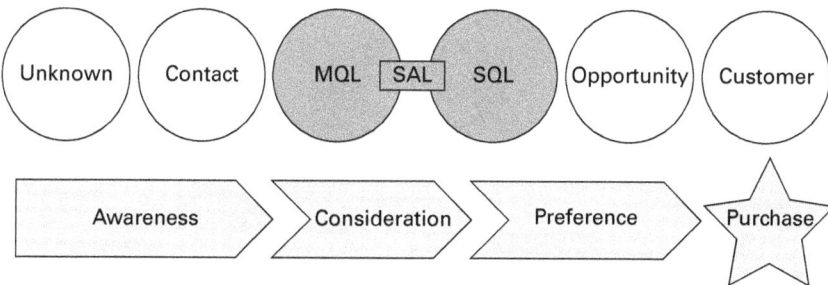

As we discussed in Chapter 2, the key stages in the contact journey are from an unknown user to a contact; this process normally involves a primary value exchange or communication, where data is initially collected. This Contact becomes part of the marketing database and enters a nurture programme. Once the Contact performs certain actions and achieves specific scores, as defined in your lead scoring model, they then become a marketing qualified lead (MQL). The lead scoring model you as a marketer use depends on your business. An example model is seen in Table 8.1.

TABLE 8.1 Lead scoring model example

Channel	Behaviour	Score
Email	Opened email	+2
	Click	+4
	Unsubscribe	−10
Website	Completed contact form	+10
	Visited product page	+5
	Deep engagement (pages + time on site)	+5
	Completed benchmark tool	+5
Webcast	Completed registration	+10
	Attended	+10
	Engaged in survey	+15
Trade show	Visited stand	+5
	Completed contact form	+10

Demographics/firmographics	Selection	Score
Role	Buyer (CIO, etc)	+20
	Influencer (procurement, etc.)	+10
	Graduate	−5
Company size	0–100	+2
	100–999	+5
	1,000–99,999	+10
	100,000+	+20
Industry	Target industry	+30
	Influencing industry	+15
	Competitor	−50

FIGURE 8.2 Lead scoring matrix

	Unsuitable Very active	Suitable Very active MQL	Highly suitable Very active MQL
	Unsuitable Active	Suitable Active	Highly suitable Active MQL
	Unsuitable Inactive	Suitable Inactive	Highly suitable Inactive

Behavioural activity — 100 to 0

Demographic suitability — 0 to 100

The lead scoring model example in Table 8.1, when paired with a lead scoring matrix like the one in Figure 8.2, starts to show where your contacts become MQLs and where you need to submit them to the sales team. Recency of behaviour should be built into your scoring model depending on when the actions take place and how long your sales cycles normally are. Waning or fading MQLs are when the recency is starting to fade.

These score examples need to be worked through with your sales teams so that the model works for both teams. Contacts can remain in a nurture programme until they perform the relevant BOFU actions to drive interest from your sales team. TOFU actions will likely mean the lead is not ready to speak with the sales team and can continue to be nurtured. Looking at members of the buying group in totality will help you understand where the account is as a whole and who might be involved in the decision-making process. Specific B2B customer data platforms allow you to look at the engaged buying group at both the individual and account level which is key to enterprise-level sales.

Referring to the contact journey in Figure 8.1, you can see that there is a step in the process noted as SAL – the sales accepted lead. This is the point in the journey where your sales team have reviewed the MQL and determine it to be of significant interest to them to bring into the sales process. Once accepted, the MQL becomes an SQL (sales qualified lead). There needs to be a service-level agreement (SLA) as to what constitutes acceptance and what it means. The timeliness of a follow up needs to be decided, and a feedback loop established, so that marketing can optimize their lead scoring models and matrices based on the realized value of the MQL, ensuring the effectiveness of their leads deliver maximum impact. This handover is incredibly important as the marketing team have driven – what they consider to be – a deep level of engagement with a contact and are passing it on as a perceived contender as a future customer. Without the feedback loop, the relationship between sales and marketing is likely to flounder. Marketing will think sales does not care about their leads and sales will think marketing does not know what a lead looks like.

An SQL is one that has gone through the SAL process and is determined by sales to be a fruitful lead to follow up. It then becomes the responsibility of the sales team to ensure there is a timely follow up, using all information available, with the aim to move the lead to an opportunity and then close to become a customer. This process is solely owned by the sales team but, depending on the nature of the opportunity, marketing may continue to be involved and help nurture through to sale.

There are times that inside sales teams are used to validate MQLs ahead of acceptance, engaging with the potential buyers to continue to nurture them more closely to a sale. This will often include personalised content, webinars with product specialists and deeper dives on relevant features and benefits. Sometimes the inside sales team continue to nurture from MQL through to customer. They may then continue to be involved throughout the opportunity phase. This ensures the SQL has an optimal experience throughout the process.

Account-based marketing (ABM)

We covered the topline of account-based marketing in Chapter 2 that referred to Brilliant Basics, but – considering the revenue focus – it is worth revisiting it with this specific goal in mind. ABM strategies align with large-scale opportunities, focusing on developing the *right* leads, instead of *more* leads. It often includes a consultative sales approach where initial conversations involving specialists are made at a loss to create a long-term relationship.

Success is not just about closing deals – not all revenue is equal. It is about building the right long-term strategies with individuals within accounts that drive towards long-term growth. Many enterprise B2B strategies look to move from one-off sales to larger multi-year annuity service-level contracts that can drive a guaranteed revenue stream for the life of the agreement. The role of marketing in this space is to ensure that the sales teams are aware of the progression through any self-navigated steps in the customer journey and share details of what the account is engaging with holistically, while also communicating relevant and timely messaging across the prospect account.

Accounts can span a range from new to existing customers. Net new clients, or greenfield accounts, are where you are starting from nothing with no relationships at all, whereas known customers, or brownfield, are where you have a level of relationship already. You need to work with the sales team to understand the purchase pathway to the optimal sale (potentially your flagship annuity product or service) within each industry you operate within. Having a defined 'door opener' on the road to the ideal sale helps you lay the groundwork to build the relationship, looking for it to pay off in the long run.

ASSESS THE RELATIONSHIP STRENGTH

As a first stage of any ABM, you need to assess the individuals within the account to understand what your relationship strength is with any known prospects, whether there are any ex-employees or alumni and if you have any connection points within the buying group. Using tools like LinkedIn will help you to see what primary and secondary connections you might hold across the account and where you might look for warm introductions. There may also be dormant leads currently in your CRM, who you might be able to reactivate.

Due to the high cost and resource intensity that ABM requires on a 1-to-1 account basis, this strategy should normally only be employed where you have incredibly high-potential accounts showing significant growth opportunities. Sales and marketing teams should align with the account team to build one approach where each member plays a distinct role in furthering the identified opportunities. Marketing can expand the footprint within an account, warming up fresh players in the buying group alongside driving a greater cohesion with the influencers the account leans on. Collectively the team treats the account like a single market and looks to deepen relationships with buyers across the account with messaging, content and creative executions all tailored to the required experience of the account.

BUILDING AN ABM STRATEGY WITH SALES AND MARKETING

It is particularly important to think about ABM with regards to enterprise-level sales. At professional services firms servicing businesses from the S&P 500, it is not unknown for more than 1,500 individuals to be working within an account delivering products and services. At this scale, coordinating around new opportunities is increasingly difficult. This is where B2B customer data platforms (CDPs) come in as extremely useful so the ABM team can see the buying signals across the clients as both individuals and, importantly, at the account level, across multiple geographies around the same topic. With unified data driving aligned strategies targeting the account, you can have greater connectivity with your sales colleagues and collectively make greater impact and move closer to realizing a sale.

Within ABM the three steps to any strategy include:

1 Identify – ensure you know the business you are targeting. What are its concerns and issues? What problems might it be trying to address? Do you know the right people in the buying group? What is the strength of your relationship?

2 Engage – building on the information and understanding of the account that you have uncovered in Step 1, build relevant strategies to engage the right people around the client issue. How can you help them achieve their goals?

3 Land and expand – can you help define the solution to the client's problem as a door opener into the broader opportunity? What might enable you to build a pathway to the optimal sale? How can you prove yourself on a low-risk project?

One-to-few campaigns might take the second tier of your account segmentation, where you might be nurturing a group of accounts towards similar opportunities, and build campaigns around their specific client issues. You can target these at multiple accounts, normally between 5–15 at a time. This could be around new regulations in a particular geography or industry and might involve outreach through channels with MOFU content.

One-to-many campaigns go further still and will target your priority accounts or those with high potential and will likely use various content types around a specific issue, powered by technology solutions. With the opportunity to personalize content and, particularly with the advent of Generative AI, 1-to-many should be the norm for your sales and marketing campaigns, targeting those individuals within an account's buying group who are able to accelerate opportunities.

Communication to the sales and account teams is key throughout the deployment of ABM strategies, as all members of the selling group need to be as aligned as the buying group. We need to make it easy to buy so that all contacts across an account are up to speed with the current stage of conversation around a live opportunity.

Optimizing ABM strategies relies on feedback from the account team. There needs to be full transparency around deals won and lost, an understanding of what any customer objections might have been and where any gaps might be in the content across the customer journey.

At targeted events the experience is key. If you are bringing your strategic accounts together either for a customer advisory board or for other forms of networking and insight sharing, ensure you build in moments that surprise and delight; memorable experiences that show you know the individuals who buy from you personally and not just as a client. 'Money cannot buy' experiences are commonplace within the technology world, as they are often part of sponsorship packages that only the biggest spenders can afford. The caveat here is that many clients can no longer accept expensive gifts down to their own internal bribery/gift-and-entertainment policies, so it is worth reviewing how many can attend as you start to build out any targeted high-value programmes.

Selling is not a dirty word

Marketers sell every day. You sell campaigns and initiatives internally; you sell the creative that brings your briefs to life; you work with the sales teams to sell to customers and clients. Embracing sales means you have an eye on revenue at all points of the funnel and buyer journey.

However you work with your sales teams, the bottom of the funnel should always have an account-first approach with teams working together to optimize the opportunities across your portfolio, tracking buying signals and pipeline data at an enterprise level. Both sales and marketing have distinct roles to play and while there is normally tension as to who leads, there are clear roles for both teams to play, with both being of equal value. Building the right teams on both sides and enabling collaboration is key.

Lead generation and opportunity identification are something that should be an imperative at all levels of your organization, so that even the most junior members of the team are trained to spot potential sales. Encouraging your teams to build networks across their own peer groups both in-house and at your clients also sets the foundation for long-term relationships. Many trusted connections made today will grow with you, enabling longevity as you move through your careers and organizations.

Upsell and cross-sell

As we have mentioned before, current customers are your most valuable asset. Maximising the return on your existing client base is the most cost effective means of driving revenue. Understanding your share of your customer's available spend, who the competitors are within an account and who you might need to unseat to take share is important when building your marketing strategies. By analysing the behaviour of your customer base, you can look at the propensity of your buyers to purchase the next product, understand what the next best product might be and start to communicate with them individually. This crosses over from B2C marketing where Amazon has driven the expectations for companies to share the next best item or the potential to buy in bulk, within your customer journey. It is also a well-trodden path by fashion e-tailers, showing you clothing items that might 'make your outfit' and suggesting the next item to purchase.

These upsell and cross-sell opportunities exist in B2B.

Upselling: Get close to your product teams to understand what items might complement the portfolio, what might your customers want to buy as an add-on and ensure that these accessories are built into the journey. You should also think through the premium and value purchases of the same product lines – do you have a basic package and upgrades that can be sold throughout the relationship? As you build out your campaigns, ensure that there is the ability of your customer to self-navigate to additional upsell opportunities.

Cross-selling: Selling across product lines means you need to understand the full spectrum of what is on offer and demonstrate the breadth of your portfolio to your customers. For instance, in professional services, you might look to sell tax services as well as transformation. It is your responsibility as a marketer to build strategies that expose your customers to the entirety of what you sell.

At the bottom of the funnel, individuals are likely to have selected their own preferences so it might feel at odds to include content that aligns to products and services that they have not stated they are interested in, but it is worth driving any targeted content with space for serendipitous discovery. For instance, within an email you might feature a block of content aligned to their behavioural preferences, including content regarding the last topic they engaged with across your channels. Another block might align to their stated preferences but there should always be a wildcard element that shows something additional that may pique their interest.

Data-driven content at the bottom of the funnel is the norm and is ripe for disruption and optimization through AI and Generative AI. The ability to dynamically optimize content during a campaign based on real-time metrics will be a game changer. Adjusting promotions, ensuring tests are continuously performed and incorporated on the fly and driven by the effectiveness of content, formats and channels will ensure that marketing's impact on revenue is maximized.

SUMMARY

Throughout this chapter we have seen the entwinement of sales and marketing.

- For optimal impact you need to balance investment in long-term brand building and short-term revenue activation
  - Work through what is right for your audience, industry and business.
  - Long-term focus will build brand equity.
  - Revenue marketing has a focus on ROI versus performance marketing which is focused on the specific performance of direct channels.
- Working together with your sales teams is the key to success
  - There are specific roles for marketing and sales to play at each stage of the funnel with separate but interlocked responsibilities.
  - Understand how field and inside sales teams are interacting with potential prospects.
- The power of lead generation can be optimized using technology platforms across channels with a clear understanding of your customer journey
  - Appropriate channels include search, social media, all aspects of content marketing and events.
  - Consider the value exchange at each point of data collection.
  - Build your own lead scoring model to help elevate the quality of leads you share with the sales and account teams.
- Account based marketing plays a crucial role in large enterprise sales
  - Work with your account leaders to understand their appetite for, and expectations from, the potential relationship with marketing.
  - Understand what the upsell and cross-sell pathways are within your portfolio so you can help drive greater opportunities for your business.

Coming up next:

Internal communications, how you need to think about activating your internal advocates.

AN EXTERNAL PERSPECTIVE
Hyper-focused customer marketing unlocks the power of relationships

The power of strategic ABM often goes untapped. When done well, it accelerates building relationships with clients and acutely illustrates the financial value of marketing.

ABM programmes come in different forms. Approach and execution differ based on industry, product/solution/service, resource models, scale, appetite/buy-in and skillset. On one end, ABM is more about a one-to-many approach which often includes AI-powered automated lead generation campaigns to named accounts, direct marketing and targeted advertising to drive customers through a nurture cycle, sending signals to sellers and client-facing teams. For others, it's more hyper-focused customer marketing with marketing teams working with large, high-revenue generating accounts to build trusted relationship with C-Suite and key clients. In some organizations, this latter 1-to-1 ABM approach may sit in a GTM or business development function; at its core it is customer marketing so where it sits will depend on organizational structure and resources.

Fundamental to the success of strategic, relationship building 1-to-1 ABM needs buy-in from senior leadership, marketing, sales, key accounts and across the whole organization. This ABM approach requires the marketer to work directly with account leadership and to ideally sit on the account leadership team. The marketer strategically coordinates marketing efforts, aligned with sales, becoming the strategic marketing business partner. The marketer then has full visibility of pipeline, is involved in account planning and is part of the relationship build with key clients. Primary focus here is account growth; the marketer will look to understand the account's and client's challenges, concerns, pressures, successes, desires, next career move and beyond. The marketer should then be equipping the account leadership team with personalized communications, executive profiling, bespoke event engagement, bespoke marketing campaign activity, in-depth research, insight and intel and beyond. It's about building authentic and valued relationships where doing the right thing by the client is always number one.

Across my career I've seen this 1-to-1 ABM approach executed well across a range of industries including energy, technology, retail and consumer. While investment was made to help build relationships, they were by no means over engineered – the account leadership teams spent time and invested in building trusted relationships with the clients. They would always advise the client on the right path for them over short-term revenue gain for themselves. The relationships built would be valued, long lasting and ultimately translate into long-term revenue growth.

Results don't happen overnight. You can have quick wins, for example, a senior client agreeing to speak at an event or dual-branded marketing. The true revenue growth, however, is seen further down the line once trust is built with ongoing authentic interactions.

It requires patience, tenacity and the right strategic marketing skillset: a strategic mindset and talent who can zoom in and out of detail. A rewarding place for seasoned and senior marketers, I cannot stress enough how fundamental leadership buy-in truly is to the success of ABM programmes. I've seen very few successful, strategic ABM executions when the leadership team isn't fully invested. Any success in these situations will often be short lived.

From the marketer's perspective, it can be hugely rewarding. They sit at the heart of addressing senior client issues and can see the impact of their activity. It's one of the best ways I've seen marketing drive commercial impact.

Sophia Kakabadse
Marketing Director, Microsoft

A CIM-qualified, commercially minded, marketing, communications and business development professional. Focused on driving results. Proven success in leading global and regional strategic marketing projects, global account-based marketing programmes, large-scale campaigns and C-Suite relationship development programmes.

References

1   Binet, L and Field, P (2013) *The Long and the Short of It: Balancing short and long-term marketing strategies*, IPA, London. ipa.co.uk/knowledge/publications-reports/the-long-and-the-short-of-it-balancing-short-and-long-term-marketing-strategies/ (archived at https://perma.cc/D4K5-3DRD)

2   Arnold, J, Selheimer, M, with Sridharan, S, Bruce, I, Chien, M, Contreras, K, Moore, C, Pattnaik, S, Salehi, R, Schmitt, C, Scipio, H, Doyle, A and Pierpont, K (2024) Budget planning guide 2025: B2B marketing executives, Forrester Report. go.forrester.com/wp-content/uploads/2024/08/Budget-Planning-Guide-2025-B2B-Marketing.pdf?_gl=1*me32jh*_gcl_au*MTI4MjkzMTY0MC4xNzI0OTE0ODk4*_ga*MjAwMjAxNjIyMS4xNzI0OTE0ODk4*_ga_PMXYWTHPVN*MTcyNTIwMjMwNS41LjEuMTcyNTIwMjcyNC42MC4wLjA (archived at https://perma.cc/V7WL-AGPA)

3   Walter, D (2024) Kantar BrandZ 2024 Most Valuable Global Brands. indd. adobe.com/view/publication/c21c3b44-92cb-4386-848e-c1641347979b/3arw/publication-web-resources/pdf/Kantar_BrandZ_2024_Most_Valuable_Global_Brands.pdf (archived at https://perma.cc/TB5K-RP9Q)

4   System 1 (2024) Methodology. system1group.com/methodology (archived at https://perma.cc/KWD8-2NTF)

5   Lombardo, J and Weinberg, P (2023) The 'circles of doom': Quantifying the misalignment of B2B marketing and sales, Marketing Week 28 September. www.marketingweek.com/the-circles-of-doom-quantifying-the-misalignment-of-b2b-marketing-and-sales/ (archived at https://perma.cc/SLU4-5CTW)

9

Internal communication: Activating internal advocates

What is internal communication?

Internal communication underpins both your culture and your brand. Bringing the style, tone and authenticity of your brand to life with your people ensures that they live and breathe the brand in their day-to-day experience. This will influence how they deal with your customers and clients, and therefore underpins the experience your end users receive. They are your ultimate brand ambassadors. When done well, increased affinity with your internal audiences will enhance greater productivity, lowering employee attrition rates and increasing commercial success.[1]

Prospective employees will look for evidence that a company aligns with their values and is a place they want to work. This is often authenticated through the individuals they meet in their recruitment journey, the culture they perceive and their experience of the recruitment process, including the technologies and systems they must use. Your communications team, just like the brand team, should be involved in helping your talent and human resource (HR) professionals define the optimal process and communications practices within your business to ensure that the experience of your organization aligns with your brand and purpose.

This is increasingly important in B2B and particularly so where your people are your product: professional, legal, financial services, commercial construction etc., or where they enable your service delivery, e.g. technology or retail. You must ensure that your internal teams are fully aware and conversant in new product detail and know the part they need to play to drive your company growth.

Thinking through your internal audiences is just as important as your external approach. You need to ensure that you have appropriate internal content for the individual's role within your business, the operational detail they need to survive and the information that they need to thrive and focus on their own personal development. These multiple layers make it a varied and interesting role as a communicator to weave the right messages into the right communications that will ultimately have huge impact on the employees in your business.

We must not confuse change management with communications. Sending an email or holding a webcast is a communications tactic and not a change strategy. As a communicator it is important to be involved in defining and telling the story but the responsibility to drive change should not rest solely with the communicator themselves. Managing change is a profession in its own right; change communications sits alongside this as an important lever but should not be mistaken as the driver for change. It is commonly understood that most transformation projects fail, with BCG first citing that 70 per cent of digital transformation projects failed in 2020.[2] Oxford University's Saïd Business School has recently shared research which uncovers that the complex factors that influence the pivot from success to failure of a business transformation are rooted in human emotions, and by focusing on the human impact at these turning points an organization increases the chance of a transformation significantly, improving performance by up to 12 times.[3]

Both communications and change communications, more specifically, can help build those workforce emotions through appropriate targeted messaging.

Types of internal communications

Not all communications have the same weight nor purpose. There are a myriad of communications that can be sent or shared with your internal audience. Before we start to look at the audience definition, let's first walk through the different types of communications. The purpose and objectives of communications can cover the following.

Leadership

Communicating the business strategy to all employees. These communications help your employees see where they play their part in delivering growth. Using regular communications can help you align your teams to the strategic imperatives that you need them to deliver. These communications can be used to enable your cultural norms, embody your brand and drive one cohesive approach moving in unison towards the business vision and purpose.

Subcategories of leadership communications will follow your operating model so you might have different geographic leaders, business unit or specific office leaders. There will also be functional and team leader communications that are used to cascade messaging and ensure the business is fully aligned to the overall strategy.

Internal marketing

When your business model depends upon your internal teams understanding the newest products, the most up-to-date services and support models for both the products and services, you will need to drive an understanding of these internally to your business development, account management and after-sales support teams.

If your account teams can choose what they put in front of your clients, opportunities exist to market internally so that the account team is fully aware of the complete suite of products and services available to the end customer. This is often facilitated through internal knowledge functions and maintained databases of searchable information.

Operational

There is a slew of operational communications that will cover everything from your office party to the opening hours of your retail units. This category covers the messages needed for people to know how to function in your business and do their jobs as best they can. They include functional policies and procedures relating to the business unit and role the individual plays. There are also communications aligned to specific projects and day-to-day work routing. Some of which might be distributed through a workflow tool – designed and deployed to drive efficient project management with feedback loops, overall governance and approval processes built-in.

The latter form of operational communication is being accelerated by AI and Generative AI, anticipating project journeys and enabling suggested content at speed. As we move to fully embrace the potential of AI in all its forms, we will see greater disruption in operational communications as the anticipatory nature of AI-driven project management moves from work routing to suggestions of improvement based on previous results and experience.

Crisis communications

When something unexpected happens, the communications team are key to steadying the ship. Your people need to know that the business will continue to operate, that teams are all still in place and that any issues will be resolved. Maintaining open lines of relevant communication across the business will help to drive a sense of calm.

Change communications

Change management and communications are different but connected, with change communication playing a role in the overall portfolio. These types of communications are leveraged to drive the adoption of new strategies and initiatives. They build an understanding of the benefits and impacts of the change but will need to contain detail around any asks of the audience and align the individual impact with the business strategy.

As humans we do not embrace change equally. Understanding the blockers and motivational drivers that might stop necessary change is a first step. Working through the different personas, messaging and formats required by specific audiences will help you plan the right approach to embed the messaging and drive engagement.

Individual

There is always a high demand for standardized discrete communication to target the individual. These are likely to combine both personalized templated forms of communication alongside personally crafted manager-driven messaging. They will include a selection of performance-related communications covering the recipients' objectives, managing personal expectations of their role and will likely also include requests for feedback on colleagues' performance. While these should be detailed for the recipient, they should follow the overall brand and cultural positioning to ensure that there is resonance.

There will often be third-party-driven communications around benefits and loyalty programmes that will be managed by others, so clear internal branding needs to be defined and shared to bring these externally owned messages into the same branded look and feel.

According to Workshop, in their Internal Communications Trends report 2024,[4] the top four goals of a company's internal communications strategy are:

1   Engaging employees and creating a better place to work (80.4 per cent)

2   Creating alignment across the organization (74.1 per cent)

3   Supporting overall business goals (70.4 per cent)

4   Informing employees of major changes (61.4 per cent)

All four of these goals look to drive engagement and understanding between employees and the overall business strategy, however the same report shows that there is an increase in lack of employee engagement from 2023 to 2024. This aligns with the broader trends we are seeing with competition for attention increasing both internally and externally. It is therefore an absolute imperative that you must think about how you drive the right experience for your employees in the same way as you do for your customers and clients.

Employee value proposition (EVP)

Just as we look to define the value proposition of the overall brand, business units, products and services, we need to look at the internal manifestation with the same level of detail and develop the employee value proposition (EVP) so that your teams understand the benefits of working with you and your business.

DEFINING YOUR EVP

Using the same tools we have developed in this book for external audiences, now consider your internal audiences.

- What do your employees think of you as a brand?
- Do the brand values resonate internally?
- What do your employees think of you as an employer?
- What is the value exchange outside of compensation – why do your employees choose to work for you?
- What is the differentiator between you and your competitors?
- Why do your employees choose to stay?
- How likely are they to recommend you to their networks? This aligns with Net Promoter Score metrics – are they a promoter or a detractor?
- What do they think of your business strategy? Does it resonate and drive a sense of belonging?

Answering these questions at scale will lead you towards being able to build your own internal employee value proposition. To get the broadest understanding of your employee's opinions, you should ask these questions directly through an ongoing feedback tool. You will need to enable anonymity but include enough information about the individual respondents so that you can slice the data by rank, role, geography and business units. This will ensure that you can see any differences that might arise through your operating model that you may need to build into the nuanced deployment of the proposition.

Once you have the detail, you should be able to unravel the answers to understand why people work for you and why they stay with you rather than moving on. It may be that you need to move from quantitative data to qualitative to understand the detail. Moving to a qualitative understanding through focus groups or one-on-one interviews will help you really get to the 'why'. Digging into this will give you a greater understanding of the unique reason your people engage with you both as a brand and as an employer. This unique reason will drive your EVP and should then be used as the basis for all your internal employee communications. It should drive the values of the business, be embedded within your employee review process and be a key part of your compensation and benefit proposition.

Once you have built your EVP you then need to focus on how you will communicate with your teams. To secure a clear understanding of their needs, work through the audience types and their engagement preferences so that you provide the messaging to drive the necessary actions.

Audience definition

Defining your audience for internal communications is an important step to take to ensure that the right message lands with the right person at the right time – it's a lot like using direct marketing principles to drive the right outcomes. Each audience will require enough information to understand their business or functional role in the outcomes your messaging is trying to drive. The types of internal audience can include:

Leaders

The different groups of leaders need to be defined. There will likely be different types: executive leadership, business unit leaders, functional leaders, office or country leaders and team leaders who all operate within different functions in a business. They can then cascade the messaging translated into their own styles and aligned with their individual priorities to their segment of the internal audience.

Employees

You will contact different employees in different ways depending on the channels available to them. For instance, lab technicians or those working in manufacturing or engineering who are away from a traditional desktop would require different outreach compared to those who sit opposite a computer all day. All employees are potential advocates for your brand and business – ensuring that your messaging delivers what is needed for the individual staff member to do their job with access to the right tools and information is key.

Recruitment

Potential employees are another key audience. Your communications with them will influence their view of you as a prospective employee. These communications need to feature the benefits of working within the company and embody the brand. You must embed prospective employees in your company's purpose and culture by welcoming them and starting to embed them as a team member well ahead of their start date – you need the process of recruitment, and its messaging, aligned to drive the individual to advocacy from the very first contact.

Alumni

In some industries alumni are key and there is a crossover between those who have previously been an employee and external audiences. Alumni can move into a client role or back to an employee and need to be thought of as a separate audience.

Planning your messaging

Messaging for employees will cover different levels of information. Taking Maslow's hierarchy of needs as a rough guide to the needs you should look to satisfy (Figure 9.1), we can see the form of messages that can be built over time.[5] You should start by laying the foundational messaging that addresses basic physiological and safety needs, answering any questions in this space, then layer in the psychological needs that cover belonging and esteem, giving your audience the feeling of accomplishment, before communicating methods of self-actualization where your recipient is enabled to reach their potential.

As you move through the different layered needs of your audiences it allows you to think through what you should include in your message and

FIGURE 9.1 Using Maslow's hierarchy of needs for communications

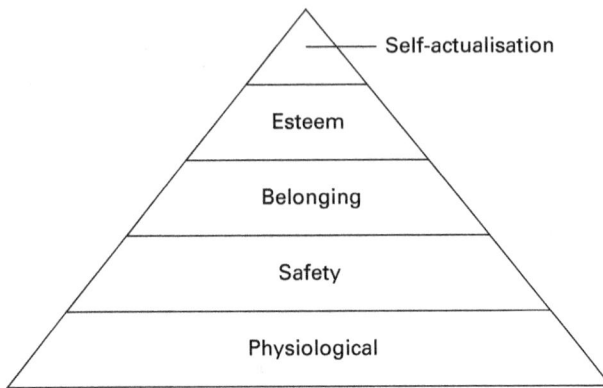

how you can drive the next best action from each group. Each communication campaign should then approach the internal audiences in a similar way to the external audiences.

- Who are you targeting?
- What do you need them to do? What is the ask? Is this to inform or drive action?
- How regularly will you need to communicate with them? Will there need to be a layered communications message?
- What types of content will you need to share with them?
- What channels do you have to use to target this internal audience?

The default form of communication is often email, but with increased competition for attention both internally and externally, inboxes tend to become oversaturated.

Push and pull communication channels

Within a business you need to think through all possible formats and channels available to you. Mapping out what you have to hand and doing a full audit will help you understand where the opportunities lie. Then think through where your audiences spend their time to help uncover new potential channels. You should think through the *push and pull* options – where might you *push* communications to your people and where might they need to access information to *pull* down when they require something specific. Current types of communication formats available include the following.

- Emails – both business and personal (the latter as the primary recruitment channel)
- Webcasts – broadcast filmed messaging, either live or replays
- Events – face-to-face, virtual, hybrid and metaverse-enabled interactive sessions
- Static and digital signage – within your real estate signage that can carry your messaging, often within the reception, lifts and offices, but also in cafeterias and restrooms
- SMS – direct mobile outreach, often used for emergencies or immediate information sharing
- Direct mail (DM) – where employees do not have easy access to digital channels in the workplace, DM is the key channel to share longer form messaging

Often *push* content is not relevant to recipients at the time they receive it, which is why it is important to also think about the information and knowledge management portals, such as your intranet, as the home of your internal content. You should treat your internal content as you would your website for external audiences. The potential channels, platforms and technology available include the following examples.

- Internal social community platforms – these enable community build, broadcast leadership messaging and facilitate cross team collaboration
- Teams/Slack/IM – often a day-to-day tool, with broadcast messaging features that can be pushed to individuals
- Intranet/portals – sites accessed through employee authentication that can be targeted to you as an individual or segmented appropriately, e.g. geographically
- Mobile app – specific company apps for your employees to access the right information at the right time, these might be specific to a business unit or functional need
- Podcast – company podcasts specifically to communicate strategic messaging or deeper levels of content, e.g. market insights and thought leadership
- External socials – often anonymized community sites that look to compare employers, frequently looking at compensation and benefits, e.g. platforms like Glassdoor

Your audiences will engage with messaging and media in a similar way to their consumer behaviours. You therefore need to think about your messaging and alignment in a similar way to your external content marketing. There is convergence across channels seen primarily in social media and PR where the messaging pushed externally has absolute relevance to the internal audience. There are now several providers building closed company groups so that you have specific content and contact with your employees.

Table 9.1 is a worked example. The scenario we are looking at is for the rollout of a new project. There is currently a lot of noise in the system. Middle layers of management feel disconnected from the details and are unable to answer queries from their team members.

TABLE 9.1 Internal communications, worked example

Audience	Current 'feel and do'	Required 'feel and do'	Messaging	Relevant channels
Functional leaders	They're not aware of the strategy detail relevant to them. Feel disconnected and unheard, not able to answer their teams' questions.	Owning their role in the strategy with enough confidence in the details to share with their teams.	Delivering the talking points of executive leadership briefings including FAQs that can be shared with their teams. Align the talking points with their personal motivations.	Webcast with a follow up email.
Team leaders	Stuck. They are hearing all sorts of rumours and noise but can't squash it.	Confidently share and communicate the messaging with their teams.	Cascade the talking points and messaging, answering the most common questions.	Functional face-to-face team leader briefing that is then shared.
Team members	Frustrated and confused. Not sure what is really going on.	Connected and able to do their job knowing their role is part of the bigger picture.	Messaging known to date, answering the latest questions, showing their role in the strategy and encouraging a culture of open dialogue.	Team meeting and ongoing internal social channel for Q&A. External socials that show the broader direction of travel that authenticates the messaging.

Going external with internal messaging can help to build credibility with your employees and help build pride in their role with you. Outdoor advertising posters can also be purchased as individual sites, which can make outdoor signage around your real estate and offices (for example) an interesting addition to your internal communication campaign. It solidifies the internal asks and messaging to your teams.

Driving relevance

Making the messaging relevant to the individual will increase the level of engagement. If the messaging resonates, it will be better received and have a greater chance of driving the actions and behaviours your business needs.

Relevance is often driven through proximity, which is why – in large global organizations – you often defer to message cascades, providing toolkits, talking points and messaging that each of the teams or functions can translate into locally appropriate messaging. A message received from your team leader lands better than from someone on high that you have little knowledge of and little likelihood of ever meeting. Tailoring the details so that it shows an understanding of the needs of your people at different levels of the business makes for more impactful messaging that is much more likely to resonate with your employees.

In my time at GE Capital, we developed an EVP that resulted in badged communications. These were useful as they gave audiences shortcuts around the type of messaging we were sharing: MyCapital, YourCapital, OurCapital etc. For example, MyCapital referred to the individual and any specific messaging that was relevant to them.

Looking back at Maslow's hierarchy of needs, once you have established the foundational physiological and safety messages, you can then move into the psychological ones – initially to drive a sense of belonging. Messaging at this level needs to show that you, as an individual, are part of the company and that you are personally understood. It is also important for a sense of belonging to drive a feeling of community – *we* work together to drive the right impact and outcomes for *our* customers. Both established and informal employee networks, sports and social groups should be celebrated through your communications channels as it will drive this sense of community.

Employee advocates and influencers

As part of any communication plan, it is important to identify the natural ambassadors in your internal networks. Employees that advocate have a high chance of landing a message with their peers due to their personal relationships and mutual trust. Influencing 'water cooler moments' helps you drive the conversation around the topics relevant to your organization. This is often seen as 'gossip' but you can positively influence the informal communications channels in much the same way you do formal ones. Planning your messaging with an advocate and influencer strategy will help you fill the void that a lack of information often creates that gossip and speculation would normally fill.

Working with advocates who are brought into your communication strategy and tasked with testing your early-stage messaging and sharing any information back to their teams is a good way of formalizing this approach. Identifying those individuals with influence who can carry the right message provides an additional channel for internal communication. These ambassadors have huge potential to influence the culture and drive a collaborative approach. The informal networks within an organization have the power to drive change, you just need to openly work with them to facilitate a mutually beneficial approach. The ambassadors gain access to additional information, and you can pre-test communications messaging to ensure that it resonates ahead of mass broadcast.

A piece in *Harvard Business Review* from 1993, authored by David Krackhardt and Jeffrey R. Hanson, focuses on 'Informal Networks: The Company Behind the Chart'.[6] This article details three types of relationship networks:

1 The advice network – prominent players in an organization that help solve problems.

2 The trust network – employees that share delicate political information and have each other's backs.

3 The communication network – employees who share work-related information on a regular basis.

Once mapped and identified, all three of these networks can be activated for communications use and help you land messaging that travels through your business in the right way. The difficult part is understanding who powers these networks, which can be uncovered through specific surveys as detailed in the article referenced.

Employee advocates and influencers, as the informal network mapping examples show, are often not in positions of formal power or influence, but instead are hugely trusted individuals who have the informal power and influence to help you drive communications.

Change communications

Not all communications messages can drive change, but all channels can carry change messaging. It just needs to be designed with that in mind, by thinking through the behavioural change you are trying to impact and the actions you are trying to illicit.

There are two change frameworks that I have used throughout my time in communications: Self-Determination Theory (SDT) and COM-B model for behavioural change. While being cornerstones of traditional theory, these can both be applied today, as they centre on the behavioural science of change.

SELF-DETERMINATION THEORY

This theory is based on the work done by Edward L. Deci and Richard M. Ryan on motivation in the 70s and 80s which resulted in their book *Self-Determination Theory* published in 2017 and still in print today.[7] It focuses on the basic psychological needs of an individual, looking at how competence, relatedness and autonomy affect an individual's development and well-being.

BASIC PSYCHOLOGICAL NEEDS

- **Competence** refers to the need to have the right skills, tools and intellect to complete a task

- **Relatedness** refers to the need to have relationships with others, a sense of community

- **Autonomy** refers to the need to feel that you have a choice, some sense of control in the outcome

---

If these basic needs are fulfilled, then the individual motivation will lead to a feeling of self-determination, driving a greater sense of fulfilment and well-being.

It is important to think about this theory as you look at your target audiences and understand how you might increase the perception of self-determination as you communicate and drive change.

COM-B MODEL FOR BEHAVIOURAL CHANGE

This model was developed by leading psychologists Susan Michie, Robert West and Maartje van Stralen in 2011 and simplified a number of larger more complex frameworks.[8]

This is an incredibly simple model, but one that has been proven to work time and time again. It is also easy to remember!

COM-B MODEL

Capability (C), opportunity (O) and motivation (M) need to be considered if you are trying to change behaviour (B).

Capability: in a similar way to SDT, it refers to the individual need to be able to be successful. Do they have the right skillset, can they access the right tools, have they had the right training?

Opportunity: a need for the individual to have the potential to change. Are they well placed to be able to make the leap?

Motivation: the need for the individual to want to change. What are the benefits, what is the upside versus the cost of standing still and not changing?

It is only by considering all three factors that you will be able to build the right behaviour and drive the change you need. These factors should all be considered as you build the messaging and communications targeting your audience segments, built around both their needs and their role in your organization. Communication without behavioural consideration is highly likely to be ignored and not drive the results you need.

High versus low context communication

It is important to understand the notion of high or low context communication when planning your messaging. Cultural norms will dictate what is needed in different geographies. High and low context are at opposite ends of a spectrum that refers to how important it is to understand the nuance of the context of the communication.

High context communication is where the context has huge importance. There is less emphasis on the content itself and more on how it is communicated, the environment and cultural assumptions that are the norm in that context. In high context cultures, what is unsaid has huge implications. In

Japan, for instance, *kuuki wo yomu* literally means 'to read the air or atmosphere' and underlines the importance of social intelligence in the Japanese culture. It aligns closely with collectivist cultures, where the focus is placed on making decisions for the good of the many.[9]

Low context communication is where the context itself is insignificant as the delivered content covers everything you need to know and there is nothing added from non-verbal or indirect content. The content leaves nothing to chance, everything is included in detail and there is no room for interpretation. Low context communication often aligns with individualist societies where people are out to protect themselves and need all details documented.

If working in a global organization that might cover countries that require both high and low context, it is worth really understanding how your messaging lands and ensuring you build in capacity to creatively translate the communications so they can land appropriately in each market.

Employee surveys

Employees who feel heard are typically more engaged and more productive, so surveys that enable your people to have a voice and an opportunity to share their opinion and experiences should be built into any strategy. A formalized feedback loop that is shared back with the teams helps you deliver to their needs and drive towards self-determination.

Understanding the specific needs of your employees is often uncovered through different methods of formalized listening. This is often an HR or talent strategy that is communicated through the relevant channels as needed. Different employee groups may need additional care, and you may want to set up ongoing employee voice surveys that are smaller focus groups or listening circles where you can dig into the specifics of a particularly emotive topic. You may consider holding one-on-one conversations with some of your sample groups as needed.

Defining the issues and topics you want to understand quantitatively and qualitatively will ensure that you get the information that you need to be able to act on them. The overlap and interplay with your HR and people leaders are fundamental to ensuring that employee feedback is used as effectively as possible. One topic that you, as a communications leader, will always want to know is whether the messages are landing and whether your channel usage is appropriate to the needs of the broader employee base.

The future impact of AI

AI and Generative AI are likely to disrupt the internal communications function in the near future, enabling first drafts of communication to be completed in seconds, producing AI-generated internal communications assets and targeting messaging through the employee lifecycle experience through all channels. Knowledge management which sits adjacent to communications but is often the source of the information that resides on intranets or employee portals will be able to be searched and surfaced once the relevant information is fed into large language models. Many organizations have plans in place to move to ringfenced versions of ChatGPT and other similar models, which would allow the model to be trained on internal information and then easily delivered through an employee-facing interface. The human element of creativity, strategic thinking and understanding will be augmented through AI, elevating communications professionals out of the day to day and enabling them to add further strategic value.

High-impact internal communications are a strategic imperative. Getting your employees to play their part in your overall business strategy is key to long-term business success. You need to understand your teams, their needs and the channels available to you, keeping one eye on the future and the potential opportunities and disruptions that may appear.

SUMMARY

- Internal communication is a strategic imperative
  - It underpins your culture and your brand.
  - Employees are your ultimate brand ambassador.
- There are a myriad of communication types
  - Leadership – communicating the business strategy to all employees.
  - Internal marketing – driving an internal understanding of newest products, most up-to-date services and support models.
  - Operational – everything from the office party to the opening hours of your retail units.
  - Crisis communications – business continuity to help steady the ship and manage the internal message.
  - Individual – personalized communications regarding performance, benefits and objectives.

- It is important to focus on the development of your employee value proposition to share the benefits of working with your business
  - o Think this through like the development of your external value proposition.
  - o Focus on how this can be embedded and activated through the business.
- Audiences require enough information to understand their business or functional role in the outcomes your messaging is trying to drive
  - o Types of audience include: leaders, employees, recruitment and alumni.
- Plan your messaging aligned to the needs of your audiences
  - o Think about the messaging – What will resonate?
  - o Think about the channels – Which are the right ones to use?
  - o The formal and informal networks within your business are key to driving engagement.

Coming up next:

Marketing management – what skills you should build to drive the strategic change you need and how do you get the business behind you?

AN EXTERNAL PERSPECTIVE

Why, when done well, corporate cheerleading is your most powerful business tool

Trust is hard-won and easily lost, especially in business-to-business environments. Employees are trusted to do their jobs; customers trust an organization to provide a product or service; and employers are trusted to pay their staff and provide the right tools and environment for them to be successful. In B2B, relationships are typically long term, involve multiple stakeholders and require extensive sign-off. The result is complex and, often, what can feel like unnecessary faff to both your people and your clients.

Countering all this is strategic communications. Managed well, communication strategies nurture and sustain critical internal and external relationships, maintaining trust throughout the cycle of business bureaucracy. Clear, consistent messaging, coupled with impactful updates, provide meaning to an organization's ambitions and objectives. The importance of all this is that ambiguity, which should be feared above all else, has nowhere to hide.

With clever oversight, content is subtly – and importantly – tailored for the many different internal and external audiences within a B2B ecosystem. However, the singular goal remains true: build understanding to cultivate trusted relationships that are motivated and productive.

Corporate communications teams are at the epicentre of shaping and maintaining an organization's reputation. In today's world, where customers have infinite choice, reputation is everything. A strong reputation can boost the bottom line via a more productive workforce and open doors to new business or partnership opportunities, while a dent to a company's credibility can close doors – sometimes forever and often in an instant.

As with most examples of B2B audience segmentation, the split between internal and external is intrinsically blurred. However, there are important nuances to consider. Internally, a good communication strategy that feels authentic to employees can transform an organization's culture. An employee's contract with their employer is no longer just a financial transaction. Today, people go to work to feel recognized, to work at a place where the company's stated values are reflected in its day-to-day operations and where they feel proud to be ambassadors for the company – enhancing its reputation from within. Imagine that internal cheerleading emanating externally to your customers? It's a win–win for an organization. And all this hinges on a communications strategy that delicately balances truth (how it feels on the ground when you show up for work each day) with ambition (the mission-driven north star goal we all want to achieve). Involving internal stakeholders in the decision-making process and key initiatives will result in a messaging framework that feels achingly apt for each organization.

Meanwhile, your company's communication strategy will also create consistency with key external stakeholders. Done well, the expertise within the business will shine, backed up by evidence points demonstrating a high say–do ratio of delivering on promises and illustrating how your organization stands apart from competitors. And when the worst of times become reality and you need to switch into crisis-mode, there is never a more important time to stand behind the pillars of promise and delivery. Your communication strategy – and the talented team that executes it – should never let these tenets fall. During a crisis, this can result in uncomfortable challenges and push back on lofty corporate jargon or trying to duck for cover. Yet trust in a well-considered communications approach will mean the company's reputation will be better for it.

In conclusion, effective communication is the lifeblood (or 'the red thread') of any B2B organization. Dismissing the significance of communications is perilous. It is essential for relationship management, reputation building and stakeholder engagement. Although often unseen and intangible, promise and progress hinges on it. In today's metric-driven world, corporate communication strategies are littered with data-driven insights, giving organizations the accountability to centre their strategies and growth plans around communications as the foundation for long-term success.

Becca Watts
Strategy | Communications | Financial Services

Becca has stepped outside of the world of comms to lead corporate strategy for a number of financial services companies. She recognizes the difference internal and external communications can make to execution and excels at delivering with clarity and insight. She is recognized for her commercial counsel and highly valued as a specialist in strategic communications.

References

1 Gallup (2024) Q¹² Meta Analysis, 11th Edition: The relationship between engagement at work and organizational outcomes. www.gallup.com/workplace/321725/gallup-q12-meta-analysis-report.aspx (archived at https://perma.cc/C9ZA-TNLK)

2 BCG (2020) Digital Transformation Report: Flipping the odds of digital transformation success. www.bcg.com/publications/2020/increasing-odds-of-success-in-digital-transformation (archived at https://perma.cc/F4Y4-SF22)

3 Oxford Saïd Business School (2024) Transformation Leadership: Navigating Turning Points. www.sbs.ox.ac.uk/sites/default/files/2024-04/2024-ey-report.pdf (archived at https://perma.cc/DVH6-YNLA)

4 Workshop (2024) Internal Communications Trends Report 2024. 7815671.fs1. hubspotusercontent-na1.net/hubfs/7815671/Workshop_24_TrendReport.pdf?__hstc=201231985.377ba175e7b30137d071cb734b8b43f0.1724685768856. 1727541541169.1728115024589.4&__hssc=201231985.1.1728115024589&__hsfp=3485190257 (archived at https://perma.cc/72AH-QGXY)

5 Maslow, AH (1943) A Theory of Human Motivation, *Psychological Review*, 50, 370–396. psychclassics.yorku.ca/Maslow/motivation.htm (archived at https://perma.cc/Y4DQ-E3E8)

6 Hanson, JR and Krackhardt, D (1993) Informal networks: The company behind the chart, *Harvard Business Review*. hbr.org/1993/07/informal-networks-the-company-behind-the-chart (archived at https://perma.cc/N7CH-KK9T)

7 Deci, EL and Ryan, RM (2017) *Self-Determination Theory*, The Guilford Press, New York

8 Michie, S, van Stralen, MM and West, R (2011) The behaviour change wheel: A new method for characterising and designing behaviour change interventions, *Implement Science*, 23 April, 6(42). pubmed.ncbi.nlm.nih.gov/21513547/ (archived at https://perma.cc/S2UQ-7J3J) [Last accessed 1 November 2024]

9 Tokhimo (2022) Kuuki wo Yomu: How Japanese read the room. www.tokhimo.com/post/kuuki-wo-yomu-how-japanese-read-the-room-2 (archived at https://perma.cc/VHU7-RPD5)

10

Marketing management: Getting the business behind you

Marketing leaders act as a connection point in most businesses. You represent the voice of the customer and translate the external market demand signals into insight that your supply side can use to optimize product and service delivery. You are at the forefront of client experience and often own the external channels that connect with your clients and customers. You will influence after-sales care, account and business development teams, alongside the human resource or talent function. If you own the communications function too, then you also hold the pen for the messaging and delivery methods internally.

Connecting the dots

By connecting the dots across your organization, you will likely have more influence and impact than you are fully aware of.

You need to wield your power wisely.

The hardest part of a marketer's role is to get the whole business behind you. It will be unlikely that you will have the funding you need to deliver on all asks you are given. So, while connecting the dots, you will need to build relationships that can take the strain of a 'no' as well as be buoyed up by a 'yes'.

In this final chapter, I am going to touch on the essential skills and thinking that I believe you need to develop to thrive in your role. We will cover both the soft and hard skills, with the former often giving you more of an advantage than the latter.

Demonstrating the power of marketing

For marketing to step into its true power, it needs to be seen as a grown-up growth lever that is commercially cognisant and fiscally responsible while being absolutely aligned to the objectives of your business. It is vital that you know how you will deliver against the asks placed at your door, are able to communicate delivery with the broader business and show how you are adding to the top- and bottom-line revenue.

You need to build, own and communicate a consistent vision for the function with a scorecard that aligns with the vision for the business. You should demonstrate that you are enabling both brand growth and demand generation. The function needs to support the priority business-led metrics including the long-term revenue growth and short-term sales increases.

We all know that if you measure something it drives behaviours aligned to that metric, so it is important that the marketing measures line up with the business. Do not use marketing jargon in your scorecard. Look at the business scorecard and work out what your role in each metric is so that you can demonstrate the full range of your impact. Ensure that you balance *leading* and *lagging* indicators, where *leading* help you predict future performance and *lagging* measure the past.

For instance, your business might be looking to move into new markets or target new audiences. The marketing insights that your team can derive from behaviours being displayed online through untapped keywords and ignored demand signals can help to show where your business might land and capitalize on the latent demand. By speaking with potential customers in the market, you will be able to help uncover the value proposition that you would need to deliver to be successful.

Ensure that you are vocal about your marketing objectives, make sure you report on them to your stakeholders and use them at the start of your functional meetings to show where you are against your goals and how you are delivering against the business objectives. Be the voice of the customer – walk in their shoes regularly, be curious about any changes or unusual signals you might start to see and address them. Marketing is the 'canary in the coal mine' where behavioural signals show future areas of interest for your customers.

Efficient growth and transformation

Proactively defining the future transformation of your function will enable you to drive growth efficiently. Embrace transformation and disruption. You need to know where the human ingenuity and human intelligence in your systems and approaches should be protected and where augmentation should be embraced. For instance, communication is seen as an area which is ripe for AI and Generative AI transformation, while the creation of brand and marketing assets is seen as an area for total disruption. Look across your full scope of services and build in this disruption to your operating model.

Staying ahead or even up to date with new developments can be a challenge, so continually assessing the optimization of your resources must be part of your ongoing objectives. Look at how you might embrace pooled resourcing so that different groups across your function can learn from a pool of early adopters, either through a Centre of Excellence (COE) or shared service model. The imperative for staying at the forefront of innovation needs to be within a manageable hub or group. This will enable you to think through proof of concept projects and deliver a minimum viable product that can be adopted at scale and will ultimately help you keep your function in a leading position.

Consider how you grow into new markets with new audiences. You do not need to have a functional footprint that aligns directly to your buyers but should be able to understand their collective needs. Your organizational structure might demand teams on the ground, but ensure you consider how you might build the right functional structure to deliver what is required by your business and ultimately your customers. This should include your agency structure which can augment your marketing function as well as reduce fixed overheads by operating a flex model using both agency and pooled resources.

Hard skills

It is imperative that you understand the business of your business. How does your organization make money, what is the operating model and what does success look like? We have talked at length about understanding and aligning with your company objectives, driving to common goals and outcomes, but what do the financial terms actually mean?

In a corporate world there are three main reports that will help you understand how your business is performing; these are issued both quarterly and annually to the market. Ensure you understand your own business and any additional regulatory reporting requirements that might be required by your industry or geographic footprint. The three main reports are as follows.

Profit and loss statement (P&L)

Sometimes known as an income statement, it shows the revenues, costs, expenses and profit or loss during a specific period of time. It also helps you to see what your expenditure is versus your revenue over the same period. It can be used to help identify where efficiencies might be made to reduce your costs, or where you might be able to see growth potential.

Top-line growth is revenue growth only – gross sales show how effective a company is at driving sales growth. Marketing can enable demand and drive sales, and by doing so contributes to the top line.

Bottom-line growth is the net income after all costs have been deducted from the revenue and shows how efficient a company is at managing its costs. Marketing can reduce the cost of sale by optimizing spend and driving more efficient lead generation.

Balance sheet

The balance sheet is literally that, a balance of a company's assets against the company's liabilities plus the equity the investors hold through share issuance.

$$\text{Assets} = \text{liabilities} + \text{shareholder equity}$$

It must balance. The value of all the things (assets) a company owns must be paid for by borrowing through liabilities or through investor injections by issuing additional shareholder equity.

The balance sheet is a snapshot showing what a company owes and owns at a specific moment in time, normally it shows the end of the fiscal reporting period for the company. It is important to note that intangible assets like brand value, if generated internally rather than through an acquisition, will not be shown on the balance sheet, so will likely be undervalued.

Cash flow statement

A cash flow statement shows how a company is operating, where its cash or cash equivalents are coming from and how the money is being spent.

It shows liquidity – how much cash is available – for the company to fund its operations and service any debt. It is used to determine whether a company is financially solid.

You should understand the fundamental financial metrics that your company uses, how it operates and whether it is financially sound. Looking at these statements will also help you understand what role your team can play in driving both top- and bottom-line growth.

EBITDA

Earnings before interest, tax, depreciation and amortizations (EBITDA) is another measure of profitability. It is a measure that shows how a company is performing on a day-to-day basis and takes into account the expenses incurred for running the business. It is a metric that is often used by private equity firms and investors to judge the potential investment success of a business.

Learning the basics will mean that you can have more useful conversations. It will allow you to make friends with your CFO and their team so that you can get into the detail of the metrics and know the performance they are driving towards and where marketing plays its role. As we heard from Elliot Moss at Mishcon de Reya, being seen as a lever for growth will protect investment in the marketing function.

Other hard skills include proficiency in more technical aspects, like IT, AI and other advanced technologies, alongside project management, data and analytics skills. Make sure you invest in your learning as you move through your company and role model spending time on these elements and encourage your teams to do the same.

Soft skills

Strong interpersonal skills drive relationships both across your stakeholders and your own teams. Getting to grips with a number of underlying skills will help you to be successful.

Stakeholder management

Stakeholder management is a continual process of monitoring your stakeholders' needs and requirements to understand what they need from the marketing function.

The higher you rise in your business, the more important it is to manage your stakeholders. The balance of project execution versus strategic socialization will shift with your seniority, with the former falling away to the latter as you rise up the ranks.

Getting the business behind you and supporting your recommendations requires you to build trust with those who are part of your leadership group.

Ahead of any management or leadership meetings where you are seeking support and approval, you need to ensure that you have socialized your plans with all those individuals you will require backing from. You will need to know what position each will take and have managed any objections and solidified support ahead of the meetings themselves. It is advisable that all formal ideas or initiatives are managed in this way – new ideas launched into meetings without known sounding generally do not land well.

STAKEHOLDER MANAGEMENT

The four-step process to follow is below:

1 Stakeholder identification – Who are they? What communication cadence do they need?

2 Stakeholder analysis – What interest do they have in your plans? What ownership or power do they have?

3 Stakeholder planning – Creation of the plan in consultation with the individual stakeholders.

4 Stakeholder communications and engagement – execution of your communications and engagement plans to drive alignment.

You should build a deep understanding of your business stakeholders, their personal and professional objectives, how they interact with your team and what they need from you to be successful. These elements will each play a valuable role in your understanding of what might be able to be traded or negotiated as you try and agree how you will collectively drive business growth. Marketing, as one of the connecting functions, needs to understand the motives of its audience which internally includes the full bench of business stakeholders.

If you are anticipating a difficult or lengthy project, you will need to make sure you consult early and often, involving your stakeholders in the creation of the plan so they have some ownership or 'skin in the game'.

Feedback loop

To maintain an open and transparent relationship with your stakeholders, you need to build in a feedback loop. It makes sense to align this to your quarterly financial cycle reporting against your plan and scorecard with time for you to make in-year adjustments as needed and then annually as a full round-up with transparent planning for the year ahead. It is at these points in the year that you need to prove the worth of your function, your teams and ultimately get the chance to shine yourself.

Showing what marketing can do does not mean solely featuring a series of photos of assets, but it doesn't mean ignoring them either. A lot of marketers discount the creative as it doesn't feel as important as the financials while others are happy to be the ad break at the ExCo meeting. Instead, you need to marry both the art and science in your report outs, bringing your vision to life and showing how you are driving both top- and bottom-line growth *creatively*. You need to amplify how you are aligned to the commercial performance of the organization to demonstrate why there should be further investment in marketing as a growth lever. You will need to manage your story with your leadership so that the value of marketing is understood.

To better understand the direction your business is taking, it is wise to build relationships with your board members and non-executive directors. It is a great way to both understand their opinion on how marketing plays a role in the future growth of the business and get advice on what they are seeing across their full portfolio. Many will have numerous board positions and through these roles will have access to a great amount of information that can help you with your own journey. The two-way relationship you will build will also help you personally, and it is worth finding someone that can help you as a mentor.

NEGOTIATION

By understanding what drives your stakeholders you will be well positioned to build in their views to ensure you prioritize where your investment should be targeted and align to what you collectively agree on. Where you are misaligned often requires deep consultation, and ultimately compromise, for the good of your business. Pitching your ideas to different functions will require putting yourself in their shoes, understanding and managing their objections to persuade them to reach agreement on the path forward. There are several steps that you may formally or informally take to reach agreement.

Preparation

You need to go into any negotiation knowing what your minimum path forward entails, what you are prepared to give up and what you see as non-negotiable. As you prepare, you should consider the value of the concession points. Think through the order you might concede them and think about how you might bring them into the conversation.

Presentation

When you face the other party, understanding their position is just as important as your own. You need to know what is important for them to understand where you are coming from and, if they have a different operating language, make sure you come to them in a way that they will understand.

Bargain

It is at this point that the give and take starts – what are you each prepared to concede to get to an agreeable outcome?

As an example, it could be that you are looking to combine a marketing campaign across several stakeholders to drive an outside-in approach aligned to a buyer's needs. In this case, I would try to demonstrate the buyer's current challenges to the stakeholder, looking to solve their issues at an enterprise level rather than simply directing them to buy a point solution. By doing so you can build a connected approach that would work for the good of the business overall.

You might concede that there needs to be greater focus on specific products with specific accounts or in certain geographic areas, but that the combined investment would be beneficial for all as it would open-up new economies of scale for media options. If the individual wanted to drive their personal agenda and be seen as a thought leader, I would also offer to feature them within the campaign (where relevant).

Close

The close, as in a sale, is where the final terms are worked through, what period will the agreement be delivered in and with what additional requirements etc. At this point, I would document the outcome and circulate over email to ensure that all are on the same page. It is only after this is agreed that an aligned plan would be shared with the leadership team.

By negotiating a mutually beneficial outcome, a win–win, you will gain the respect of your stakeholders. Sharing your strategic plans, aligned to the objectives of the business and demonstrating that you are thinking about the success of the company helps build a reputation for commercial astuteness. Every discussion and negotiation therefore moves you closer to the role of trusted adviser.

TEAM LEADERSHIP

Leadership starts with listening. Being a strong team leader means understanding each team member, their individual needs and enabling them to reach their full potential. Each will need varying levels of coaching, mentoring and managing – it is down to you as their leader to work out the balance that will optimize the individual's performance.

The approach that resonates for me is that of servant leadership which is known as a style of leadership where the goal of the leader is to serve the team, sharing power and putting the needs of the individual first to help each develop and perform as highly as possible. This philosophy was originally articulated by Robert K Greenleaf and published in his seminal essay, *The Servant as Leader*, published in 1970.[1]

Teams learn by mimicking the management styles visited upon them, which in turn builds the culture of the team as they then perpetuate the same style with their own sub-team members. It is important to manage as you would wish to be managed – for me, this is with a culture of openness, where consensus is driven through conversation and collaboration. I hold myself to account and know that high performance is essential to drive high standards of execution. The teams around me know this and, while it is not a stated expectation, it has become a cultural norm.

I have worked with fantastic leaders over the years and an important learning for me was 'to be kind, not nice'. Being kind means being honest, not shying away from the truth and sharing constructive feedback quickly while being mindful of the feelings of an individual. It is not quite as well-honed an approach as Kim Scott details in her book *Radical Candor*, but it aligns well to her thinking and I would highly recommend her book to work through a more formal framework.[2]

Allowing challenge and accepting two-way constructive feedback in open meetings can help drive a more open culture where team members feel able to do the same. The key word in all of this is constructive – kindness is king (or queen). All feedback *has to be delivered with care for the individual recipient.*

Personal leadership style

As a leader you need to understand what drives you, defining your personal purpose and underlying motivation. You should be fully aware of your strengths and weaknesses and know the impact they can have if they are amplified in situations of stress. Owning your weaknesses and demonstrating to your team members that you are working on them helps to model the vulnerability needed for your direct team members to do the same with the teams they lead. It is also good to call out those beliefs that do not serve you as an individual or as a team. You need to be comfortable with the honest conversations to really give yourself the opportunity to grow.

As you shape your team, you need to build diversity into your selection process. It is too easy to employ those whose skillsets you recognize and those you personally get along with. By doing so you risk hiring solely in your own image and shaping a team that does not represent a diverse opinion. Instead, you should recruit the best people you can, give them brilliantly interesting challenges and help them grow.

Your role as a leader is to unblock the roads ahead of your team, enable them to thrive and coach them to even greater heights.

Personal focus and leadership

In the coming section we will touch on a number of areas that will help you manage your own role and career as part of the overall approach to managing your function.

Growth mindset

This belief resides in the approach that with a growth mindset a person's capacity to learn and grow can change, whereas with a fixed mindset the individual will not change and is stuck in their current intelligence and lived experience. It was first introduced by Carol Dweck in her book *Mindset: The New Psychology of Success*.[3]

With a growth mindset we lean into challenges, we work hard to overcome obstacles and fail forward, learning from mistakes. We are happy to show and admit we don't know the answer and are building new skills, manifesting new intelligence and enabling self-determination. This too aligns with how we can drive to self-actualization as part of Maslow's hierarchy of needs. With a growth mindset, anything is possible through hard work and bravery.

I have two primary school aged children and love that they are being taught to embrace a growth mindset at school by adding 'yet', for instance, 'I can't ride a bike' versus 'I can't ride a bike yet'. The latter statement gives the opportunity for growth for the individual to learn and fulfil greater potential. This same approach can enable your team members to think differently about their own potential, driving resilience in the face of adversity and moving forward in times of disruption.

Decision paralysis is often an outcome of a fixed mindset, where the individual is afraid to fail and unsure of what to do next. Colin Powell was often noted as saying that with less than 40 per cent of the information it was too soon to make a decision, but with anything over 70 per cent the decision was made, and the outcome was already certain.[4] We need to be comfortable operating between 40 and 70 per cent, knowing that this is where informed decisions are made with incomplete information. We must rely on our instincts and experience to make the right choice.

Imposter syndrome is another term often used where people are operating uncomfortably in the grey. They feel uncertain of their choices and are not confident in their performance, wondering when they are going to be found out. This is a feeling most of us have at some point and is something that can be quite debilitating if not dealt with and overcome. Turning the mindset from imposter to challenger helped me work this through. When I am in a space where I am vulnerable and not totally in control, I can feel like I shouldn't be there to take up the space, but, if you pivot this feeling into one of openness to challenge, you can start to feel like this is a moment of intense growth. It doesn't make the feeling of the moment any easier, but it turns it into a positive. Rather than dealing with the negativity of imposter syndrome, it is instead about new potential and your own personal evolution.

Build your personal brand

It is important that you define and then build your personal brand. The visibility of your personal brand plays an important role in building trust and increasing confidence in your expertise. Your personal brand also contributes to the brand of your business. The combined alignment will help you to be collectively successful.

Personal brands evolve over time and do need regular investment and management to stay relevant and memorable. It represents the essence of you – your expertise, experience, passions and personality. Your uniqueness is always your superpower and one you should build into your personal value proposition.

PERSONAL VALUE PROPOSITION

It is important to work through what defines you in much the same way as we have worked through for the business, the brand and your employees. Think about three areas of messaging and what you want to be known for:

- Expertise and talent – what are you famous for?
- Current focus – what are you working on now?
- Personal passion – what difference do you want to make in the world?

Then weave in your purpose and tone of voice to define your value proposition. This should then be used as the filter for all your messaging and be communicated through everything you say and do.

CULTIVATE YOUR EXTERNAL AND INTERNAL NETWORKS
People buy from people, particularly those they know and trust.

A focus on building lasting connections and relationships built on shared experiences and interests will help you increase your visibility, giving you access to opportunities and personal growth.

- Identify influential networks and industry bodies and join them.
- Stay up to date with what is going on across your areas of expertise and passion.
- Find both internal and external initiatives that allow you to amplify your personal brand.

A good place to start is by attending events that are focused on your areas of interest and from there you will start to be aware of what might be available as deeper specialist groups or specific networks emerge for you to connect with.

YOUR BRAND TAKES WORK
You need to dedicate time to concentrate on engaging both on and offline, across all relevant channels:

- Lean into offline asks – which are often more daunting – like networking, speaking opportunities and judging panels, alongside online channels and podcasts.
- Book time in your diary to work on your brand.
- Create and share relevant thought leadership.
- Sign up to newsletters and follow those that interest you.

Just as you take time to build the brand of your business and your function you need to focus on how you personally show up.

Building your own personal brand is useful for both building external credentials for the business you work in, with a forward-thinking marketing team, but also internally as you begin to be seen as an accepted expert in your own subject matter.

Extrovert versus introvert

There are expectations that leaders need to be extroverts and that only a certain type of person can lead. Most often the adjectives used to describe leaders – outgoing, assertive and bold – are those also associated with extroverts.

The fundamental difference between the two is where each gets their energy from: introverts energize internally by recharging by themselves and extroverts by spending time with others.

Both leadership styles have pluses and minuses and both can be brilliant leaders. Introverts are more likely to show not tell people about their achievements and lead through steady communication and by setting examples, whereas extroverts provide clear direction, motivating others and building lasting relationships easily.

As with anything, there are shades of extrovert and introvert in all of us, and it is not as clear cut as being one or the other. Knowing how you operate, where you get energy from and what helps you thrive will give you strong foundations to build from.

Knowing when to leave

While you might try your best, not every role is, or can be, right for you. And if you get to a point where you have done your best to work within the culture and align to the company objectives and your plans are still not landing with your stakeholders, it might not be the right role for you.

Explore your options by looking at roles that are adjacent to yours in the same company or by looking externally to find new opportunities. Make sure you keep your LinkedIn profile up to date and connect with recruiters. Brief them on what exactly you are and, importantly, are not looking for. Great recruiters understand that sometimes a role doesn't fit personally or professionally, so finding someone you can trust will help you manage changes throughout your career. They will get to know you and your long-term goals, helping you be successful.

CAREER CHOICES

I am often asked about the balance of agency- and client-side roles; which is best? I do think it is unique to the individual, however my time working in agencies across my career gave me a broad swathe of foundational skills that I have been able to apply client side, but it has been the jump to client side that enabled me to develop further. Agency life builds resilience, hustle and agility, balancing multiple projects with looming deadlines alongside the fun of being at the creative cutting edge. On the inside, seeing a project through as a client, gives you further perspective and insights into the business of marketing. This is often the gap I see in those with a pure agency focus – executing the final delivery and understanding how a project truly lands. Whatever your career choices, understanding the power and commercial potential of marketing and being able to translate it for those in financially focused roles will enhance your skillsets.

The best advice I was ever given was from one of my first bosses: 'you work for your CV and not for me.' This remains an adage I live by – looking across my skills for the gaps that a new role, opportunity or project might help me fill. This will ensure that you maintain the knowledge and agility to embrace the exciting opportunities of an ever-changing career in marketing.

SUMMARY

- Make sure you think about how you connect the dots across your stakeholders. Marketing is often the mediation point as you think about exposing the needs of the business externally.
- Demonstrate and wield the power of marketing wisely
  - Align your marketing scorecard with the business KPIs.
  - Embrace disruption for efficient growth.
- Focus on both the hard and the soft skills
  - Hard: the business of your business – finance, IT, technical skillsets.
  - Soft: stakeholder management, negotiation, team leadership.
- Develop your own personal leadership
  - Demonstrate your leadership skills.
  - Embrace your development areas.
  - Focus on building a growth mindset.
  - Build your personal brand.
- Know when to move
  - Drive your career through curiosity.
  - Look at your CV as if you were hiring you – work to fill the gaps.

Coming up next:
Conclusion and key takeaways

References

1 Greenleaf , R K (1970) *The Servant Leader*, Center for Applied Studies, Cambridge Massachusetts, USA. More information available at www.greenleaf. org/ (archived at https://perma.cc/Y4FF-ET3D)

2 Scott, K (2019) *Radical Candour: Be a kick-ass boss without losing your humanity*, St Martin's Press, NY USA

3 Dweck, C S (2006) *Mindset: The new psychology of success*, Random House, New York

4 Powell, C. Quotations from Chairman Powell. govleaders.org/powell.htm (archived at https://perma.cc/5DMQ-5EZM)

Conclusion: Marketing means business

Throughout this book we have looked at how to elevate B2B marketing, moving the function from a back-office service function to the boardroom table by embracing the fundamentals and going back to the brilliant basics.

Looking at the macro-context, things are on the up. In the 12 months leading up to 25 September 2024, 62 per cent of B2B marketers surveyed by Marketing Week said their role is becoming more strategic.[1] I would urge you to embrace the increased strategic nature of your role but remember to have fun. You are in the most creative and transformative role in your business, and you can do great things that will really help drive future success for your organization.

So, where do you start?

Start with the confidence that B2B and B2C are more similar than they are different but know that, by using the fundamentals we have walked through, you will start with solid foundations particularly relevant to your role as a business-focused marketer. Continue to build your B2B learning and understand best practices from both business models in order to help you increase the holistic value you drive.

We have worked through how you might approach a marketing plan from start to finish, looking at building the business' distinctive brand, defining your target audience, building out your value proposition and starting to think through your messaging and the channels to connect with your prospective customers. We have looked at the balance of the four key areas of focus – brand, reputation, relationships and revenue – touching on the methods of optimization for each area.

If you are in a role with a plan already in place, optimization is key. Take a pause and review what you are doing, the plans you have in flight and where the gaps might be. Make sure you understand the current commercial impact your plans are achieving and where there might be room for improvement.

Futureproof your function

Ask your stakeholders how they see your function. What is their current perception of the work that you do and the impact that you have? What story are you telling your business?

Ask your customers and clients what they need. What does your business and brand mean to them? Get a foundational understanding of their requirements from providers like yours. What do they buy and why do they buy it? How do you stack up against your competitors? Would they consider you? If not, why?

What can you improve within the year? What do you have budget for that you can pivot to anything new? What can you set as foundations for the future?

Next, set your objectives for the year ahead.

Study the business of your business

Make sure you know how money is made, what success looks like today and the current plan for a successful tomorrow.

Learn to love data. Focus on speaking the language of finance and have it as an ongoing objective. Make friends with your finance colleagues.

Align your functional objectives with the commercial outcomes the business is trying to achieve. Look at the scorecard the business has set itself. How can you deliver against each of the metrics? What role can marketing play?

Build a distinctive brand

Remember to balance the long and the short of it. Long-term brand investment drives short-term revenue gains. The opposite is **not true**. This will enable you to survive for years to come. Do not behave like a commodity.

Ensure that you measure the overall time audiences spend with your brand – the aggregate attention – and the depth of engagement throughout the journey at both individual and account level. Ignoring the account level insights will leave money on the table.

Not all customers are equal

Look for the high value customers and clients. Make sure you optimize journeys to build more look-a-like audiences.

Embrace disruption. Whether it be AI, Generative AI or something else, make sure you know what the potential impact on your business and your function will be. But, more importantly, make sure you understand the impact on your customers, their clients and their business models.

Work across your industry

Build a better understanding of what the future might bring. Hold hands with your competitors as needed to drive the right levels of regulation that will enable you to continue to operate and thrive.

Make sure you accept all opportunities and stay curious. Continue to foster a growth mindset and look for the upside of disruption. Be Netflix, not Blockbuster.

Give back. Sign up to be a mentor for those rising through the ranks. Ensure you share what you know, your networks and give tips on how to navigate the profession.

Join the organizations that help represent our industry. Continue to work with those that look to professionalize marketing to give it the same credentials as other chartered vocations.

Do not pull the ladder up. Make sure that those behind you can climb up, too. Offer a helping hand to those who do not have access.

Enjoy the journey

Find a mentor you can rely on and ask them to hold a mirror up to you, so that they can help you navigate the journey through our profession as best as possible.

Find your tribe. Alongside using networks to further your personal brand, make sure you find some likeminded friends along the way. We spend a lot of time at work and it needs to be fun; finding the right folk to spend time with is half the battle.

Above all else, be kind not nice.

Reference

1 Rashbass, H (2024) Over half of B2B marketers say role becoming 'more strategic', Marketing Week, 25 September. www.marketingweek.com/b2b-marketers-more-strategic/?cmpid=em~newsletter~weekly_news~n~n&utm_medium=em&utm_source=newsletter&utm_campaign=weekly_news (archived at https://perma.cc/5BCF-TJD3)

INDEX

Note: Page numbers in *italics* refer to figures.

Looking for another book?

Explore our award-winning
books from global business
experts in Marketing and Sales

Scan the code to browse

www.koganpage.com/marketing

More books from Kogan Page

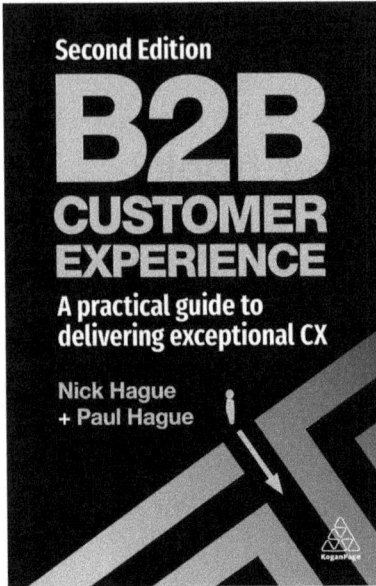

Second Edition

B2B CUSTOMER EXPERIENCE
A practical guide to delivering exceptional CX

Nick Hague + Paul Hague

ISBN: 9781398608511

2ND EDITION

B2B DIGITAL MARKETING STRATEGY
HOW TO USE NEW FRAMEWORKS AND MODELS TO ACHIEVE GROWTH

SIMON HALL

ISBN: 9781398610170

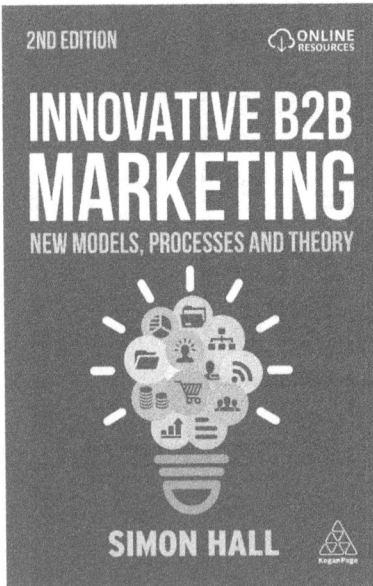

2ND EDITION

ONLINE RESOURCES

INNOVATIVE B2B MARKETING
NEW MODELS, PROCESSES AND THEORY

SIMON HALL

ISBN: 9781398604766

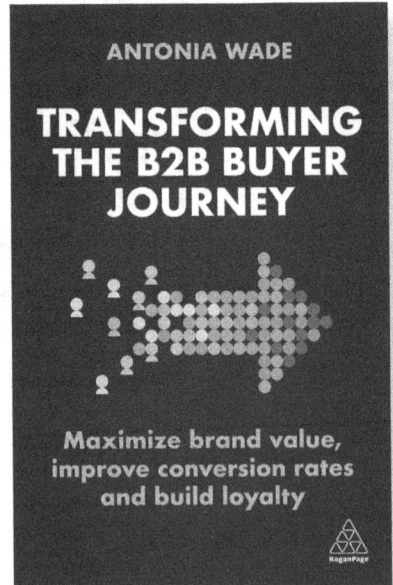

ANTONIA WADE

TRANSFORMING THE B2B BUYER JOURNEY

Maximize brand value, improve conversion rates and build loyalty

ISBN: 9781398606807

www.koganpage.com

From 4 December 2025 the EU Responsible Person (GPSR) is:
eucomply oÜ, Pärnu mnt. 139b – 14, 11317 Tallinn, Estonia
www.eucompliancepartner.com

www.ingramcontent.com/pod-product-compliance
Lightning Source LLC
Chambersburg PA
CBHW071553210326
41597CB00019B/3227

9 781398 619647